FINANCIAL
RESTRUCTURING TO
SUSTAIN RECOVERY

T0326594

MARTIN NEIL BAILY
RICHARD J. HERRING
YUTA SEKI
Editors

FINANCIAL RESTRUCTURING TO SUSTAIN RECOVERY

NOMURA INSTITUTE OF CAPITAL MARKETS RESEARCH
Tokyo

BROOKINGS INSTITUTION PRESS
Washington, D.C.

Financial Restructuring to Sustain Recovery may be ordered from:
Brookings Institution Press, 1775 Massachusetts Avenue, N.W.
Washington, D.C. 20036
Telephone: 1-800/537-5487 or 410/516-6956
E-mail: hfscustserv@press.jhu.edu; www.brookings.edu

Library of Congress Cataloging-in-Publication data

Financial restructuring to sustain recovery / Martin Neil Baily, Richard J. Herring, and
Yuta Seki, editors.
    pages   cm.
Includes bibliographical references and index.
ISBN 978-0-8157-2524-4 (pbk. : alk. paper)
    1. Finance. 2. Economic development. I. Baily, Martin Neil. II. Herring, Richard.
III. Seki, Yuta.
    HG173.F51465 2013
    332—dc23   2013038841

9 8 7 6 5 4 3 2 1

Printed on acid-free paper

Typeset in Adobe Garamond

Composition by Cynthia Stock
Silver Spring, Maryland

Printed by R. R. Donnelley
Harrisonburg, Virginia

Contents

1   Introduction: Financial Restructuring to Speed Recovery   1
    Martin Neil Baily, Richard J. Herring, and Yuta Seki

PART I. THE U.S. APPROACH

2   Restructuring the U.S. Housing Market   25
    Franklin Allen, James R. Barth, and Glenn Yago

3   Bankruptcy and Economic Recovery   97
    Thomas Jackson and David Skeel

4   Reenergizing the IPO Market   123
    Jay R. Ritter

PART II. THE JAPANESE APPROACH

5   Reconstructing and Revitalizing Japan's Financial Sector   149
    Yuta Seki

    Contributors   171

    Index   173

MARTIN NEIL BAILY
RICHARD J. HERRING
YUTA SEKI

1

Introduction:
Financial Restructuring
to Speed Recovery

THE FINANCIAL CRISIS of 2007–08, which led to what is now known as the Great Recession, caused more widespread economic trauma than any other event in the postwar era. This experience has raised wide-ranging questions about how to reform the financial system to enhance its resilience and prevent the reoccurrence of such episodes. And, because the recovery has been disappointingly slow and uneven, attention has also turned to possible reforms to markets and the financial infrastructure that might speed recovery.

This volume focuses on some of those potential reforms. The Nomura Institute of Capital Markets Research, the Brookings Institution, and the Wharton Financial Institutions Center organized the conference, held in late October 2012, on which this volume was based. This volume contains the revised presentations made at the conference. After this introductory chapter, the second chapter examines potential reforms to the U.S. market for housing finance, the collapse of which played a central role in the crisis and has impeded economic recovery. The third chapter focuses on reform to the U.S. bankruptcy process, which is essential for the efficient reallocation of capital and labor. The fourth chapter considers the market for U.S. initial public offerings, which facilitates the growth of new firms, which are often believed to be the main source of growth in employment and productivity, and has been very slow to revive. The volume concludes with an examination of Japan's experience in attempting to reform the financial sector to resume growth. Japan's real estate market collapsed in the early

1990s and has struggled to recover for the past twenty years. Financial reform has been a central focus of policy and continues to be a challenge. Japan's experience may well hold lessons for the current plight of the U.S. economy. As this conference series has demonstrated over the years, contrasts between the experiences of Japan and the United States can often be illuminating regarding both what to do and what not to do.

In this introductory chapter we provide a summary of the book. A broad theme running throughout is that each of these aspects of the financial services industry can play a useful role in facilitating recovery and the resumption of growth, but the necessary reforms are sometimes subtle and often difficult to implement. Just as the financial sector was the source of many of the problems that caused the Great Recession, it may also have a crucial role to play in economic recovery.

Mortgages

In chapter 2, Franklin Allen of the Wharton School, University of Pennsylvania, James Barth of the Auburn University College of Business and the Milken Institute, and Glenn Yago of the Milken Institute discuss the restructuring of the U.S. housing finance system in a very broad context including both how the system has evolved from historical precedents in Europe and how the United States compares with other leading industrial countries. They begin by noting that the housing sector is an important part of the U.S. economy, with residential investment averaging about 5 percent of gross domestic product (GDP) and housing services averaging about 12–13 percent of GDP. It has always been subject to boom and bust cycles in new construction, but these cycles have not caused widespread problems since the Great Depression of the 1930s. This time, however, the boom and bust in the U.S. housing market contributed to a global financial crisis and the Great Recession. The bust was *not* widely anticipated in the United States, other countries also failed to see it coming, and so this failure to anticipate the bust cannot explain the unusually painful impact on the U.S. economy. What went wrong? Where was the problem, and how can we fix the system?

Early on, the United States developed a system of housing finance that was similar to that in the United Kingdom. U.S. homeownership was greatly expanded with land grants so that by 1890 two-thirds of farm housing was owner occupied. The early introduction of savings-and-loan institutions (S&Ls) distinguished the development of housing finance in the United States, with the first S&L organized in 1831. The S&Ls were granted tax advantages (and later interest rate advantages relative to other financial institutions) so that the sector developed differently from the banking system. During the Great Depression, the S&Ls did not suffer classic bank runs because they had not issued demand deposits. They suffered withdrawals, nonetheless, as customers tried to maintain their level of consumption by withdrawing their savings. This caused widespread failures. The U.S. government tried to revive and sustain the S&L industry during the Great Depression by establishing the Federal Home Loan Bank system in 1932 and setting up the Federal Savings and Loan Insurance Corporation in 1934.

After World War II, the S&L sector prospered, growing from 3 percent of private financial assets in 1945 to 16 percent in 1975. Interest rates increased sharply in the 1970s, however, which put enormous strain on the S&L sector. By charter, S&Ls held mainly long-term fixed-rate mortgages that were funded largely by short-term obligations. Short-term interest rate increases in the late 1970s and early 1980s caused widespread insolvencies. Despite massive government support and an explicit policy of forbearance, many S&Ls failed. This led to a fundamental change in regulations that enabled S&Ls to become much more similar to commercial banks, and in time the insurance funds for S&Ls and banks were combined and administered by the Federal Deposit Insurance Corporation.

Since the 1930s, the federal government has played an increasingly important role in the allocation of mortgage credit in the United States. This has included loan insurance and guarantees, with the establishment of Fannie Mae, Freddie Mac, Ginnie Mae, and the Federal Housing Administration as well as some provisions of the Community Reinvestment Act. Indeed, the United States is one of a handful of countries in which government plays the major role in the provision of residential mortgage finance, with roughly 50 percent of outstanding home mortgages financed by government-sponsored enterprises. Measured in terms of the ratio of mortgage debt to GDP, government support appears to have succeeded in expanding the availability of mortgage finance. Apart from the special case of Switzerland, the ratio of mortgage debt to GDP is much higher in the United States than in other high-income countries. Yet despite the heavy involvement of the U.S. government and bipartisan emphasis on increasing homeownership rates, the United States has lagged the median for other countries with similar income per capita.

During the 1980s, the United States shifted from reliance on S&Ls for the provision of mortgage finance to reliance on the securitization of mortgages in capital markets. This feature distinguishes the U.S. housing finance system from that of other high-income countries. In most other countries, housing finance is funded largely through deposits held in financial institutions or—especially in Denmark, Germany, and Spain—by covered bonds, which differ from securitized mortgages in one important respect. The holder of covered bonds can rely on the guarantee of the issuing bank in the event that defaults in the underlying portfolio of mortgages jeopardize servicing of the bond. The holder of a securitized claim, however, must rely on the subordination structure of the securitization, which was often opaque, or on the guarantee of a thinly capitalized private mortgage insurer rather than that of a depository institution with access to the safety net.

During the housing bust, the U.S. system was severely tested and found to be much more fragile than most market participants had anticipated. Even though the decline in U.S. housing prices was not substantially greater than that experienced by several other countries or Hong Kong from 1992 to 2008, the impact on the U.S. financial system (and on several major foreign banks, which held large amounts of securitized U.S. mortgage debt) was disproportionately damaging. Although other factors undoubtedly contributed to the Great Recession, many analysts believe that the collapse of the U.S. market for securitized mortgages was at least a proximate cause.

Allen, Barth, and Yago note that, over two centuries, U.S. housing finance markets have worked reasonably well. We have had three great disruptions, but these were more likely caused by unanticipated macroeconomic factors than by weaknesses in the U.S. system of housing finance. Nonetheless, this raises an important question about how housing finance should be redesigned in the United States: what kinds of macroeconomic disruptions should the system be expected to withstand in the future? If the macro environment is expected to be more volatile in the future, the mortgage finance system must be restructured to adapt.

Within North America, housing finance in Canada and the United States has many similarities, but also some important differences. In Canada, more housing finance is provided on the balance sheets of financial institutions than through capital markets. The norm in Canada is the five-year fixed-rate mortgage (versus the typical thirty-year fixed-rate mortgage in the United States), with recourse to the borrower in the case of default (versus no right of recourse in much of the United States) and some prepayment penalties (versus no prepayment penalties in most U.S. mortgages). Canadian residents do not receive a mortgage interest rate deduction in computing taxable income. And, although the Canadian government does provide some mortgage insurance and guarantees, direct government involvement in the housing sector is considerably less than in the United States. Nonetheless, Canadian homeownership rates are similar to those in the United States, and the boom-bust cycles in Canadian housing have been much less pronounced.

Even though we lack robust models of fluctuations in real estate pricing, Allen, Barth, and Yago believe that it should be possible to enhance the resilience and efficiency of the U.S. housing finance system through several innovations. For example, mortgage contracts could be improved to provide risk sharing in the event of unanticipated macroeconomic conditions. They argue that the dominance of large financial institutions could be curbed to reduce the threat to financial stability. Government involvement in the housing sector should be rolled back because it cannot be sustained and has caused serious distortions in the allocation of resources. Eliminating the bias against renters in the U.S. tax code and other federal programs would lead to greater diversification in the U.S. housing stock and provide a better range of options for the highly mobile U.S. society. In the near term, they argue, it is urgent to restore confidence in the structure of securitization and to develop a role for covered bonds in the U.S. market.

Conference participants raised a wide range of questions stimulated by the presentation. How can securitization be restored without some way of ensuring that the risk is not redistributed to institutions that cannot afford to bear a loss? Can prudential regulations aimed at the provision of mortgage finance, such as policy-determined limits on loan-to-value ratios, improve the stability of the financial system? What causes housing bubbles? To what extent did the large current account deficits in the United States contribute to the problem? Is the role of the U.S. government in the housing market really different in substance from the implicit (and, often, explicit) support that foreign governments provide for their key financial institutions? To what extent did the internationally agreed Basel II risk weights on the mortgage lending of banks contribute to the problem by reducing prospective capital requirements?

Bankruptcy

In chapter 3, Thomas Jackson of the University of Rochester and David Skeel of the University of Pennsylvania extend the discussion to the underlying institutional infrastructure that stimulates growth and recovery. They make a strong case that bankruptcy policy can play a crucial role in economic growth, including recovery from recessions. Indeed, they argue that the efficient operation of markets depends on the existence of an effective bankruptcy process.

In their view, the primary role of bankruptcy law is to reduce the frictions that would otherwise impede the reallocation of assets to their highest-and-best use in the case of firms facing financial failure. They argue that a properly functioning bankruptcy law neatly separates the issue of "who gets what" from the issue of "what is the highest-and-best (most efficient) use of the assets." Two features are particularly important.

First, bankruptcy reduces the coordination problems that would occur if each individual creditor took independent actions against a borrower who was generally defaulting because liabilities exceeded the borrower's assets. Although piecemeal liquidation of a firm's assets may be appropriate in some cases, the rush to seize assets (caused by creditors seeking payment before the assets run out) may, nonetheless, reduce the total value of the firm's assets to be distributed among all creditors. If the firm's difficulties are purely financial rather than reflecting an underlying economic failure, then piecemeal liquidation is not appropriate and the grab for assets may cause the destruction of going-concern value, thereby inflicting a loss on the creditors as well as society more broadly. In effect, attempts by individual creditors to protect the priority of their claims may prejudice decisions about the overall allocation of resources.

Second, bankruptcy facilitates the shift in control (and ownership) from the old owners of equity to the creditors. This is important because as the firm approaches insolvency—and especially once it has become insolvent—the old equity owners (as recipients of upside value but protected by limited liability against downside losses) are likely to make excessively risky decisions. Indeed, they may forgo projects that have a positive present value, but low risk, in favor of much riskier projects with equivalent—or lower—expected returns. The opportunity to gamble for resurrection means that old equity owners have strong incentives to obstruct a change in control as long as possible and to increase the riskiness of the firm's business. Bankruptcy rules address this problem by enabling creditors to initiate (or force) a proceeding in which control is shifted from the old equity owners to the creditors.

Jackson and Skeel argue that American bankruptcy law is probably the most successful in the world in preventing the consequences of insolvency from impeding the allocation of assets to their most productive uses. In addition to the certainty brought about by our nation's long experience with bankruptcy law—and the advantages of a judicially based process adhering to rules known in advance—American bankruptcy law has five key features:

—Once a bankruptcy proceeding has been initiated, an automatic stay is imposed, requiring that creditors cease all efforts to claim the debtor's assets. Creditors are obliged to shift from asset-grabbing mode to negotiation mode. In several other countries, the imposition of a stay is the result of a vote among creditors or some other mechanism that is not automatic.

—Preference rules permit the debtor to retrieve repayments made to creditors within ninety days before the filing for bankruptcy. This is intended to curb the temptation of creditors to "cut and run" rather than to renegotiate their claims on the troubled debtor. Although creditors may still believe that they will do better by withdrawing credit, they must take account of the fact that they may be forced to return the payment if the debtor files for bankruptcy within the next ninety days.

—The debtor is permitted to assume executory contracts—contracts for which performance remains on both sides and that potentially have a net value to the debtor. These contracts are treated like potential assets of the firm, and counterparties are prohibited from terminating them unless the debtor decides not to continue with them, in which case the contract terminates and the counterparty is left with a claim.

—Priority of creditor claims must be honored in any distribution of the firm's assets. The ability of potential creditors to rely on the priority of their claims in bankruptcy enables them to price claims on the borrower more efficiently ex ante and enhances the flow and reduces the cost of credit.

—U.S. bankruptcy law differs from that of most other countries in that managers continue to run the firm in bankruptcy. The objective is not to punish borrowers in default (beyond their economic loss), but rather to keep the business operating until the appropriate final disposition can be determined. Consequently, bankruptcy does not carry the stigma that it does in many other countries. It is framed as a financial choice, not a moral failing.

Not all firms have access to the bankruptcy courts. Depository institutions and insurance firms are resolved through administrative processes, while securities firms must be liquidated. Financial holding companies, however, may file for reorganization under the bankruptcy code, as can most other nonfinancial firms.

Although Jackson and Skeel praise many features of the U.S. approach to bankruptcy, they believe that it can and should be improved to enhance its effectiveness in speeding the reallocation of resources to the most productive use. They highlight two problems in the existing arrangements.

First, bankruptcy is likely to occur too late—after the incumbent management has had an increased incentive and a prolonged opportunity to waste resources. Stronger corporate governance is not likely to solve this problem. In principle, so long as the corporation is solvent, the board has a fiduciary duty to the existing shareholders—but not to the creditors. At the point of insolvency, however, its duties must expand to include the creditors. Unfortunately, the "point" of insolvency is unclear ex ante. Although courts and experts increasingly have relied on the looser notion of the "zone" or "vicinity" of insolvency, courts have significantly restricted creditors' ability to enforce the duty outside of bankruptcy. Although there are good reasons for the restrictions, they contribute to delays in initiating bankruptcy proceedings.

Jackson and Skeel argue that bankruptcy proceedings should begin before the point of insolvency, ideally just as the incentives for the shareholders to take greater risks begin to increase. They argue that a legal rule needs to be established to determine when the reshuffling of ownership claims against the debtor's assets should occur in order to reduce the scope for delays. The rationale for a rule to determine when the shift in ownership claims should take place is essentially the same as that for bankruptcy. The bankruptcy process reduces the scope for individual creditors to make a grab for the troubled debtor's assets. A rule for determining when a change in ownership should take place reduces the challenges that a heterogeneous group of unsecured creditors faces when initiating action to shift control from the existing shareholders. While the firm is organized to facilitate collective action on behalf of the shareholders, creditors have no such mechanism. Indeed, individual creditors may believe that they are likely to get a higher repayment by acting individually against the borrower than by cooperating with other creditors to wrest control of the firm from the current shareholders. Thus shareholders (and managers acting on their behalf) will prefer to delay filing for bankruptcy as long as possible in order to preserve their option to capture a large future upside return, and individual creditors may prefer to take individual actions than to initiate a bankruptcy process. The result is that the firm's assets may be invested in increasingly risky ventures.

If both existing shareholders and creditors lack strong incentives to initiate bankruptcy proceedings, why do they occur at all? Jackson and Skeel conjecture that the initiative is usually taken by new creditors. New creditors are likely to be willing to lend to a firm in financial distress only if shareholders (and management) file for bankruptcy. A bankruptcy filing automatically gives priority to the claims of new creditors over all previous unsecured creditors. While shareholders and managers will resist this pressure as long as possible, the need for liquidity may give them no choice. Because managers in the United States can usually continue to operate a firm that is restructuring, they may be somewhat less reluctant to file for bankruptcy than managers in other countries. Nonetheless, bankruptcy is still likely to be initiated too late, largely because of the difficulties in valuing a firm's assets. While illiquidity is unambiguous, insolvency may occur earlier and be much more difficult for outsiders to detect.

Jackson and Skeel make several suggestions for encouraging more timely filings for bankruptcy. First, large firms should be required to file a living will, similar to (but simpler than) those required under the Dodd-Frank Act for systemically important financial institutions. These documents would specify how a bankruptcy proceeding would unfold. This would reduce the uncertainty about what would happen if a firm were to file for bankruptcy and speed the process if such a filing were to occur.

Second, they believe that a balance sheet insolvency standard should be reintroduced and added to the current cash flow test as a basis for an involuntary filing. The increased scope for filing an involuntary bankruptcy petition would reduce the problem of delay. While they acknowledge that balance sheet insolvency may be difficult to ascertain, they believe the potential benefits outweigh the possibility of abusive filings.

Third, they advocate permitting the Securities and Exchange Commission (SEC) or some other primary regulator to file an involuntary petition for bankruptcy on the same basis as a firm's creditors. They believe that the SEC should not be subject to the same inhibitions that delay filings by managers (on behalf of existing shareholders) and creditors, and they conjecture that giving the government a potential role at the commencement of a bankruptcy may reduce the tendency to improvise a bailout outside the court-supervised process.

In addition, they suggest some incentives that could be introduced to reduce delays in bankruptcy filings. First, an incentive could be given to shareholders to initiate a timelier filing for bankruptcy. For example, shareholders might be given a small percentage of the difference between the going-concern and the liquidation value of a firm's assets. Timely filings would protect some value for the old shareholders, while filings that are unduly delayed would wipe them out. Second, an incentive could be given to the creditors who file an involuntary bankruptcy petition. This would enable them to benefit (to a modest extent) relative to those creditors who simply press for individual repayments from the debtor. Third, to curb a tendency by large, influential creditors to delay a bankruptcy filing to just over the ninety-day period after they have received payment that is subject to preferences, they suggest imposing a modest penalty on any creditor who receives a preference with the intent to avoid a bankruptcy proceeding. Fourth, they suggest removing exemptions from key bankruptcy provisions, such as the automatic stay for some counterparties or creditors. Protection from the consequences of bankruptcy weakens the incentives that some institutions would otherwise have to monitor the firm's creditworthiness most effectively. They argue that the wholesale exception of qualified financial contracts from bankruptcy's stay and preference provisions may reduce the incentives of counterparties to monitor a firm and generate market signals that can be used by other creditors.

They also note some procedural reforms that could reduce the scope for delays in the bankruptcy process. These include shortening the exclusivity period in which the debtor has the sole right to formulate and file a plan of reorganization and shortening the period for soliciting acceptances and voting on the plan.

Jackson and Skeel conclude with a discussion of the tension between their view of the role of bankruptcy, which emphasizes that the main objective should be to facilitate the highest-and-best use of assets, and the view that bankruptcy should also be employed to save jobs. They note that so long as the conclusion with regard to the highest-and-best use is to keep the firm's assets together, both goals can be achieved. But, when the firm's assets are worth more broken up and sold separately, the two goals appear to be in conflict.

They argue that the political pressures to favor reorganization rather than liquidation can be enormous, but can lead to perverse outcomes. While it may be possible to "save" jobs at the firm in distress, this may be only temporary if the firm's problems are the result of economic as well as financial failure. Moreover, the jobs that are "saved" may come at the cost of jobs that are lost at more efficient firms, although this job loss is an opportunity cost experienced by workers who are difficult to identify and thus much less likely to mobilize political pressure. They note that this policy may well result in shielding inefficient firms from productivity gains that could be achieved by shifting resources to more efficient firms, with damaging implications for economic growth. While recognizing the validity of government support for displaced workers in some instances, they argue that this issue should be evaluated on its merits rather than be subjected to opaque (and undemocratic) trade-offs in the bankruptcy process.

Jackson and Skeel cite the two Chrysler bailouts as examples of the dangers of trying to use the bankruptcy process to save jobs when the debtor is suffering from both economic and financial distress. They argue that, by 2009, capacity in the automotive industry appeared to be at least 25 percent greater than steady-state demand, and so the question was not whether jobs in the industry would be lost, but rather whose jobs would be lost. By "saving" jobs at Chrysler, the government increased the pressure on more efficient producers to reduce capacity. Chrysler, they conjecture, would have been more valuable sold piecemeal—for example, the sale of the Jeep brand, much of Chrysler's real estate, and some of its most efficient plants—than maintained as a going concern. Although they are champions of the role of bankruptcy in enhancing economic growth, they warn that expecting it to achieve additional objectives can diminish its effectiveness in this central role.

Discussion focused primarily on two issues: the idea of requiring living wills and the interpretation of the Chrysler bailout. Some participants questioned whether living wills could serve a useful function for large, nonfinancial corporations not subject to prudential supervision. In other words, they questioned whether the benefits exceeded the costs that would be placed on corporations. Moreover, they raised concerns about whether the SEC should play a role in enforcing safety and soundness requirements on firms and whether it has the expertise to force an involuntary bankruptcy filing.

In addition, some conference participants questioned whether the reallocation function had much of a role to play in the Chrysler case, since the liquidation value of its assets would be quite low. Skeel replied that the most serious distortion of the process was structuring an auction for Chrysler's assets in such a way that only the government could bid. While he acknowledged that there may be a case for suspending bankruptcy rules during a crisis, this period should be clearly distinguished from normal times. Intervening on behalf of an industry, he continued, is much less worrisome than favoring a particular firm. He emphasized that the government should not be in the business of picking survivors.

Initial Public Offerings

In chapter 4, Jay Ritter of the University of Florida analyzes the challenge of reenergizing the market for initial public offerings (IPOs) in a new context. He questions whether the observed decline in IPOs deserves the attention it has received in Congress and the financial press—or, indeed, whether it is a significant policy problem at all.

Conventional analysis starts from the presumption that firms that go public are major creators of jobs and that the marked decline in the number of operating companies going public since 2000 may have contributed to the relatively sluggish rate of growth in jobs over the last decade. This line of reasoning usually attributes the decline to three factors: the impact of the Sarbanes-Oxley Act of 2002 (SOX) on smaller firms, a decline in analyst coverage of small firms since the imposition of the Fair Disclosure Rule in 2000, and the Global Settlement that imposed constraints on sell-side analysts.

The number of jobs that would have been created with a higher volume of IPOs is a counterfactual that can never be proven, but Ritter notes that the estimate of 22.4 million jobs that has been widely quoted in the press, in congressional hearings, and by industry trade associations is certainly too large. He shows that the estimate made by industry consultants relies on three unrealistically optimistic assumptions: first, that the record volume of IPOs that occurred in 1996 would have been sustained throughout the subsequent period; second, that the firms that did not go public would have added jobs as rapidly as twenty-five of the most successful IPOs; and third, that the shortfall of IPOs (relative to the record level achieved in 1996) began in 1997 rather than after the collapse of the high-tech bubble in 2001, as analysts usually assume. These implausible assumptions lead to the conclusion that the number of jobs lost due to the cumulative shortfall in IPOs was nearly double the actual number of unemployed workers in August 2012.

Ritter presents an alternative estimate, based on less extreme assumptions that reflect period averages rather than high-water marks. These assumptions imply that as many as 2.03 million jobs may have been "lost" through the end of 2012.

He cautions, however, that this mechanical estimate may also be too high because it implicitly assumes that the workers who would have been hired by the additional IPOs would otherwise have been unemployed and that investors who would have invested in the "missing" IPOs would have made no alternative investments.

Ritter also examines the reasons advanced for the decline in IPOs—mainly involving the costs of being a public company. First, Section 404 of SOX requires publicly traded companies to undergo external audits of their internal systems to ensure accurate financial reporting. Because such audits have a relatively large fixed-cost component, this regulation falls especially heavily on smaller companies. Ritter does not disagree, but he notes that this cannot explain a significant part of the decline in IPOs because IPO volume has continued to be low after most of the provisions applying to small companies were repealed in 2007. Moreover, European IPOs have followed a similar downward trend even though SOX never applied to them.

Second, the SEC's attempt to level the playing field regarding disclosures by public corporations (Regulation FD in 2000) and its attempt to reduce the conflicts of interest facing security analysts employed by underwriters of publicly traded shares (the Global Settlement in 2003) may have contributed to a decline in coverage of small stocks by security analysts. Ritter agrees that a decline in coverage could reduce the number of potential investors in small-cap stocks and lead to a decline in their prices relative to those of large-cap stocks (which continued to be covered by security analysts). He questions the quantitative impact, however, and breaks the question into two parts: How much does coverage by analysts boost a stock's price? What is the sensitivity of IPO volume to increases in public market valuation? Using estimates from previous work, he concludes that if small-stock share prices were 5 percent higher due to greater coverage by analysts, the volume of IPOs might have increased by as many as ten IPOs a year. In fact, the average market-to-book ratio for small-cap stocks was about 73 basis points lower from 2001 to 2009 relative to the period from 1990 to 2000. This decline in market valuations would also account for a drop of forty-two IPOs a year. Ritter is reluctant to put much weight on this explanation, however, because in the period from 1980 to 1990, when analyst coverage of small-cap stocks was not restricted and the average volume of IPOs was higher, the market-to-book ratio for small-cap stocks was lower than in the period from 2001 to 2012.

Third, some analysts attribute the decline in IPOs to the high direct and indirect costs of making a public offering. Direct costs include fees to investment bankers (which are typically about 7 percent in the United States relative to 4 percent in Europe), costs of printing, legal services, and auditing, as well as the opportunity cost of firm managers' time. Indirect costs result from the under-pricing of IPOs by the underwriters to facilitate distribution. On average, this amounted to about 11 percent of the first-day closing price during 2001–12. Thus scaling for the size of a typical IPO, going public may cost nearly 5 percent of the post-issue market price of the firm. In addition, publicly traded firms have higher ongoing legal costs due to higher insurance premiums for directors (rela-tive to private firms) and the costs associated with discovery and legal defense of class-action lawsuits against public firms. Ritter, however, questions whether these factors can explain the decline in IPOs because they did not change signifi-cantly compared with the previous decade, when the average volume of IPOs was much higher.

Fourth, Ritter has little patience with the argument that the relative value of small-cap stocks has dropped because of a decrease in the minimum increment in which securities can trade (tick size). Following the move to decimalization, tick size did fall to $0.01 from the increments of $0.125 that had prevailed earlier. Although the decrease in tick size is evident, Ritter shows that the implied drop in small-cap valuations did not occur. Small firms tend to have a higher price-to-earnings ratio than large firms, and these ratios have not deteriorated since 1996, even though the tick size has decreased markedly.

Congress passed the Jumpstart Our Business Startups (JOBS) Act in April 2012 in an attempt to generate more IPOs and more jobs. The JOBS Act attempts to encourage the funding of small firms largely by easing the burden of several investor protection measures for the benefit of firms making IPOs. These include (1) encouraging "crowdfunding" to facilitate the access of new firms to small investments by large numbers of investors; (2) permitting the advertis-ing of securities offerings to the general public; (3) creating a new category of "emerging-growth" firms that are exempt from SOX and other regulations for their first five years as public companies; (4) increasing the permissible number of shareholders "of record" (and exempting the firm's employees from this count) before public disclosure requirements are triggered; (5) easing disclosure require-ments for community banks; (6) eliminating the "quiet period" regulations that had restricted analysts working for underwriters from making buy and (rarely) sell recommendations at the time of an IPO; (7) raising the Regulation A limit from $5 million to $50 million; and (8) conducting a study on the impact of the reduction of tick size on issues of IPOs.

Ritter warns that the unintended consequences of the JOBS Act may be per-verse. By making it easier to raise money privately, increasing liquidity for some private firms, restricting shareholder access to information, constraining the abil-ity of shareholders to challenge management after an IPO, and reducing the incentives for research on new firms by independent analysts, the net impact of the act may be to reduce the flow of capital to small start-up firms and to diminish the number of IPOs. In any event, he expects the impact of the JOBS Act to be quite limited because it does not address the main detriment to higher investment in IPOs: a marked decline in the ability of small high-growth firms to generate sustainable profits. For similar reasons, he does not expect the JOBS Act to have much impact on job creation or economic growth.

What then accounts for the decline in IPOs? Ritter introduces an alternative explanation based on the advantages of growing large quickly. He believes that the economy has undergone a structural change in recent years so that, especially in some important high-technology industries, big firms have an increasing advantage relative to small firms. Thus a strategy of organic growth (which may lead to an IPO) is often inferior to a strategy of engaging in mergers and acquisitions, either as a target or as an acquirer. This is a much more innocuous interpretation of the decline in IPOs by small firms. In Ritter's view, the decline in small-cap IPOs has been the result of profit-maximizing decisions driven by the changing structure of the economy than by restrictions that place a disproportionate burden on small firms that go public. He supports his argument by noting that small firms now have a much greater tendency to engage in mergers and acquisitions than in earlier decades and that small-cap firms do not appear to have attempted to avoid the costs of a public issue in the United States by making use of alternative European markets that have lower costs, which would be expected if IPOs were a more profitable strategy. Moreover, the average flow of venture capital into new technology has been higher since the collapse of the high-tech bubble in 2000 than in the late 1990s, indicating that venture capitalists have not been deterred by the decline of activity in the market for IPOs.

Does it follow that the decline in the volume of IPOs is irrelevant? Ritter notes that we cannot determine whether the volume of IPOs is too low because we do not know what the optimal volume of IPOs should be. We do know, however, that it should be expected to vary over time. Public policy toward IPOs, he believes, should be framed as part of a broader attempt to enhance the efficiency of all capital markets. Tax and investor protection measures should not be designed to channel subsidies to small-cap firms.

Ritter favors three broad kinds of policies that should boost the efficiency in the allocation of capital more generally and lead to higher rates of growth. First, he favors policies that lower the costs of going public, which, on average, reduce the value of a firm by 5 percent. He believes that the costs of distribution by investment banks through book building are too high, in part because the SEC does not require all of them to be disclosed. He sees this asymmetry in the disclosure requirements for direct and indirect costs (respectively, explicit fees and underpricing) as shielding an important conflict of interest between small firms and their underwriters. Underpricing of IPOs may facilitate the initial placement of shares, but it also enables underwriters to benefit from the allocation of IPOs to hedge funds and other lucrative clients, who, in return, are willing to overpay on their own commissions. Ritter believes that the extent of underpricing would decrease if the SEC were to require disclosure of these indirect costs in the same way it requires disclosure of the direct costs of underwriting. In addition, it might lead to greater experimentation with IPO auctions, an alternative to book building, which might also reduce the underpricing of IPOs.

Second, Ritter believes that the cost of operating as a publicly traded firm could be reduced if liability laws were reformed to limit class-action lawsuits and redirect sanctions from firms to the executives responsible for the alleged misdeeds. This would reduce the cost of liability insurance for directors, legal expenses, and the costs incurred in complying with discovery motions. The shift might also prove a more effective deterrent to malfeasance than the current system in which corporations are the targets of class-action suits.

Third, Ritter argues that the pace of innovation could be increased if copyright and patent laws were reformed to enable the creator of an innovation to capture some of the benefits of the innovation by creating a *temporary* monopoly. He would like to eliminate the current U.S. practice of extending the monopoly long after the death of the creator, a period when the harm done to the distribution of knowledge is likely to be greater than the enhancement of incentives to create innovations. At the same time, he warns that lack of enforcement of intellectual property rights can undermine the appropriate incentives to invest in innovation.

In the discussion following Ritter's presentation, several participants expressed surprise that the decline in IPOs could have had such a minimal impact on investment in high-growth start-up firms. Ritter noted that his argument applies mainly to IPOs in certain industries such as biotechnology firms, communications firms, and other high-tech start-ups, which are likely to have a positive impact on growth and employment. In these industries, becoming large very quickly appears to have strong advantages. At the same time, he emphasizes that start-ups in other kinds of industries are much less likely to have such a large positive impact on overall employment and economic growth. For example, the growth of a restaurant chain may be profitable to its owners but have little impact on overall employment because its growth comes largely at the expense of competing restaurants. Questions were also raised about the extent to which auctions of IPOs could substitute efficiently for the traditional book-building approach to distributing the shares of investment banks.

Lessons from Japan

In chapter 5, Yuta Seki of the Nomura Institute of Capital Markets Research reflects on lessons learned from Japan's two-decade-long attempt to reform its financial system to facilitate economic recovery. He begins by discussing current economic conditions in the United States, characterized by the recovery of share prices and earnings at large lenders but lingering issues in the real economy. In his view, this situation is reminiscent of the Japanese economy in the 1990s.

Seki proceeds to discuss the events surrounding the collapse of the Japanese real estate bubble in the early 1990s. Sharp appreciation in land prices during the bubble years encouraged excessive and speculative lending practices, with, for instance, typical loan-to-value ratios climbing from 70 percent to upward of 120 percent before the bubble burst. Further, Japanese banks often assumed loans based on junior liens, which eventually served to hamper them in seizing or selling collateral once the market started to turn. Without the capacity to sell collateral, it became impossible to determine the amount of uncollectable loans, disturbing the confidence in markets.

After the collapse of the real estate bubble, Japanese financial institutions had a difficult time disposing of nonperforming loans, which contributed to the extended length of the economic malaise. Seki attributes Japan's slow progress in disposing of nonperforming loans to four factors. First, the sheer depth of the crisis complicated the recovery: the Nikkei Average plunged approximately 78 percent from its peak, and commercial land prices dropped a precipitous 85 percent. Second, there was no established framework for resolving large financial institutions. The Deposit Insurance Corporation of Japan had only envisioned needing to resolve small lenders and was not prepared to handle bank failures on the magnitude of the crisis. Therefore, the resolution process implied that depositors were likely to take a haircut, and regulators feared the substantial risk of bank runs. Third, there was no legal or financial framework for restructuring debt. The Japanese had no reorganization procedures akin to those of Chapter 11 of the U.S. Bankruptcy Code, and thus there was no way of passing ownership of nonperforming loans onto distressed debt funds or other specialist institutions. Consequently, real estate loans locked up on balance sheets, which prevented redevelopment and reuse of real estate and had pernicious effects on the real economy. Fourth, as markets seized, banks had difficulty raising capital, which further depressed their share price and credit, creating a vicious cycle. Simultaneously, pressure from investors, counterparties, and regulators led banks to record the minimum allowable loan loss reserves in order to preserve their capital ratios. Altogether, these factors contributed to delaying the disposition of nonperforming loans.

As asset prices began rising in the late 1990s, the Japanese economy seemed to be improving, but after the collapse of the tech bubble in mid-2000, the nascent recovery stagnated. Widespread belief that the nonperforming loan problem was the root cause of the poor state of financial markets pressured the government to address the issue. This prompted the administration of Prime Minister Junichiro Koizumi and his two successive ministers responsible for the financial services industry, Hakuo Yanagisawa and Heizo Takenaka, to take measures aimed at facilitating financial institutions' disposal of nonperforming loans.

Yanagisawa, who had been appointed minister of state for financial services by Yoshiro Mori in January 2001, built a platform with Prime Minister Junichiro Koizumi focused on broad structural reform of the financial sector and supply-side-oriented policy. To this end, Yanagisawa proposed direct write-offs and final disposition of nonperforming loans in place of the indirect write-off methods that the banks preferred, namely increasing loan loss reserves as the quality of loan assets deteriorated. Direct write-offs entailed court-ordered liquidation of borrowers, loan sales, and debt forgiveness based on borrowers' restructuring plans. Additionally, in an effort to make the nonperforming loan problem more transparent, Yanagisawa led the Financial Services Agency in conducting special inspections of banks' internal assessments of major borrowers. The inspections focused on the management of credit to large borrowers that posed systemic risks and sought to create a consistent system of loan categorization so as to ensure that different banks would not categorize loans to the same borrower differently. Banks responded to these policies by aggressively disposing of nonperforming loans and coping with the associated losses. But the stagnating economy, coupled with the ongoing special inspections, caused the amount of nonperforming loans held by the major banks to increase a significant 47 percent year-over-year. The ensuing criticism of Yanagisawa led to his dismissal in September 2002, and the minister of state for economic and fiscal policy, Heizo Takenaka, took on the additional role of minister of state for financial services.

In October 2002, Takenaka presented his Financial Revival Program, which became nicknamed the Takenaka Plan. The plan set a target of cutting the non-performing loan ratio from 8.4 percent in fiscal 2002 to half of that by fiscal 2004. The program involved various policies aimed at providing support for troubled lenders and incentivizing the major banks to write off nonperforming loans. The Takenaka Plan set dual goals of revitalizing financial institutions in order to regain the trust of markets and corporations and to promote sustainable financial positions and better business models. In the absence of private equity and securitization markets, the plan also set about instituting the legal infrastructure, markets, and personnel needed to revitalize distressed companies.

Altogether, the Takenaka Plan called for three new frameworks: one for the financial system, one for corporate reorganization, and one for financial regulation.

Seki then outlines the three prongs of the Japanese government's solution to the nonperforming loan problem: promoting the final disposition of nonperforming loans, creating a system to encourage borrowers to recapitalize, and facilitating real estate market liquidity.

The Japanese government created various incentives to encourage financial institutions to dispose of nonperforming loans. First, they required banks that received public injections of capital to submit business improvement plans that were subjected to quarterly reviews. Furthermore, passage of the Rapid Recapitalization Act authorized the Financial Services Agency (FSA) to issue business improvement orders to banks that failed to meet the targets for return on equity and net profit; typically, when results fell short of targets by 30 percent or more, the FSA would respond with a business improvement order, a practice that became known as the 30 percent rule. Since the issuance of a business improvement order implicitly expressed disapproval of bank management, it often led to the installation of a new bank management team. Therefore, the 30 percent rule put significant pressure on the banks, creating incentives for them to dispose of nonperforming loans quickly in order to protect management autonomy.

The Japanese government also sought to unify the disclosure standards for nonperforming loans and to establish a special inspection scheme. Japanese policymakers had difficulty assessing the scale of bad assets when the bubble first began to collapse, partially due to the lack of unified and transparent loan classification standards. Although the Financial Reconstruction Act of 1998 settled on a definition of nonperforming loan categories and disclosure requirements, discrepancies persisted between the banks' internal assessments, public disclosures, and assessments by foreign investment banks. The special inspection scheme and its corollary parts finally changed the situation. First, the scheme served as a real-time check on banks' borrower classifications and helped to restore the confidence of market participants. Second, the scheme prevented banks from using different categories for borrowers with large loans from multiple lenders. Third, the special inspections yielded synergies with earlier rules for removing nonperforming loans from bank balance sheets. Fourth, the special inspections scheme complemented the backstop of public funds that the Takenaka Plan facilitated.

The second prong of Japan's financial restoration sought to encourage borrowers to recapitalize. The Civil Rehabilitation Act was instrumental in establishing a system of support for corporate reorganization procedures. The act provided for speedier and more flexible reorganizations and created incentives for business managers to pursue strategic restructurings. Additionally, the Resolution

Collection Corporation (RCC) and the Industrial Revitalization Corporation of Japan (IRCJ) both played important roles in facilitating the disposal of distressed debt. The RCC, modeled after the Resolution Trust Corporation, established during the S&L crisis in the United States, coordinated corporate reorganization and assisted companies in working through complicated debt claims. The RCC, however, lacked the resources to deal with large corporate borrowers, which led to the establishment of the IRCJ, which was authorized to purchase debt claims for up to two years and was mandated to close after five. Funded by the DICJ and Norinchukin Bank, the IRCJ received guarantees on its loans from the Japanese government for up to ¥10 trillion and provided assistance in forty-one cases. The IRCJ effectively acted as a buyout fund with government guarantees and received high marks for its success and the earnings that it was able to generate. The experience and human capital built up at the IRCJ contributed to the development of Japan's buyout market after the organization was disbanded.

The third and final prong that Seki discusses, the revival of liquidity in the real estate market, was largely accomplished through the introduction of real estate securitization and real estate investment trusts (REITs). The securitization of real estate loans and other types of debt began in 1998 with temporary legislation authorizing special-purpose companies to securitize assets, while the legal framework for doing so was established by the Asset Securitization Act of 2000. That same year, the Revised Investment Trusts Act authorized the formation of REITs; by September 2001, two REITs were listed on the Tokyo Stock Exchange. As the market was forming, securitized assets were composed primarily of operating properties with relatively favorable locations as opposed to traditional nonperforming assets such as land set aside for failed development projects. Hence, although real estate securitization itself did not contribute directly to cutting the amount of nonperforming loans, the securitization market fueled a gradual increase in real estate transactions and restored liquidity in the market, indirectly creating an environment more conducive to the disposal of properties by large borrowers and lenders.

Seki concludes by expounding on relevant lessons for policymakers from Japan's experience. First, he argues that when a collapsed asset bubble affects the real economy, a solution is unlikely to be reached by focusing exclusively on lenders. Japan's financial revival depended on policies that revitalized corporate borrowers in addition to policies geared toward incentivizing financial institutions to remove nonperforming loans. Second, he argues that the Japan case demonstrates the effectiveness of policies tied to market mechanisms. The Financial Revival Program in Japan, for instance, encouraged banks to dispose of nonperforming loans and recapitalize voluntarily, thereby beginning the process of revitalization with those banks favored by the market. Additionally, Japan's success in laying the groundwork for markets in securitization and reorganization was essential for reviving corporate borrowers and restoring liquidity.

Discussion focused on possible parallels between the Japanese experience during the 1990s and the more recent U.S. experience. On the surface, the similarities are striking. The Japanese financial crisis began with the collapse of a massive real estate bubble after which the Japanese government tried to offset the shock with a huge fiscal stimulus that failed to kick-start the economy. It also experimented with unconventional monetary policy that had negligible impact on restoring growth. Business proved unwilling to make new investments despite very liquid balance sheets, and the government lacked a framework for restructuring large, complex financial institutions that held much of the bad debt and were obliged to deleverage rather than resume lending. The Japanese economy has languished over two decades and is only now showing signs of more robust recovery. Some participants argued that these similarities were more apparent than real. In particular, they noted that the U.S. government had moved much more quickly to restructure bad debts and that the bankruptcy system had facilitated the reallocation of resources. Other participants felt that the Japanese experience could not be dismissed so easily, noting the Fed's fear of falling into a Japanese-style deflation, the meager evidence that quantitative easing is working, and the disappointingly sluggish U.S. recovery. One participant noted that many of the structural reforms introduced in Japan to hasten recovery—securitization, bankruptcy proceedings that can result in reorganization, and mechanisms for resolving financial institutions—did not prevent the United States from falling into a deep recession and an agonizingly slow recovery.

Conclusions

The Brookings, Nomura, Wharton conference papers spanned a range of vital issues for restructuring the financial sector and aiding the recovery of the real economy following the crisis. Problems in the mortgage market in the United States were at the heart of the near collapse of American financial institutions and the spread of the crisis around the world. Redesigning that market and the role of government-sponsored enterprises remains a huge and uncompleted task that will be easier as a result of the paper by Allen, Barth, and Yago, which uses both an historical and a comparative approach and draws out clear policy recommendations.

One of toughest lessons learned in the crisis is that no effective mechanisms were in place to resolve financial institutions that got into trouble. Policymakers were scrambling to decide whether to bail out failing institutions or let them fail.

Taxpayer funds were put at risk, and there was inconsistent treatment of different players. Jackson and Skeel make a powerful case for bankruptcy as the most effective and fair mechanism for resolving troubled institutions, emphasizing the importance of having a predictable path for such cases. Such a path takes away concerns about moral hazard, protects taxpayers, and makes sure that market participants know what risks they are facing.

The revival of the real economy depends heavily on innovation and the growth of young companies and the ability of the economy to fund that segment. Ritter's paper helps us to understand what has been behind the sharp drop in the number of IPOs and which policies may be effective and which may be ineffective. Ritter argues that, for many young companies, merging into larger existing companies has become more attractive than growing organically through an IPO.

Seki's paper has offered important lessons about why the Japanese financial crisis lasted so long and what was needed eventually to turn the corner. The failure to recognize and deal with bad debts dragged down the economy, a heavy weight that was finally lifted by courageous policy efforts. Both the United States and, perhaps especially, Europe would do well to study this history as they continue to struggle in their own economic recovery efforts.

PART I

The U.S. Approach

FRANKLIN ALLEN
JAMES R. BARTH
GLENN YAGO

2

Restructuring the U.S. Housing Market

HOUSING PEOPLE IS one of the most important businesses in the world. The value of global housing reached a record high of slightly more than $90 trillion in 2008.[1] In the United States, residential investment averages roughly 5 percent of gross domestic product (GDP), while housing services average between 12 and 13 percent, for a combined 17 to 18 percent of GDP.[2] In other big countries such as China and India, housing makes up 15 and 5 percent of GDP, respectively. Housing, moreover, is an important component of wealth for its owners. Indeed, in countries such as Finland, Germany, Italy, Sweden, and the United Kingdom, housing accounts for more than 60 percent of household wealth, while in countries such as Spain it accounts for as much as 75 percent. In China and the United States, the corresponding figures are 41 and 26 percent, respectively.[3] In the United States, housing accounts for between 77 and 85 percent of tangible household assets. Changes in such a large portion of household wealth due to changing housing prices can potentially have significant effects on consumer spending and therefore on overall economic activity.

This paper is based on our book, *Fixing the Housing Market* (Allen, Barth, and Yago 2012). We gratefully acknowledge the excellent assistance provided by Nan (Annie) Zhang, a research assistant at the Milken Institute.

1. McKinsey & Company (2009).
2. National Association of Home Builders (www.nahb.org/generic.aspx?genericContentID=66226).
3. Peterson Institute for International Economics (2012).

In recent years, too much credit flowed into the housing market in many countries, contributing to housing price booms and busts. As a result, the housing markets in the United States and other countries suffered severely when housing prices collapsed. Among thirty-nine countries surveyed, twenty-six recorded home price declines and eighteen experienced accelerating rates of decline in recent years.[4] Given the importance of housing for the financial and real sectors in countries, this situation contributed to the global financial crisis and economic recession. The United States suffered a severe credit crunch and its worst recession since the Great Depression. In this regard, Robert Shiller has noted, "Residential construction as a percentage of gross domestic product has had a prominent peak before almost every recession since 1950."[5]

In this paper, we look beyond the booms and inevitable busts of real estate markets to examine prospective ways to promote better-functioning housing finance systems to support homeownership. As always, though, before moving forward, we have to understand the past.

Some Early History

The first evidence of the existence of mortgages was *horoi,* or "mortgage stones," in ancient Athens. These were markers used to indicate that a property was mortgaged and to identify the creditors.[6] By the late twelfth century, mortgages had reappeared in England in the form of common-law financial instruments to enable the purchase and sale of property. Real estate debts that were not paid could be recovered by lenders in property sales.

In the eighteenth century, early land developers designed financial contracts in which real estate investors would buy not an entire large tract, but a segment for development and resale accompanied by an option to purchase the adjacent segment. The pioneers in this effort were John Wood and his son, whose projects in Bath, England, used this method to integrate individual housing units and related commercial space to develop the city. Wood went beyond the city limits of Bath to an area unencumbered by regulations and leased land for ninety-nine years, with each lease based on the performance of the development of the previous one. By utilizing options, he was able to circumvent land laws, raise debt and equity financing, and lease and manage related properties.

---

4. Global Property Guide (2011).
5. Shiller (2007).
6. Fine (1951).

This was the beginning of urban real estate development and residential housing finance as we know it today.[7]

Presidents Jefferson and Lincoln and Promoting Homeownership

Even as urbanization and residential development grew in the eighteenth and nineteenth centuries throughout Europe and the United States, agriculture remained the most important contributor to economic growth. Homeownership accompanied reform and expansion of landownership for farming. By 1890 in the United States, two-thirds of all farm housing was owner-occupied, increasingly so throughout the 1900s. At the same time, homeownership was less prevalent in urban areas. Over time, however, the overall homeownership rate increased from 45 percent at the beginning of the 1900s to between 60 and 70 percent in 1960. As figure 2-1 shows, it has remained at that level ever since.[8] The costs associated with homeownership have represented an increasingly larger portion of consumer spending, especially since the turn of the twentieth century, as the homeownership rate increased, the size of homes expanded, and home prices trended upward. Possession of land and property, especially homes, reinforced some main drivers of nation building—thrift, industriousness, occupational mobility, citizenship, and economic security.

There was a surge in the demand for housing brought about by increased commercial activities in cities and population growth and the westward expansion of settlements for thirty years after the American Revolution. Providing access to capital in the form of land for individual owners, opening markets globally for their products, committing funds to internal improvements, and opposing fiscal measures that hurt taxpayers were all part of Jefferson's policies. Limiting formal authority, deferring to individual freedom, and committing to growth through access to economic opportunity were the keys to economic and political democracy. These notions were the very definition of "Americanism"—a term coined by Jefferson and which he counterposed to "aristocracy." He argued consistently against the dominance by a new elite group of wealth and privilege and gave high priority to laws that would prevent the concentration of landed wealth. It was in

---

7. Rabinowitz (2002).

8. According to Collins and Margo (1999), "In 1900, only 16 percent of all white male household heads held a mortgage and only 6 percent of blacks did, but by 1990, 57 percent of whites held a mortgage compared to 43 percent of blacks." The rate of owner occupancy for African Americans was 8 percent in 1870 and 54 percent in 2007 (Collins and Margo 2011).

Figure 2-1. *Homeownership Rate in the United States, 1900–2012 Q2*[a]

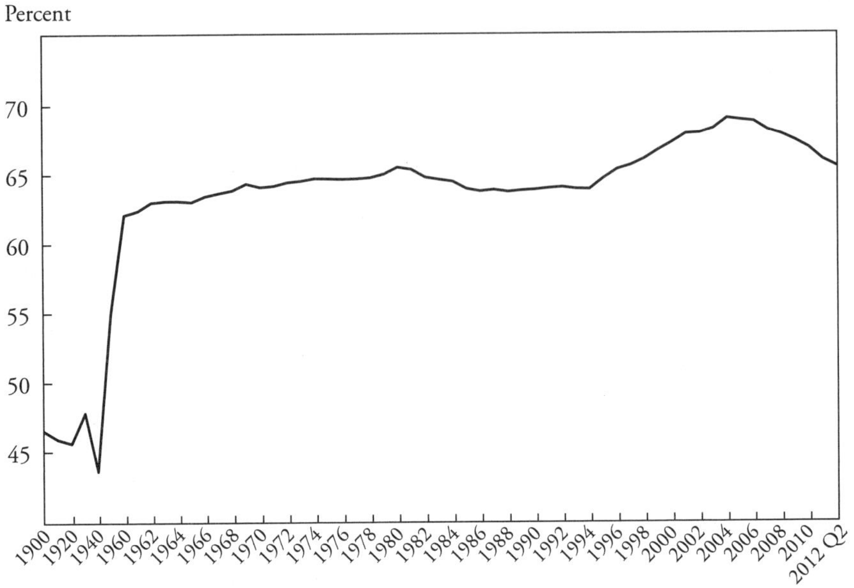

Percent

Source: U.S. Census Bureau.
a. Data from 1910 to 1960 are for decades; annual data are given thereafter.

this context that land reform and home finance merged in public and financial policies and programs.

Focusing on land and homeownership, the Homestead Movement was geared to opening opportunities for would-be farmers in an age when this occupation was still considered the norm. Ever since passage of the Land Ordinance of 1785 and the Land Act of 1796, the federal government provided assistance to settlers in the form of low-priced land. Other acts followed with regularity, such as the Pre-emption Act of 1841, which permitted would-be settlers to stake claims on most surveyed lands and to buy up to 160 acres for a minimum price of $1.25 per acre.

In 1862, Lincoln signed into law the Homestead Act. Under its terms, any citizen or person intending to become a citizen who headed a family and was over the age of twenty-one could receive 160 acres of land, clear title to which would be conveyed after five years and payment of a registration fee. As an alternative, after six months the land could be bought for $1.60 an acre. This established housing and landownership as common American goals.

On January 1, 1863, Daniel Freeman and 417 others filed homestead claims, and more pioneers followed. By 1934, over 1.6 million homestead applications had been filed, and more than 270 million acres representing 10 percent of the U.S. land mass passed to individuals in the largest capital distribution measure in public policy.[9] The ethos and purpose of this transfer infused housing policy for years to come.

Considerable restrictions were placed on the ability to access capital and asset markets for agricultural and industrial workers throughout the nineteenth century. Aside from savings accounts and insurance policies, real estate in the form of houses and lots was a new investment objective of savers.

Without large-scale pension plans, homes were a major way to accumulate wealth, and owner-occupied homes could also be a source of income through rentals and boarding. The choice of home tenure—between renting and owning—emerged in this social, political, and economic context as property markets grew in the nineteenth century with industrialization. Wealth accumulation became concentrated in real property as society became more urban and less rural, with the associated increase in homeownership. These developments set the stage for the genesis of modern housing finance.

For many, homeownership is the "American Dream" as well as an indicator of status, position, and individual identity. But for most, the dream could not come true without taking advantage of lending practices that have evolved in the United States since pre–Civil War days, with the birth of the savings and loan industry.

Modern Housing Finance in the United States

The financial system in a modern economy facilitates the transfer of resources from savers to borrowers. This allows the productive sectors to invest in capital necessary for growth. The financial system also allows consumers to adjust to variations in income over time so as to smooth consumption. Homeownership, of course, requires financing given the price of housing relative to the typical homeowner's income. The modern financing of housing largely began with the savings and loan industry in the United States.

Origin and Development of Savings and Loan Associations

The first American savings and loan institution was organized in 1831 to enable its member shareholders to pool their savings so that a subset of them could obtain financing to build or buy homes. Every member was to be afforded the opportunity, over time, of borrowing funds for this purpose, with the association terminating after the last member was accommodated. Association membership

9. National Archives and Records Administration (2010).

was geographically restricted: no loans were made for homes located more than five miles from the institution.

This first savings and loan was organized as a mutual institution and therefore owned by its shareholder members. Shareholders were expected to remain with the institution throughout its life, but those wishing to withdraw their shares were allowed to do so if they gave a month's notice and paid a penalty of 5 percent of their withdrawal. The association's balance sheet consisted of mortgage loans as assets and ownership shares as liabilities, with relatively little net worth. These shares were the precursor of the savings deposits held today.

These institutions served the important role of consolidating the savings of a group of local individuals and rechanneling the funds to these same individuals in the form of mortgage loans. Thus savings and loans filled a niche that was woefully underserviced by other financial institutions at the time. Only much later did borrowers and savers become separate and distinct customers of these institutions.

Originally, institutions of this type were called building societies because they bought land and built homes. When they began lending to members to build their own homes, they were referred to as building and loan associations. After the 1930s, they tended to be called savings and loan associations.

Perhaps it is not surprising that the need for financing for home purchases went largely unfulfilled by commercial and mutual savings banks.[10] These financial entities preceded the development of savings and loans, but neither catered to the housing market. Commercial banks issued liabilities consisting primarily of currency and demand deposits that were acceptable to their customers because they were meant to be backed by self-liquidating commercial loans. These banks catered to the short-term business loan market.

Mutual savings banks did not issue currency or accept demand deposits, but were involved with the savings of the general public. Unlike savings and loans, however, they were originally philanthropic. Their intent was to provide financial services for the small saver, which required that their deposits be more flexible in terms of amounts and maturities and correspondingly required a much more flexible asset portfolio than just mortgages. Each type of institution specialized in a particular market, and the specialization was reflected in the balance sheets of these financial firms.

After the organization of the first savings and loans, similar institutions spread throughout the United States—for example, entering New York in 1836, South Carolina in 1843, and what is now Oklahoma in 1890. As these associations spread throughout the country, innovations began to occur. For example, the

---

10. Credit unions did not come into existence until the early 1900s.

self-terminating type of institution was replaced by a more permanent type, and the borrowers were separated from the savers. Thus these firms began to operate with a long-term horizon in mind, and they began to accept shareholders who were not obliged to take out mortgage loans. This not only enlarged the pool of potential shareholders but also emphasized the savings aspect of membership in an association. So the link between borrower and saver began to dissipate despite the mutual form of organization under which these firms usually operated. These institutions generally did not take deposits per se; in many states, in fact, they were precluded by law from doing so. It was not until the advent of federal deposit insurance for savings and loans in the 1930s that the taking of deposits as such became widespread.[11]

Over time, competition from commercial banks was beginning to develop. In the early 1900s, national banks were informed that they were not prohibited from accepting savings deposits. Moreover, Federal Reserve member banks were given an incentive to use this source of funds when a lower reserve requirement was placed on savings accounts than on demand deposits.

On the asset side, competition for residential mortgages was also beginning to develop between savings and loans and banks, albeit to a much lower degree. Without active secondary markets and with somewhat restrictive regulations, the two types of depository institutions found that comparative advantages in information collection and processing, as well as the favorable tax treatment afforded savings and loans, still led to fairly identifiable balance sheet differences.

Thus as the economic boom of the 1920s began, the banks and savings and loans maintained different balance sheets, competed only indirectly, and were regulated to a different degree and by different levels of government. The federal regulators were most interested in commercial banks and the payments mechanism, while the state governments were most directly involved with savings and loans and their role in facilitating homeownership.

Savings and Loan Associations and the Great Depression

In the first 150 years of their existence, savings and loans have only suffered two large-scale failures. The first was the Great Depression of the 1930s, and the second was the severe economic downturn of the 1980s.

During the depression, savings and loans did not accept demand deposits and therefore did not suffer the runs that plagued commercial banks. Nevertheless, their members had to draw on their savings to maintain consumption. Savings and loans were hard-pressed to cope with these withdrawals because their assets

11. Bodfish (1931, pp. 95–96).

were almost entirely mortgages, and they prided themselves on maintaining low liquidity levels. Moreover, reserves for losses were relatively low because "many state laws . . . discouraged the accumulation of reserves and some supervisory authorities practically forced the distribution of all earnings."[12] As withdrawals mounted and assets declined in value due to delinquencies and defaults, savings and loans failed. These failures severely limited the flow of funds to housing.[13]

This disruption in the housing market finally changed the role of the federal government in the regulation of the savings and loan industry.

First, on July 22, 1932, the Federal Home Loan Bank Act was signed by President Hoover. This act set up the Federal Home Loan (FHL) bank system, consisting of twelve regional FHL banks under the supervision of the Federal Home Loan Bank Board (FHLBB) in Washington. The main purpose of the system was to strengthen member savings and loan associations financially by providing them with an alternative and steady source of funds to promote homeownership. The system was designed so that the FHL banks could issue bonds in the capital markets and thus be able to provide advances to healthy and reasonably safe institutions.

Second, the Home Owners' Loan Act was signed on June 13, 1933. Although the main purpose of the act was to facilitate the refinancing of mortgages in distress cases, many borrowers seeking the more favorable interest rate and other terms offered by the government were also able to obtain loans. This led many borrowers deliberately to default on their existing loans, thus exacerbating the problems of savings and loans.[14] Another purpose of the 1933 act was to allow the FHLBB to charter federal savings and loans. The aim was to establish savings and loans in places where the state institutions were providing insufficient service.

Finally, the National Housing Act, enacted on June 27, 1934, created the Federal Savings and Loan Insurance Corporation (FSLIC) to provide deposit insurance for savings deposits at savings and loans. Membership in the FSLIC was made compulsory for federal associations and optional for state-chartered associations. With the establishment of the FSLIC, the savings and loans were placed on an equal footing with commercial banks, which were insured by the Federal Deposit Insurance Corporation (FDIC). Eventually, the FDIC would become the administrator of federal deposit insurance for savings and loans as well. On March 31, 2006, the FDIC merged the Bank Insurance Fund and the

---

12. Bodfish (1931, p. 7).

13. According to Bodfish (1935, p. 22), "One-half of the counties in the United States as a result of the Great Depression now had no mortgage loan institutions or facilities."

14. Bodfish (1935, p. 21).

Savings Association Insurance Fund to become the Deposit Insurance Fund. The merger was mandated by the Federal Deposit Insurance Reform Act of 2005.

Postwar Growth and Diversification in the Savings and Loan Industry

Following the Great Depression and World War II, savings and loans experienced tremendous growth for close to four decades. They surpassed mutual savings banks in terms of total assets for the first time in 1954 and grew to half the size of the commercial banking industry by the end of 1980. This expansion was spread throughout the entire industry, with large and small institutions participating.

The magnitude of the redistribution is remarkable. Private financial assets in 1945 totaled $247 billion. Of this amount, savings and loan associations held a meager 3 percent, compared to 65 percent for commercial banks. By 1975, however, savings and loans had increased their share of the total to 16 percent, while the share for commercial banks had dropped to 37 percent. Mutual savings banks and life insurance companies also lost considerable ground during this period. Moreover, although the share of total financial assets accounted for by all of the depository financial services firms declined to 51 percent from 76 percent, the share of savings and loans quintupled.

Tax law in the savings and loan industry came into play in 1951. Before the Revenue Act of 1951, savings and loans were exempt from federal income taxes. Although this act terminated their tax-exempt status, savings and loans nonetheless were able to avoid paying taxes because they were permitted essentially to deduct up to 100 percent of taxable income through a bad-debt reserve.

In 1962, however, another revenue act was passed that reduced the bad-debt deduction to 60 percent of taxable income, subject to a qualifying asset restriction. This restriction stated that for a savings and loan to be eligible for the maximum deduction, 82 percent or more of its assets had to consist of cash, U.S. government securities, and passbook loans, plus one- to four-family residential property loans. The deduction was zero if these assets fell below 60 percent. The Tax Equity and Fiscal Responsibility Act of 1982 further reduced the bad-debt deduction to 34 percent in 1982 and then to 32 percent in 1984. The Tax Reform Act of 1986 reduced the bad-debt deduction as a percentage of taxable income to 8 percent in 1987. Thus, over time, the tax laws have provided a large but diminishing incentive to invest in eligible mortgage-related assets.

In addition to the tax laws, there were regulations pertaining to FHLBB-member associations, FSLIC-insured associations, federal associations, and state associations. The Interest Rate Control Act of 1966, for example, gave the FHLBB the authority to set rate ceilings, which until then had been nonexistent, on the savings deposits of member associations. This ceiling was set initially at one-half of 1 percent but later was reduced to one-fourth of 1 percent above the ceiling rate that commercial banks were permitted to pay on savings deposits. The ceiling represented an attempt to provide a competitive edge to savings and loans to garner funds for the residential housing sector. This differential was abolished in January 1984, and all rate ceilings for depository institutions were eliminated in March 1986.

The regulations for federal associations were initially quite direct in their intention to limit lending to local home mortgage loans, which meant loans secured by houses within 50 miles of the association's home office.

In 1964, federal associations were permitted to make unsecured, personal loans for college or educational expenses—the first time they had been allowed to make loans for any purpose other than acquiring real estate.

In the same year, the geographic limit for mortgage loans was extended to 100 miles. Later, Congress extended this limit to encompass the association's home state—and beyond that for the largest savings and loans. Then, in 1983, the FHLBB permitted federal associations to make loans nationwide. Unless prohibited by state law, state associations with FSLIC insurance were permitted to do the same.

Federal associations were also permitted in 1964 to issue mortgages and buy property in urban renewal areas and to buy securities issued by federal, state, and municipal governments. And then in 1968, these associations were allowed to make loans for mobile homes, second or vacation homes, and housing fixtures. Thus began the entry of savings and loans into business areas long viewed as the exclusive domain of commercial banks.

Turbulent 1980s for the Savings and Loan Industry

As interest rates rose unexpectedly and fluctuated widely in the late 1970s and the early 1980s, it became very clear that many savings and loans were ill equipped to handle the new financial environment. Their newly authorized market-rate deposits were rapidly escalating their cost of funds, while the largely fixed-rate mortgage portfolios were painfully slow to turn over.

The result was rapidly deteriorating profits and a significant increase in failures. The problems persisted—even as interest rates declined in 1982 and the maturity-mismatch problem lessened—due to a growing deterioration in the quality of assets held by many associations.

The savings and loan industry's ratio of net worth to total assets fell from more than 5 percent at the end of 1979 to 3.4 percent at the end of 1985. Over this same period, more than 500 savings and loans failed, and an additional 400 or so were left with negative net worth. By the end of the decade, approximately 500 more associations had failed, and the government had bailed out the industry. A few years later, the insurance fund for savings and loans was merged into the insurance fund for commercial banks.

The turbulence of the early 1980s, however, did more than reduce the number of institutions. It permanently affected the way savings and loans were to do business. Instead of just savings and time deposits, these institutions began to offer transaction accounts, large certificates of deposit, and consumer repurchase agreements—virtually as wide a selection as that of any commercial bank. On the asset side, these institutions went beyond mortgages to hold consumer loans, commercial loans, mortgage-backed securities, and a wide variety of direct investments. As such, savings and loans were from then on to differ from commercial banks more as a matter of degree than of kind. The distinctions among the depository financial services firms became forever blurred.

Variable-rate mortgages, which existed in the early 1970s in some states such as Wisconsin and California, were rejected by Congress on a national basis in 1974. Although federally chartered savings and loans were allowed to issue variable-rate mortgages in states where state-chartered institutions were permitted to do so, it was not until January 1, 1979, that all federally chartered savings and loans were allowed to offer variable-rate, graduated-payment, and reverse-annuity mortgages on a national basis.

Sources of Funding for Home Purchases and Homeownership Rates

In addition to savings and loans, noninstitutional sources were major providers of home finance before World War II. Frederiksen reported that in the late 1800s about 55 percent of mortgages in the country were held by local investors who made the loans or sold the property themselves, and about 18 percent were held by nonresident investors. "So that in America," he wrote, "the making of a mortgage loan is essentially a local transaction."[15] He further noted, "It is entirely satisfactory only when the investor is personally familiar with the property mortgaged, and the insurance is kept up, and when, furthermore, he is able at any time to take steps to protect himself in case of default."

Frederiksen's study indicates that the mortgages averaged less than half of the value of the mortgaged property and that less than half of the property in America was under mortgage.[16] When local investors were replaced increasingly

15. Frederiksen (1894).
16. Frederiksen (1894).

by more formal and more regulated sources after World War II, two major real estate crises occurred, one in the 1980s and the other in the late 2000s, with the most recent one more widespread and costly than the earlier crisis. Most prior instances of bubbles in the United States had been purely local in nature. Certainly regulation played a role in the recent crisis, but national markets that are to some extent facilitated by the rise of standardization and more regulated sources of funding should help to buffer local supply and demand shocks. This suggests that the management of monetary policy was an important cause of a national bubble rather than regulation per se.

As shown in table 2-1, savings and loans were a major provider of funding for housing until 1980. Afterward, commercial banks became more important than savings and loans. But in recent decades, government-sponsored enterprises have dominated the field.

As shown in figure 2-2, financing of homeownership differs substantially across countries. In the United States, securitization has clearly become very important, while in Denmark covered bonds dominate. In other countries, such as Australia, Austria, Finland, France, Germany, Greece, and Japan, homeownership has been financed largely through the use of deposits at financial institutions.

In 1769, Frederick the Great of Prussia structured the first covered bonds in the aftermath of the Seven Years' War to ease the credit shortage in agriculture. These bonds were later extended to provide funding for residential and commercial real estate. Issued by banks and secured by a pool of mortgages, covered bonds resemble mortgage-backed securities, with the exception that bondholders have recourse to the underlying collateral of those bonds because the mortgages stay on the balance sheets of issuing banks.[17] The holders of covered bonds also have recourse to the bank that issued the covered bonds if the value of the pool of mortgages should prove insufficient.

The use of covered bonds has been largely restricted to European countries, with the spread to Canada and the United States being a recent development. These bonds are the primary source of mortgage funding for European banks. As compared to the securitization used by banks in the United States, covered bonds have a cost disadvantage due to greater capital requirements.[18] In addition, the FDIC is unhappy about the use of covered bonds in the United States, as they create a class of claimants that stand in front of the FDIC in a liquidation.

Figure 2-3 shows the extent to which mortgage-backed covered bonds played a role in financing homeownership in 2010. Denmark is notable, with covered bonds accounting for 100 percent of residential loans outstanding. In the United

17. Allen and Yago (2010) and Paulson (2008).
18. For further discussion, see Bernanke (2009).

Table 2-1. *Nonfarm Residential Mortgage Holdings in the United States, by Type of Institution, 1900–2012 Q2*

Year	Total holdings (US$ billions)	Commercial banks	Savings and loans[a]	Life insurance companies	Government-sponsored enterprises[b]	Other[c]
			Percentage of total holdings			
1900	2.92	5.42	34.38	6.27	0.00	53.93
1905	3.52	8.32	36.08	7.22	0.00	48.38
1910	4.43	10.05	40.69	9.11	0.00	40.15
1915	6.01	9.41	41.82	8.68	0.00	40.09
1920	9.12	8.77	39.93	6.12	0.00	45.18
1925	17.23	10.78	40.80	8.17	0.00	40.24
1930	27.65	10.29	38.11	10.41	0.00	41.19
1935	22.21	10.02	32.80	9.91	0.00	47.28
1940	23.81	12.59	33.54	12.13	0.75	41.00
1945	24.64	13.78	34.69	14.74	0.03	36.77
1950	54.36	19.19	37.08	20.30	2.44	20.99
1960	162.11	12.56	49.77	17.73	1.79	18.14
1970	352.25	12.96	52.71	12.12	5.24	16.97
1975	574.64	14.43	53.62	6.48	11.11	14.35
1980	1,100.40	15.61	48.41	3.40	16.14	16.44
1985	1,732.10	13.60	37.58	1.94	28.15	18.74
1990	2,893.73	16.19	23.91	1.52	39.83	18.55
1995	3,719.23	18.63	14.64	1.05	48.35	17.34
2000	5,508.59	19.02	11.90	0.75	49.49	18.85
2005	10,049.21	19.21	10.47	0.50	40.74	29.08
2010	11,386.53	21.11	4.32	0.46	53.77	20.33
2011	10,034.36	21.22	4.09	0.06	58.16	16.47
2012Q2	9,844.03	21.93	3.52	0.07	59.14	15.34

Sources: U.S. Federal Reserve Flow of Funds and Census Bureau (1961).

a. Includes mutual savings banks.

b. Includes all government-sponsored institutions participating in the mortgage market (government-sponsored enterprises and mortgage pools backed by agencies and government-sponsored enterprises), both on-balance-sheet holdings and securitized mortgages.

c. Includes state and local government employee retirement funds, private issuers of asset-backed securities, finance companies, real estate investment trusts, and credit unions.

States, covered bonds are a new development and thus still relatively unimportant in financing homeownership.

How does America stack up against other nations in terms of homeownership? The answer to that question has varied over time. In 1890, the U.S. homeownership rate was at 17.9 percent compared to 6.7 percent for Europeans. By

Figure 2-2. *Sources of Funding for Home Mortgages in Selected Countries, 2009*

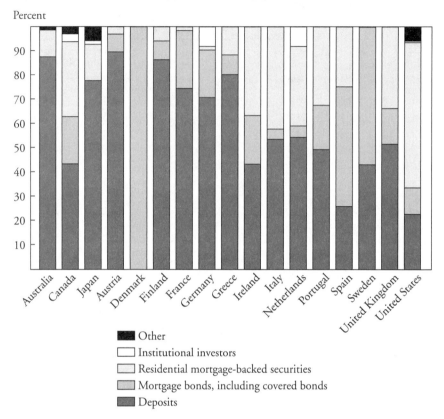

Percent

Other

☐ Institutional investors

☐ Residential mortgage-backed securities

☐ Mortgage bonds, including covered bonds

☐ Deposits

Sources: Based on the latest available data from U.S. Federal Reserve Flow of Funds (2009) for the United States; EMF (2009) for EU countries; Odaira and Takado (2008) and Government Housing Loan Corporation for Japan; and Australian Bureau of Statistics for Australia.

the middle of the twentieth century, that rate had risen above 61 percent in the United States, but European countries were gaining as well. Their rates were 50 percent for Belgium, 33 percent for France, 13 percent for Germany, 26 percent for Sweden, and 43 percent for the United Kingdom.[19]

Figure 2-4 shows more recent data, with homeownership rates varying from a low of 38 percent in Switzerland to a high of 98 percent in Romania. Of the forty-seven countries in the figure, only Switzerland and Germany (43 percent) fall below 50 percent. These low rates have been attributed to cultural factors,

19. Haines and Goodman (1991).

Figure 2-3. *Covered Bonds in Selected Countries, 2010*

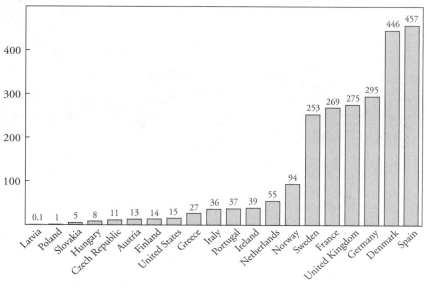

a. Amount of mortgage-backed covered bonds outstanding

US$ billions

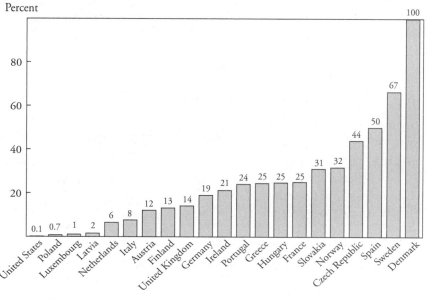

b. Share of mortgage-backed covered bonds in residential loans outstanding

Percent

Source: EMF (2010).

Figure 2-4. *Homeownership Rates in Various Countries, 2009 and 2010*[a]

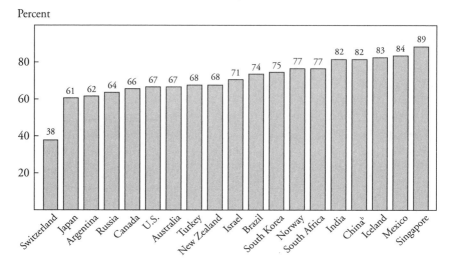

a. 2009

Percent

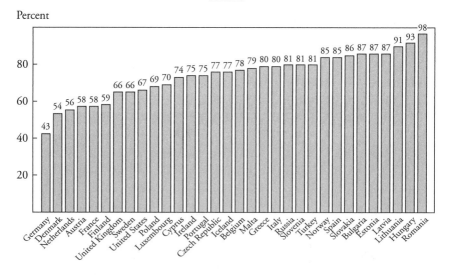

b. 2010

Percent

Source: Allen, Barth, and Yago (2012).

a. Based on the latest available data. In countries like Brazil, it is not clear exactly how favelas are treated in the homeownership rate provided. Also, it is not clear in South Africa what is included or excluded in the homeownership rate. The sources listed do not always provide sufficient detail to elaborate on these issues.

b. Includes only households that have hukou—those who are officially registered in their city of residence.

very low rents, and conservative mortgage lending.[20] Greece, Italy, and Spain have much higher rates of homeownership, reflecting cultural values, discriminatory policies toward private rental housing, and weaker support of "social" rental housing (low-cost public housing owned and managed by government or nonprofit organizations).[21] Fisher and Jaffe have found that, even though several partial factors are associated with high or low rates of homeownership, no single explanation can account for all global patterns. In their words, "Any explanation of worldwide homeownership rates must be limited from a generalizable proposition to an anecdotal explanation with limited empirical content."[22] However, given the very wide distribution of income in the United States, we should perhaps not expect the rate of homeownership to be comparable to that in other countries.

Figure 2-5 provides information on the ratio of home mortgage debt to GDP. As may be seen, Switzerland has the highest ratio at 130 percent in 2009, even though it has the lowest homeownership rate among the countries in the figure. This reflects a high cost of housing due to substantial increases in housing prices over the past decade and a sizable group of wealthy domestic and foreign-born (often transient) individuals who can afford more expensive homes. Germany has a ratio of mortgage debt to GDP that was relatively low at 47 percent in 2010, reflecting its low rate of homeownership. Overall, the ratio for the twenty-seven European Union countries was 52.4 percent in 2010 as compared to a U.S. ratio of 76.5 percent in the same year.

According to Bardhan and Edelstein, "The large differences in the national mortgage markets reflect the fact that mortgage markets retain strong national characteristics . . . as a result of the differences in the historical, demographic, political, and regulatory environments in which mortgage lenders operate."[23] In some countries, like France, mortgage interest is not subsidized, while the rental market is subsidized and heavily regulated. This policy contributes to lower homeownership rates, leading to lower ratios of mortgage debt to GDP.[24]

More generally, as urban property values increase and more developed mortgage capital markets emerge in cities, a higher proportion of homes can be financed by mortgages in areas of rapid urbanization and industrialization. In this way, homes provide not only secure shelter, but also potential income (through rentals and boarding) and serve as collateral for borrowing.

20. See "Bricks and Slaughter, A Special Report on Property," *Economist*, March 5, 2011.
21. Lea (2010b).
22. Fisher and Jaffe (2003).
23. Bardhan and Edelstein (2009) and Lea (2010a).
24. Green and Wachter (2005).

Figure 2-5. *Ratio of Home Mortgage Debt to GDP in Selected Countries, 2009 and 2010*

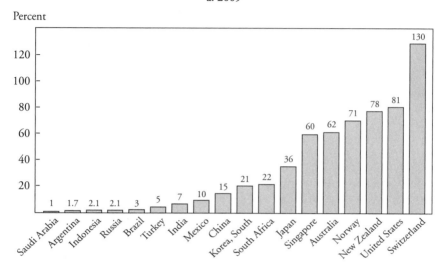

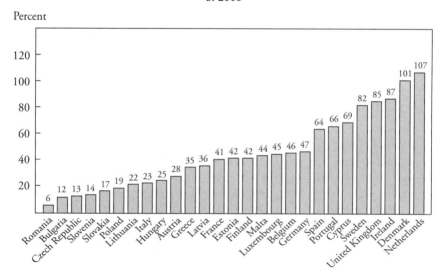

Sources: EMF (2010) for EU countries and Iceland, Russia, Norway, Turkey, and the United States; Warnock and Warnock (2008) for the other countries. Based on the latest available data. EMF (2009) provides the latest data as of 2009, and Warnock and Warnock (2008) provide the average data for 2001–05.

Federal Government Involvement in Mortgage Markets

Since the 1930s, the federal government has played an increasingly important role in the allocation of mortgage credit. Instruments of federal policy used for this purpose include or have included loans insured and guaranteed by the Federal Housing Administration and Veterans Administration; secondary mortgage transactions by the Federal National Mortgage Association (Fannie Mae), the Federal Home Loan Mortgage Corporation (Freddie Mac), and the Government National Mortgage Association (Ginnie Mae); interest rate subsidies; tax expenditures; and direct loans. Federal regulations have been enacted to affect the behavior of mortgage lenders in the pursuit of social objectives. These regulations include the Fair Housing Act (Title VIII), the Equal Credit Opportunity Act, the Home Mortgage Disclosure Act, and the Community Reinvestment Act.

Housing policies are clearly a part of the stabilization, allocation, and distribution activities of the federal government. The first major federal housing initiatives, enacted in the National Housing Act of 1934, mentioned earlier, were part of an economic recovery program implemented during the Great Depression. Although stabilization of economic activity has always remained an important objective, allocation and distribution objectives have become increasingly important. Indeed, such aims were explicitly acknowledged in the 1949 Housing Act, which proposed a "goal of a decent home and a suitable living environment for every American family."

An implicit but important goal of federal housing policies has been to encourage the acceptance of greater risk in mortgage markets. Encouraging greater risk taking may be socially desirable for reasons of economic efficiency and distributional equity. Attitudes toward risk by private lenders and federal, state, and local financial regulatory agencies, however, may prevent mortgage transactions that would be profitable for borrowers and lenders. In such cases, appropriately designed federal mortgage insurance programs may enhance the efficiency of mortgage markets. Low-income applicants for mortgages are likely, for numerous reasons, to be more risky. Improving the access of such individuals or groups to mortgage credit through government actions can be a means of achieving greater distributional equity.

Table 2-2 shows that the United States is one of relatively few countries among those listed in which the government provides support to residential mortgage markets.[25] However, most European governments have very close ties to their

25. According to Ergungor (2011), the fiscal year 2010 budget indicates that the "U.S. government will spend $780 billion in tax expenditures over the next five years to subsidize housing through mortgage interest and property tax deduction."

Table 2-2. *Government Support for Mortgage Markets in Selected Countries*

Country	Government mortgage insurance	Government security guarantees	Government-sponsored enterprises
Denmark	No	No	No
Germany	No	No	No
Ireland	No	No	No
Netherlands	NHG[a]	No	No
Spain	No	No	No
United Kingdom	No	No	No
Australia	No	No	No
Canada	CMHC[b]	CMHC[b]	No
Japan	No	JHFA[c]	Possible
Korea, South	No	No	KHFC[d]
Switzerland	No	No	No
United States	FHA[e]	Ginnie Mae	Fannie Mae, Freddie Mac, FHL banks[e]

Source: Lea (2010b).
a. NHG, National Mortgage Guarantee.
b. CMHC, Canada Mortgage Housing Corporation.
c. JHFA, Japan Housing Finance Agency.
d. KHFC, Korean Housing Finance Corporation.
e. FHA, Federal Housing Administration; FHL, Federal Home Loan

large banks and support them in times of crisis. As a result of the recent mortgage market meltdown in the United States, the role of the government in mortgage markets is being reconsidered. However, as of the writing of this paper, no legislative action had been taken to make any major changes, particularly as regards government-sponsored enterprises.

The Canada Mortgage and Housing Corporation (CMHC), which is a 100 percent government-owned and -controlled corporation, insures (guarantees) mortgage loans and securitizes some of the insured loans. Pollock points out that CMHC is "in one sense . . . a combination of FHA and Ginnie Mae." He adds that it insures roughly half of Canadian mortgages, which is the same proportion as the combined Fannie Mae and Freddie Mac in the United States in terms of the outstanding stock of mortgages.[26] In terms of the flow of issuance, Fannie Mae and Freddie Mac have guaranteed more than 90 percent of mortgages in recent

26. Pollock (2010).

years. Homeownership rates are nearly identical in the two countries, as shown in figure 2-4. Furthermore, despite government support for homeownership, Australia, Ireland, Spain, and the United Kingdom all have higher homeownership rates than the United States, with far less government support.

New Mortgage Products and Mortgage Insurance

During the 1920s, the U.S. mortgage market relied heavily on mutual savings banks, savings and loan associations, insurance companies, and commercial banks. These four types of institutions accounted for 74.4 percent of the total new mortgage loans made on one- to four-family housing from 1925 to 1930. The typical mortgage terms on loans made by these institutions during this period were quite different from those prevailing in subsequent periods, including the present. During the 1920s, mortgages were written with terms to maturity not exceeding twelve years and with loan-to-value ratios close to 50 percent. In the 1930s and 1940s, however, these mortgage terms were significantly loosened. By 1947, the term to maturity approached twenty years and the loan-to-value ratio was roughly 70 percent. In more recent years, both of these factors were further liberalized.

During the 1930s, the housing and banking industries virtually collapsed. Between 1930 and 1933, more than 8,800 banks failed. In 1933 alone, 3,891 banks suspended operations. Total housing starts fell 70 percent, from 2,383,000 in 1926–30 to 728,000 in 1931–35. It is estimated that only 150,000 persons were employed in on-site construction in 1933. At the same time, approximately half of all home mortgages were in default, and foreclosures were occurring at the phenomenal rate of more than 1,000 a day. Nonfarm real estate foreclosures reached a maximum of 252,000 in 1933.

Among the responses of the federal government to these events were the establishment of the Home Owners' Loan Corporation (HOLC) in 1933 and the passage of the National Housing Act of 1934, which created the Federal Housing Administration (FHA) mortgage insurance programs. The HOLC was established to buy mortgages in default and threatened with foreclosure. It was therefore concerned directly with mortgage debt and only indirectly, if at all, with the availability of new mortgage credit. At its peak in 1935, the HOLC held more than 15 percent of all U.S. residential mortgage debt. By contrast, the National Housing Act of 1934 was designed to increase the availability of new mortgage credit and thereby encourage the revival of the housing industry. The principal instrument was Section 203(b) of the National Housing Act.

Mortgages insured under Section 203(b) were secured by the Mutual Mortgage Insurance Fund (MMIF). The creation of the Federal National Mortgage Association (Fannie Mae) in 1938 provided additional impetus to Section 203(b) mortgage activity since it was authorized to buy such mortgages. Fannie Mae therefore made FHA mortgages extremely liquid by providing a ready secondary market for the longer-term type of mortgages offered under Section 203(b).

The main feature of Section 203(b) was the provision of mortgage insurance to all borrowers at a uniform premium. Each Section 203(b) loan was to be evaluated on the basis of economic soundness to ensure the solvency of the MMIF. Although no formal definition of economic soundness was provided in the legislation, limits were placed on the maximum mortgage amount and the maximum loan-to-value ratio. There is, however, a general consensus in the literature that the FHA implemented Section 203(b) mortgage insurance by imposing minimum values on neighborhood quality, property quality, and borrowers' creditworthiness. These criteria were implemented by conducting a property inspection, and maximum permissible values were established for monthly payment-to-income ratios.

High levels of mortgage insurance activity experienced under Section 203(b) during the 1930s, 1940s, and 1950s, along with sizable surpluses in the MMIF, indicate that, during this period, the bulk of FHA-insured mortgage loans were profitable. Indeed, as early as 1938, the maximum loan amount and the maximum loan-to-value ratio were increased based on favorable loss experience. Subsequently, these maximums were further increased. Government insurance transactions generally met or exceeded the criterion of actuarial or economic soundness. However, it is possible for the average transaction to earn a profit even though the marginal loan transaction, at the highest loan-to-value ratio, may suffer a loss.

Congress has traditionally set the maximum mortgage amount that can be insured under FHA programs. In 2008, under the basic Section 203(b) single-family mortgage insurance program, the limit was $362,790. Thirty years earlier in 1978, the limit was $60,000, which was in force since 1977. Before then, the cap was $45,000, a limit introduced by the Housing and Community Development Act of 1974. Until passage of this act, the mortgage limit was $33,000.

If housing prices rise more rapidly than these congressionally determined mortgage limits, the maximum permissible loan-to-value ratios must necessarily fall. This reduction in the real value of mortgage limits in inflationary periods induces borrowers to shift to conventional-mortgage loans.

The first private mortgage insurance (PMI) company was established in 1887. The 1950s also saw the revival of the PMI industry, which began to offer insurance for conventional-mortgage loans for the first time since the 1930s. The industry had collapsed during the Great Depression.

As the result of legislation passed in 1956 in Wisconsin, the Mortgage Guarantee Insurance Corporation began operating in 1957. Subsequently, more and more PMIs were permitted to operate as additional states passed enabling legislation.

The PMIs became increasingly important thereafter. The standard mortgage insurance policy indemnifies the beneficiary against losses in the event of default, with the amount indemnified depending on the coverage chosen.

An increase in the demand for conventional loans, of course, also results in an increase in the demand for PMI. When the U.S. housing market collapsed in 2007 and 2008, mortgage insurers paid $15 billion in claims. This, of course, was a tiny fraction of total losses.

PMI competes with FHA insurance by offering lower premiums for safer mortgages. FHA generally sets an insurance premium of 0.5 percent of the outstanding mortgage amount, amortized over the term of the loan, on all its loans. In contrast, PMI premiums vary according to the loan-to-value ratio of the mortgage, the percentage of the mortgage amount insured, and the choice of prepayment option with fixed length of coverage. Of course, these premiums are set lower than the FHA premium because the PMI companies only insure relatively low-risk mortgage loans, a practice known as "cream-skimming." The FHA is left with the rest. Increased PMI activity decreases the volume of Section 203(b) insurance activity and raises the loss rate, thereby reducing the surplus in the MMIF. Both of these outcomes have been observed.

The FHA has made several important contributions. Among these are helping to popularize and standardize the fully amortized, fixed-interest, level-payment mortgage; to lengthen the term of mortgages; to increase the loan-to-value ratios on residential mortgages; to develop minimum property standards, standardized appraisals, and standardized mortgage contracts; and to make information on risks of default available to private mortgage lenders and insurers. All of these factors, of course, have contributed to the development of a truly national mortgage market.

The introduction of PMI encouraged lenders to make larger loans because, with insurance, conventional loans could be sold to institutions such as Fannie Mae and Freddie Mac (discussed in the next section). Until these institutions were created or were permitted to buy conventional insured mortgages, however, lenders were undoubtedly reluctant to relax their loan terms, particularly when faced with usury laws or "soundness" requirements imposed by federal or state regulatory agencies.

Government-Sponsored Enterprises

The United States established three government-sponsored institutions to support the housing sector. First, as noted earlier, the Federal Home Loan Bank Act set up the FHL bank system in 1932, consisting of twelve regional FHL banks, to strengthen savings and loans by providing them with an alternative and steady source of funds to promote homeownership. It now provides such funding to

Table 2-3. *Housing Goals Set for Fannie Mae and Freddie Mac, 1997–2014*

Target	1997–2000	2001–04	2005–08 housing goals				2009
			2005	2006	2007	2008	
Low- and moderate-income families	42	50	52	53	55	56	43
Underserved areas	24	31	37	38	38	39	32
Special affordable	14	20	22	23	25	27	27

Redefined target	2010–11	2012–14
Low-income families	27	20
Very low-income families	8	7
Low-income areas	13	11
Refinancing mortgages	21	21

Sources: Federal Register, Milken Institute.

all depository institutions. Second, Fannie Mae was established in 1938 to buy home mortgages and create a secondary market for such mortgages. Third, Freddie Mac was established in 1970 to increase the availability of residential mortgage credit by contributing to the development and maintenance of the secondary market for residential mortgages.

Since Freddie Mac primarily buys conventional mortgages and then issues securities backed by those mortgages, a process known as securitization, its creation increased the liquidity of this type of mortgage loan. More important, however, is Freddie Mac's policy (required by its enabling legislation) of limiting its purchases to conventional mortgages in which the borrower has at least a 20 percent equity in the property or in which lower borrower equity is accompanied by private mortgage insurance, so that the effective exposure risk is reduced to 80 percent of the loan amount. Clearly, this policy increased the demand for PMI. About the same time that Freddie Mac was created, the Emergency Home Loan Financing Act of 1970 authorized Fannie Mae to buy conventional mortgages and securitize home mortgages.

The Federal Housing Enterprises Financial Safety and Soundness Act of 1992 established goals for Fannie Mae and Freddie Mac for financing affordable housing and housing in inner cities, rural, and other underserved markets. In 1996, the affordable housing goal was increased from 40 percent to 42 percent of their financing to go to borrowers with low and moderate incomes for each year from 1997 through 2000. This goal was boosted to 50 percent for the years 2001 to 2004 and raised still higher in some subsequent years, as shown in table 2-3.

Figure 2-6. *Total Mortgages Outstanding as a Percentage of GDP in the United States, 1900–2012 Q2*

Percent

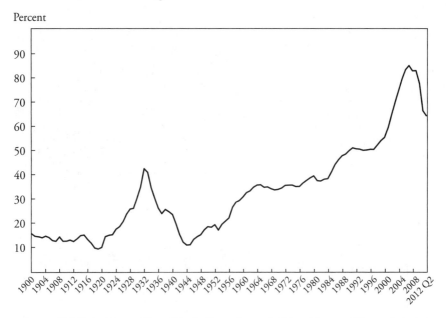

Sources: U.S. Federal Reserve Flow of Funds, Census Bureau (1961), and Bureau of Economic Analysis.

Revisions were made for 2010 and 2011 to include four separate goals and one subgoal for purchases of single-family mortgages and one goal and one subgoal for purchases of multifamily mortgages. In the revisions, goals were also set for underserved areas (low-income or high-minority census tracts and rural counties) and special affordable housing (very low-income families and low-income families living in low-income areas). In a manner similar to the previous goal for underserved areas, the revised goal for low-income areas targeted the purchase of mortgages in specified geographic areas.

Figure 2-6 shows the ratio of total mortgages outstanding to GDP over the past century, while figure 2-7 shows the growing importance of financial institutions like Freddie Mac and Fannie Mae in financing homeownership over the past three decades. (As a result of the recent mortgage market meltdown, however, their future remains uncertain as of the writing of this paper.) Like Freddie Mac, Fannie Mae can only buy conventional loans with high loan-to-value ratios if these loans have private mortgage insurance. Fannie Mae's activities and policies therefore also increased the demand for PMI. In the early 1970s, regulations

Figure 2-7. *Total Home Mortgages Outstanding and Share of Home Financing Provided by Government-Sponsored Enterprises in the United States, 1960–2012*

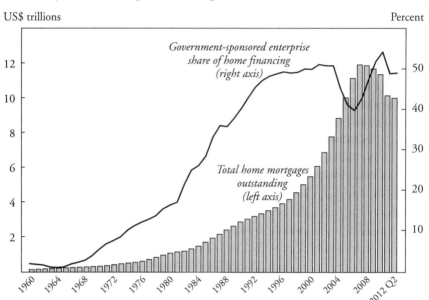

Sources: U.S. Federal Reserve Flow of Funds, Census Bureau (1961), and Bureau of Economic Analysis.

were also promulgated permitting thrift institutions to originate mortgages at 95 percent of value when the individual loans are insured.

The securitization of residential mortgages has clearly spread beyond the United States during the past thirty years, as shown in table 2-4. Other developments have also facilitated the financing of homeownership, such as covered bonds in Denmark and Pfandbriefen in Germany. Clearly, however, securitization and covered bonds are used more often in mature economies than in emerging markets due to their complex legal and financial issues.

To show the limited role of securitization in housing markets in countries around the world, we rely on data from the World Bank Survey IV released in September 2012. Figure 2-8 shows the percentage of bank assets in residential real estate loans in various mature and emerging-market economies for 2010, while figure 2-9 shows the percentage of loans that have been securitized. Comparing these two figures, it is clear that almost all the banks in the countries surveyed do indeed hold residential real estate loans on their balance sheets. However, such loans are securitized in only a relatively few countries. The vast majority of the countries in which no real estate loans are securitized are developing countries.

Table 2-4. *Date of First Mortgage-Backed Securitization in Selected Countries*

Year	Country
1970	United States
1984	Australia and Canada
1985	United Kingdom
1988	France
1989	South Africa
1991	Spain
1995	Germany and Ireland
1996	Argentina
1999	Brazil, Japan, Italy, and South Korea
2000	India
2003	Mexico
2004	Malaysia
2005	China
2006	Russia and Saudi Arabia

Source: Milken Institute, Capital Access Index 2005.

Federal Policies to Address Special Housing Problems in Inner Cities

In the 1950s and 1960s, federal housing policy focused increasingly on inner cities. This represented a basic shift from the primary emphasis placed in the 1930s and 1940s on increasing the supply of adequate housing. This change was initially reflected in the Omnibus Housing Act of 1954, which attempted to expand housing credit and production in urban renewal areas and provided mortgage insurance to families displaced by urban renewal.

In addition, the Federal National Mortgage Charter Act of 1954 established the first special assistance functions (which require government financial support) to be carried out by Fannie Mae. These new programs were established with their own statutory provisions and insurance funds to permit them to function almost independently of the FHA. This was done to insulate the original FHA mortgage insurance fund, supporting programs, such as Section 203 single-family home mortgage insurance, from the effects of the relatively permissive underwriting terms of each new program.

Relaxation of mortgage terms relative to those in effect for the regular government mortgage insurance programs was a major feature of the 1954 Housing Act and the 1954 Mortgage Charter Act. The trend toward liberalization continued, with generous insurance terms on housing for the elderly and loans at subsidized interest rates to developers of private housing for the elderly. The 1961 Housing Act further relaxed the terms of government mortgage insurance and broadened

Figure 2-8. *Percentage of Bank Assets in Residential Real Estate Loans in Selected Countries, 2010*

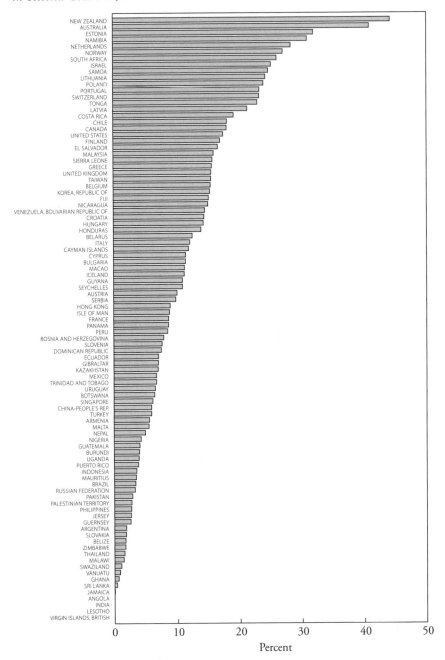

Figure 2-9. *Percentage of Securitized Residential Real Estate Loans in Selected Countries, 2010*

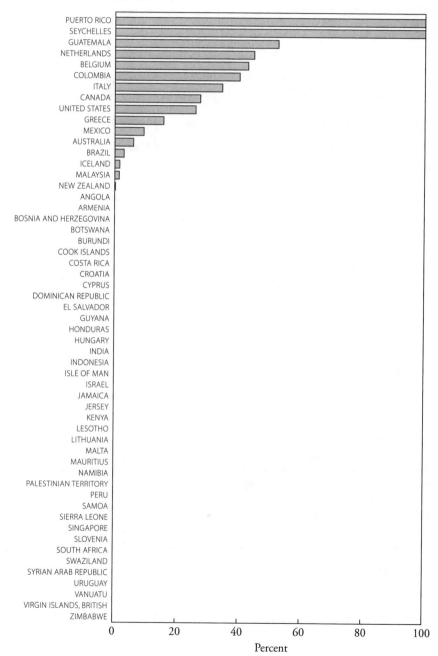

Source: World Bank Survey IV, September 2012.

the coverage of insurance to include low- and moderate-income families. The act enabled such families to acquire housing at low down payments. It provided for subsidized mortgage insurance at below-market interest rates. The Housing and Urban Development Act of 1968 designated troubled urban areas as worthy of special consideration, waiving the statutory limitations concerning loan-to-value ratio, size of unit, or maximum mortgage amount. The terms of the mortgages insured under this provision were to be designed with consideration for the needs of "families of low and moderate income in such areas."

Government Regulation of Conventional Mortgage Lenders

The expansion of FHA mortgage insurance and housing subsidies during the 1960s and 1970s was perceived as less than completely successful in achieving social objectives. Several explanations were offered. Racial discrimination was cited as one barrier to the efficient and equitable functioning of urban housing markets. Concern about discrimination in housing markets was manifested in the Fair Housing Act in 1968 and Equal Credit Opportunity Act in 1974. Both regulations defined criteria that creditors may and may not use in their lending decisions. In general, both acts prohibited lenders from denying or limiting credit solely on the basis of race, sex, creed, or national origin. In addition, the Fair Housing Act permitted lenders to take some neighborhood characteristics into account, but not others.

The Home Mortgage Disclosure Act (HMDA) of 1975 and the Community Reinvestment Act (CRA) of 1977 were aimed at increasing the volume of conventional loans in redlined areas. The HMDA required lenders to disclose the location of their loans, but not their deposits. The CRA sought to prod lenders to expand mortgage lending in older and moderate-income areas in which they have offices.

Turmoil in Global Housing Markets: Implications for the Future of Housing Finance

In the wake of the global financial crisis of 2007 to 2009, it is important to understand the implications of this economic tsunami for the future of housing finance, not just in the United States but in other countries around the world. We begin with the collapse of the housing and mortgage markets in the United States.

The U.S. Housing Crisis

The residential mortgage market in the United States has worked extremely well over the past two centuries, enabling millions to achieve the dream of homeownership. The homeownership rate reached a record high of 69.2 percent in the second quarter of 2004 before declining to 65.5 percent at the end of the second quarter in 2012 (figure 2-1), with all segments of society participating during the rate-increasing period.

To be sure, housing markets have experienced previous periods of turmoil. After the Great Depression, the first major episode was the collapse of the savings and loan industry in the early 1980s. This led to significant changes in mortgage markets.

When the Federal Reserve changed its policy to combat inflationary pressures in the late 1970s, short-term interest rates rose rapidly, and the yield curve inverted, with short-term rates exceeding longer-term rates. At the time, savings and loans were heavily involved in the mortgage market, holding about half of all mortgage loans in their portfolio. The vast majority of these loans were traditional fixed-rate, thirty-year mortgages. The inverted yield curve meant that nearly all savings and loans were insolvent if their mortgage portfolios had been marked to market because the interest rates on their outstanding mortgage loans were lower than the rates on Treasury securities of comparable maturity as well as newly issued mortgage loans. The nearly 4,000 savings and loans in existence at the time were estimated to be insolvent on this basis by roughly $150 billion (or $417 billion in 2011 dollars).

The reason for this dire situation was that the savings and loan institutions were largely prohibited from offering adjustable-rate mortgages or hedging their interest rate risk through the use of derivatives. Congress responded to the crisis by broadening the powers of savings and loans so that they could operate more like commercial banks, which largely avoided the same plight. Furthermore, savings and loans were also allowed to offer adjustable-rate mortgages.

This financial innovation enabled savings and loans to shift some of the interest rate risk to borrowers. While adjustable-rate mortgages accounted for less than 5 percent of originations in 1980, that share had increased to 64 percent in 2006, before declining to 37 percent in 2010 as a result of the financial crisis.[27]

The broader powers of savings and loans also meant a blurring of distinctions among different types of depository institutions. The share of home mortgages held by savings institutions dropped from 50 percent in 1980 to 8 percent in 2006 and to less than 3.5 percent in the second quarter of 2012, while commercial banks saw their share rise from 16 percent to 22 percent over the same period.

The percentage increase for commercial banks may seem relatively small, but the total assets of commercial banks in the second quarter of 2012 were

27. Office of Thrift Supervision (2011).

$13 trillion, compared to the $1 trillion in assets for savings institutions. Commercial banks are now more important than savings institutions for financing housing. One factor in this change was that the Basel rules set risk weights on mortgage assets that encouraged banks to hold them.

The second episode of disruption emerged in the summer of 2007, triggered by the "subprime mortgage market meltdown." The 1980s savings and loan crisis was more regional in nature, while the subprime damage was truly national in scope. Millions of households with subprime loans (loans made to less creditworthy individuals) became delinquent on their mortgages, and many lost their homes to foreclosure. Many of these homebuyers took out "hybrid" mortgage loans, which featured low introductory interest rates for two or three years but a higher rate thereafter. This financial innovation was fine as long as home prices continued to rise. With higher home prices, borrowers could build up equity and refinance their mortgage at a lower interest rate. Such individuals had the opportunity to improve their credit ratings at the same time. Another contributory factor was that loan-to-value ratios were increasing at more or less the same time. This also contributed to the overall deterioration in lending standards.

Unfortunately, home prices fell—and fell dramatically. This led to a surge in foreclosures and a tightening of credit standards by lenders that triggered the housing market meltdown and contributed to a more general financial crisis and deep recession. As of the writing of this paper, housing prices have appeared to bottom out and begun to rise in some parts of the country, which has helped to improve the overall residential real estate sector. This underscores the importance of promoting well-functioning housing markets in countries around the globe.

Changes in U.S. mortgage markets over the past three decades contributed to the most recent crisis. Before 1980, as noted, the vast majority of mortgage loans were made by savings and loans. These institutions originated, serviced, and held these loans in their portfolios. But as early as 1970, combining these three functions into a single institution began to change the funding of home purchases, as mortgage loans were increasingly securitized.

In subsequent years, Ginnie Mae, Fannie Mae, and Freddie Mac became the primary securitizers of home mortgages. These three entities securitized only 5.2 percent of all outstanding mortgages in 1970, but their share rose to a high of 49.5 percent in 2000 before declining to 40.7 percent in 2005 and then subsequently rising to 59.1 percent in the second quarter of 2012 (table 2-1).

Furthermore, financial institutions themselves began to securitize mortgages, referred to as private-label-backed mortgage pools. The share of private-label securitizers in home mortgages was less than 1 percent in 1984 and then increased to a high of 21 percent in 2006, before declining to 14 percent in 2009.

The private-label-backed mortgage pools increased significantly before the financial crisis and then declined abruptly during and after the crisis. As of mid-2012, nearly all securitization of mortgages was being done by Ginnie Mae, Fannie Mae, and Freddie Mac. The role of private-label securitizers in financing housing had become virtually nonexistent.

Beginning in the second half of the 1990s, subprime mortgage loans grew rapidly in importance. The subprime share of total originations was less than 5 percent in 1994, increased to 13 percent in 2000, and then grew to more than 20 percent in 2005 and 2006, before declining to 0.3 percent in 2010 and at the end of the second quarter of 2011. Furthermore, the share of subprime originations packaged into mortgage-backed securities (MBSs) more than doubled over the same period, from 31.6 percent to 80.5 percent, before declining to zero in 2010 and at the end of the second quarter of 2011. The subprime mortgage market essentially shut down in 2009 and thereafter. But this was not all that was happening. MBSs were put into pools, and new securities were issued, referred to as collateralized debt obligations (CDOs). The issuers of CDOs were the major buyers of the low-rated classes of subprime MBSs in 2006. CDOs were also put into pools, and still newer securities were issued, known as "CDOs-squared."

Lending institutions and investors seeking higher yields in the earlier years of the decade found the subprime market attractive but apparently underestimated the risks. At the same time, the prospect of subprime loans coupled with rising home prices undoubtedly enticed borrowers in many parts of the country.

Home prices jumped nationally at an average annual rate of nearly 9 percent from 2000 to 2006, after rising an average of slightly less than 3 percent a year in the 1990s (see figure 2-10). Stated another way, a home worth $150,000 in 2000 was worth $251,565 in 2006. This environment undoubtedly fueled optimism on the part of lenders, borrowers, and investors.

In the summer of 2007, several subprime lenders filed for bankruptcy, and other financial firms suffered heavy losses on subprime securities. The rate of foreclosures on subprime loans increased and by some estimates nearly doubled from 2000 to 2006. For loans made in 2006, the foreclosure rate was 5.5 percent just six months after origination. This exceeded the corresponding rates for all previous years. As of November 2007, there was one foreclosure for every 617 households, according to RealtyTrac.

This situation led to many condemnations of subprime mortgages, particularly hybrid loans or loans with interest rate resets. The process of securitizing loans was questioned. Some critics argued that subprime borrowers should not have been offered many of the innovative financial products that became available before the housing market collapse. It is important to remember, however,

Figure 2-10. *Home Prices in the United States, 1991–2012*

Index, 1991 Q1 = 100

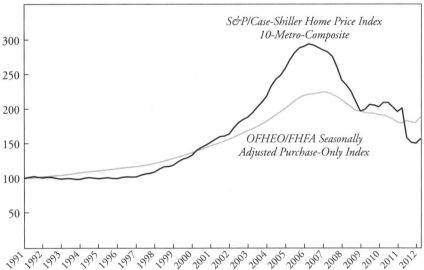

Sources: S&P/Case-Shiller (Bloomberg) and Office of Federal Housing Enterprise Oversight (OFHEO)/ Federal Housing Finance Agency (FHFA).

that the growth in this market reflected a combination of factors, including the increase in first-time homeownership attributable to less rigorous screening of loan seekers. A significant part of the problem here was in the origination process. Mortgage brokers passed on the risk and were paid by volume, so they did not have good incentives to screen properly. Subprime loans also let some borrowers improve their credit scores and then qualify as prime borrowers. Furthermore, most of the same types of mortgage products offered to subprime borrowers were also offered to prime borrowers. And the securitization of these products was important in enhancing the liquidity of mortgage loans and increasing the supply of funds for such loans. Most important, the factors that cause individuals to enter foreclosure are generally linked not to the type of product they receive, but rather to the financial straits in which they find themselves after obtaining a mortgage loan. These difficulties include unemployment, divorce, health problems, and, especially, a decline in housing prices that leaves homes worth less than their outstanding mortgage balances.

By recognizing the key role that these factors play, it becomes clear that additional legislation and regulations cannot—and should not try to—prevent subprime lending (or innovation in the mortgage markets more generally), because that will simply shut off credit to less creditworthy individuals who want to become homeowners. Instead, efforts should focus on educating consumers about complex loan products and simplifying the documents necessary for informed decisionmaking. Indeed, it is not clear that the government can even play an effective role here. Anyone who has read a truth-in-lending disclosure is likely to come away totally mystified if, indeed, they have the fortitude to read it to the end. Consumers must be allowed to choose mortgage products, even if some expose borrowers to interest rate risk. Also, investors, domestic and foreign, in securities backed by subprime loans—particularly the more exotic types—must appreciate more fully the fact that the marketplace is sometimes quite harsh in punishing those who seek ever-higher returns without taking into account the correspondingly greater risk.

Lastly, in view of the fundamental determinants of foreclosures, more thought should be given to what foreclosure rate is acceptable on subprime mortgage loans. Surely it would be unreasonable to implement regulations based on the premise that the socially desirable foreclosure rate is zero. If that were the case, hardly anyone would qualify for a mortgage.

It is difficult to distinguish between prime and subprime borrowers on the basis of measures of creditworthiness such as FICO scores[28] that provide standardized evaluations of creditworthiness. In the same way, it is difficult to distinguish between them on the basis of the mortgage products they use. Over the past decade, most—if not all—of the products offered to subprime borrowers have also been offered to prime borrowers. In fact, from January 1999 through July 2007, prime borrowers obtained thirty-one of the thirty-two types of mortgage products—fixed-rate, adjustable-rate, and hybrid mortgages, including those with balloon payments—obtained by subprime borrowers.

If the loan product itself were the problem in the subprime market, one might expect all borrowers using that product to be facing foreclosure. But this was not the case. Foreclosure rates were rising, as noted, but the rates differed widely by type of product and borrower. Most important, the foreclosure rates on all mortgage products still fell far short of 100 percent, which means that many borrowers were benefiting from them. Of course, widespread defaults and foreclosures do impose externalities that offset these benefits to some extent.

To argue that the product is the source of the problem is to ignore a fundamental truth: the ability or willingness to repay loans depends on financial

---

28. FICO scores are named for the company that developed and sells them. The FICO Company was originally called Fair, Isaac and Company.

factors. The marketplace and a borrower's financial circumstances may deteriorate, leading to serious problems, including foreclosure. In some parts of the country, for example, real estate prices fell so far that houses were worth less than the balances owed on them. In addition, borrowers lost jobs, or suffered divorce or serious illness, or otherwise faced severe financial straits. These factors, together, of course, with the bursting of the bubble, contributed to increases in foreclosures, regardless of the mortgage product.

Some products, however, did become associated with relatively high and rising foreclosure rates, especially among subprime borrowers. But both prime and subprime borrowers experienced foreclosures for twenty-nine of the mortgage products, indicating that virtually every mortgage product—whether prime or subprime—is a candidate for foreclosure.

Of course, foreclosure rates are typically higher on subprime mortgages than on prime mortgages, regardless of product type. Subprime borrowers are by definition riskier. Furthermore, loan-to-value ratios, together with the borrower's FICO score, are important determinants of mortgage loan risk. In particular, subprime borrowers received a larger proportion of loans with loan-to-value ratios greater than 80 percent as compared to prime borrowers.

So what does one conclude? Product innovation is beneficial, and attempting to curtail such innovation in the mortgage market could deny credit for borrowers who would not otherwise qualify for loans. Legislative or regulatory actions that are too sweeping and severe could limit the availability of mortgage products, denying borrowers a wider menu from which to choose the product that best suits their needs. However, this is not to say that some limitations on the range of products available are not desirable. At some point, the sheer complexity of the array of products imposes heavy costs on customers and makes the information asymmetry problem difficult to resolve. There is an optimal degree of product choice.

Of course, innovative new products require education on the part of lenders and borrowers. To the extent that problems arise for lenders, they will make adjustments in the products they offer. Borrowers, too, must educate themselves about which products are most suitable for their current and expected financial status.

The process by which lenders and borrowers decide on specific mortgage products is imperfect and can at times create difficulties for both, resulting in changes of mortgage terms and the curtailment or discontinuation of some products, as was seen in the recent market turmoil. And regulatory authorities should be vigilant against fraudulent activity.

Rising foreclosure rates are a serious issue. But as Lawrence Summers, then of Harvard University, stated in September 2007, "We need to ask ourselves the question, and I don't think the question has been put in a direct way and people have developed an answer; what is the optimal rate of foreclosures? How much are we prepared to accept?"[29] Another way to ask this question is, How many of these people were actually homeowners? If they did not have positive equity they were implicitly renting at very attractive rates with an option to buy. The important issue here is to price risk correctly and make sure that those who bear the risk can do so without creating systemic problems.

The same type of argument applies to securitization. Securitization per se is not a problem; it is the quality of the products that are securitized, and the creditworthiness of the borrowers, that can present problems. For example, to the extent that subprime loans created problems, so would securities backed by such loans.

In the first part of the 2000s, foreclosures were mainly a problem in the prime mortgage market. In recent years, they became largely a problem in the subprime mortgage market. In response to the worsening problems associated with subprime loans, lenders greatly reduced the origination of such products, particularly those with reset features. However, many subprime borrowers benefited from the product diversity, which provided access to credit and homeownership. It is, once again, important that any legislative or regulatory action not unduly curtail subprime mortgage loans.

Many subprime borrowers got financing on extremely generous terms. Lenders in many cases extended credit without requiring a down payment. Borrowers were able to take out loans on the basis of the equity that had been built up over time in their homes, especially during the period of rapidly increasing home prices. Of course, when home prices declined, many of these owners found that they owed more, including the first- and second-lien mortgages, than their homes were worth. This provided an incentive to stop making payments and allow homes to go into foreclosure. Again, the ability and willingness to repay loans are what matter, not the method of financing home purchases.

One last point is that the nonrecourse feature of mortgage lending in many states is an important difference between the United States and other countries. In most places, lenders have the legal ability to pursue defaulting borrowers and obtain repayment from their income or other assets. This is an important factor contributing to the higher rate of default in the United States than in other countries. Although in recourse states, lenders do have the option of pursuing defaulting borrowers, in practice they usually do not. The problem is one of perception: big bank, poor homeless family, and little hope of getting much money back.

---

29. Summers (2007).

Table 2-5. *Average House Price in Selected Countries, 1998–2011*[a]

Country	Boom, 1998 Q1– 2006 Q2	Bust, 2006 Q2– 2011 Q3	Overall, 1998 Q1– 2011 Q3	Similar to the United States?
United States	49.9 (15)	–22.6 (2)	16.0 (16)	Not applicable
Australia	78.5 (7)	17.7 (17)	110.1 (3)	No
Belgium	55.2 (11)	12.4 (14)	74.4 (7)	No
Canada	53.3 (13)	28.5 (19)	96.9 (4)	No
Denmark	79.5 (6)	–19.5 (4)	44.6 (13)	Yes
Finland	68.4 (8)	2.7 (11)	72.9 (8)	No
France	102.2 (4)	5.1 (12)	112.6 (2)	No
Germany	–11.4 (18)	–5.7 (9)	–16.5 (18)	No
Ireland	131.4 (1)	–25.3 (1)	72.9 (9)	Yes
Italy	53.4 (12)	–7.9 (6)	41.2 (14)	Yes
Japan	–25.6 (19)	–8.3 (5)	–31.8 (19)	No
Korea, South	4.4 (17)	6.5 (13)	11.1 (17)	No
Netherlands	61.0 (10)	–6.9 (8)	49.8 (12)	Yes
New Zealand	64.2 (9)	–1.7 (10)	61.4 (11)	Yes
Norway	53.0 (14)	24.3 (18)	90.2 (6)	No
Spain	108.6 (3)	–20.8 (3)	65.3 (10)	Yes
Sweden	83.4 (5)	16.0 (16)	112.9 (1)	No
Switzerland	10.7 (16)	14.2 (15)	26.4 (15)	No
United Kingdom	112.2 (2)	–7.3 (7)	96.6 (5)	Yes

Source: Cohen, Coughlin, and Lopez (2012).
a. Rankings of countries in parentheses.

Housing Problems in Other Countries

The United States was not the only country to endure problems in its housing sector in recent years. As table 2-5 shows, ten of nineteen countries experienced significant increases in housing prices during the decade before prices declined. The three countries that experienced the biggest declines in prices were Ireland (–25.3 percent), the United States (–22.6 percent), and Spain (–20.8 percent). The experiences of seven of the countries, moreover, were similar to that of the United States.

Why, despite the fact that some countries experienced bigger increases in home prices than the United States, did the U.S. housing market suffer far worse than did the markets in these other countries? For one thing, riskier borrowers were granted an increasingly larger share of mortgage loans, and lending standards were far more lenient in the United States. According to Lea, "First subprime lending was rare or nonexistent outside of the United States. The only country with a significant subprime share was the U.K. (a peak of 8 percent of mortgages in 2006). Subprime accounted for 5 percent of mortgages in Canada, less than 2 percent in Australia, and negligible proportions elsewhere."[30]

In the United States, borrowers with little or no documentation regarding their income or net worth were able to obtain mortgage loans. Interest-only and negative amortization loans were also made available to many borrowers. Lastly, loan-to-value ratios in some cases exceeded 100 percent. Although some of these practices existed in other countries, such as the United Kingdom, they were less prevalent than in the United States.[31] In Germany, moreover, the maximum loan-to-value ratio was 80 percent.

One might think that the country with the highest level of mortgage debt relative to GDP would also be the country with the worst-performing mortgage market. Figure 2-5 indicates that the Netherlands had the highest level of mortgage debt relative to GDP. However, home prices rose higher in the Netherlands than in the United States before the crisis, but declined far less during the period of bust, as shown in table 2-5. The fact that Dutch home prices did not collapse as they did in the United States spared the Netherlands problems in its housing market. In addition, although the Netherlands did extend high loan-to-value mortgages, they remained a small minority of total mortgages. The tax subsidy extended to borrowers, moreover, was less in the Netherlands than in the United States.[32]

In contrast to the Netherlands, Ireland had the biggest increase in home prices before the crisis and the biggest collapse in home prices during the bust. Ireland also had the third-highest mortgage-debt-to-GDP ratio in the European Union, at 87 percent. Its housing market also suffered severely in recent years.

Another difference between the housing markets in the United States and other countries is that only the United States has government-sponsored enterprises like Freddie Mac and Fannie Mae. These two financial institutions were chartered by the U.S. government and were expected not only to maximize profits for their shareholders but also to provide mortgage credit to make housing finance more affordable for moderate- and low-income households. Unfortunately, this dual mandate led to the insolvency of both of these giant mortgage institutions, which were placed into conservatorship in September 2008 by the

---

30. Lea (2010c).
31. See Lea (2010c) and Ellis (2008).
32. See Ellis (2008).

Figure 2-11. *Homeownership Rates in Canada and the United States, 1971–2010*

Percent

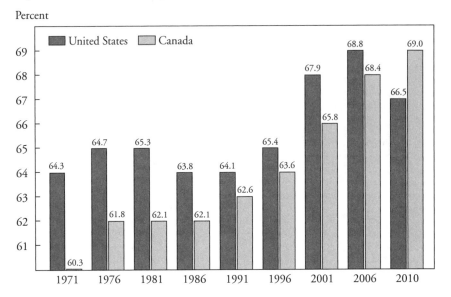

Sources: For Canada, Statistics Canada and for 2010, an estimate from Scotia Economics. For the United States, U.S. Census Bureau.

U.S. government. The actions of these institutions worsened the performance of the housing market in the United States.[33]

Lastly, covered bonds are the dominant source of housing finance in Denmark. This form of financing is an alternative to the securitization of mortgages, which has been so important in the United States. The advantage of covered bonds is that they remain on the balance sheets of financial institutions and are collateralized with home mortgages that also remain on the balance sheets. Other European countries use covered bonds, though to a far lesser degree. During the past decade, Denmark saw greater fluctuations in housing prices than the United States, yet avoided the housing problems that afflicted the United States. Covered bonds may therefore be a good complement to, if not substitute for, securitization.

Housing Problems in the United States versus Canada

It is instructive to compare the performance of housing markets in Canada and the United States. As figure 2-11 shows, these two countries have similar

33. Barth and others (2009).

Figure 2-12. *Home Prices (Year-over-Year Percentage Change) in Canada and the United States, 1993–2010*

Percent

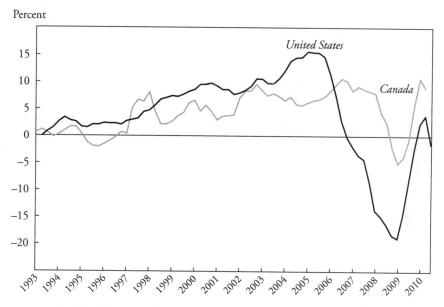

Sources: S&P Case-Shiller/Fiserv, Bank of Canada, Royal LePage, 2010 Q3.

homeownership rates, and both of these rates had tended to trend upward until the global financial crisis struck. At the same time, home prices in Canada and the United States closely tracked one another until 2003, when U.S. prices rose faster and then declined more abruptly and further than those in Canada. Home prices in both countries rose from their lows in 2009 and were increasing in 2010 (see figure 2-12).

With regard to residential delinquency rates, figure 2-13 shows that the United States performed far worse than Canada during the global financial crisis. Indeed, the delinquency rate for Canada remained relatively flat over the entire past decade. This is in sharp contrast to the tremendous rise in the delinquency rate beginning in 2007 in the United States. Why did the Canadian housing market perform better than the U.S. market, given that both countries have the same general pattern in homeownership rates? One factor is that Canada benefited substantially from a commodity boom.

Another important distinction between Canada and the United States is the extent of government involvement in the housing market. The U.S. government plays a far greater role in supporting the financing of housing than does the

Figure 2-13. *Residential Delinquency Rates in Canada and the United States, 2001–10*

Percent

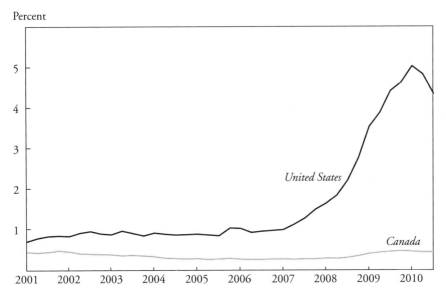

Sources: Canadian Bankers Association, Mortgage Bankers Association, 2010 Q3.

Canadian government. Financing and mortgage insurance support in the United States is provided by Freddie Mac and by Fannie Mae—both of which have specific housing goals set by the U.S. Department of Housing and Urban Development—and by Ginnie Mae.[34] These three institutions provided nearly 60 percent of the funding for home mortgages in 2006. All three have a mandate to support housing in a way that is not strictly comparable to the approach that would be taken by a firm focusing on risk-return trade-offs to maximize shareholder value. Canada does have a government-owned mortgage insurance agency, the Canada Housing and Mortgage Corporation, but the insurance is not targeted to affordable housing.[35] Canada does not have any entities similar to Freddie Mac and Fannie Mae. Furthermore, in contrast to the United States, securitization in Canada provided slightly less than 20 percent of the funding for mortgages in 2006. Banks and credit unions provided slightly more than 70 percent of funding in that year.

Canada does not have legislation similar to the Community Reinvestment Act enacted in 1977 to encourage depository institutions to help to meet the credit

34. Barth and others (2009).
35. Lea (2010c).

Table 2-6. *Key Differences in Mortgage Finance in Canada and the United States*

Indicator	Canada	United States
Mortgage interest deduction	No	Yes
Main product	Five-year fixed-rate mortgage	Thirty-year fixed-rate mortgage
Recourse	Yes	No
Prepayment penalty	Yes	No
Funding model	On-balance-sheet	Originate-to-distribute
2006 peak, subprime percentage of loans outstanding	Less than 5 percent[a]	20 percent

Source: Traclet (2010).

a. Subprime mortgages in Canada are mainly near-prime/Alt-A and are much more conservative than those in the United States.

needs of the communities in which they operate, including low- and moderate-income neighborhoods. These differences contributed to greater problems in the housing market in the United States than in Canada.

Table 2-6 shows more differences in mortgage finance between Canada and the United States. Americans benefit from a mortgage interest deduction from their taxes; Canadians do not. Also, Canadians who become delinquent on their mortgage loans and eventually end up in foreclosure are subject to recourse by lenders. This is not the case in the United States, where borrowers have a greater incentive to default on their mortgage, especially when they owe more than their home is worth.

In 2006 the subprime share of total outstanding mortgages was less than 5 percent in Canada, while in the United States it was 20 percent. In addition, Canada relies to a far greater degree on on-balance-sheet funding than the United States, which relies more on securitization. With a greater degree of subprime mortgages, a large fraction of which were securitized, the housing market performed worse in the United States than in Canada.

Lastly, Canada relies on mortgages with a fixed rate—typically for five years but sometimes as short as one year or as long as ten years. The rate is then renegotiated at the end of this period and adjusted to the current market rate. This enables borrowers to manage their interest rate risk differently by changing the length of the fixed-rate period depending on the level and trend of interest rates.

Yet another difference between the two countries is that 80 percent of Canadian homeowners with mortgages had equity that was 20 percent or more of the value of their home in 2010. Only 2 percent of mortgage holders in Canada had negative equity. In contrast, about 25 percent of mortgage holders in the United States had negative equity.

Canada, moreover, had more conservative lending policies than the United States during the past decade, with the proportion of loans with little or no down payment being far lower than in the United States. As Lea points out, while Canada "relaxed documentation requirements, there was far less 'risk layering' or offering limited documentation loans to subprime borrowers with little or no down payment. There was little 'no doc' lending."[36]

One final comment regarding housing price bubbles and their bursting: regulators in developed countries have increased focus on home prices as a source of systemic risk in banking. Of 143 countries, 49 now consider housing prices in assessing systemic risk in the banking sector, while 94 do not (see table 2-7). However, most of the countries that do consider housing prices are developed countries, while those that do not are mostly developing countries. If regulators are successful in focusing more directly on housing prices to prevent banking crises in the developing countries, which account for a very large share of world GDP, the likelihood and severity of another global financial crisis may be significantly diminished.

Challenges in the Postcrisis Housing Market

In this section, we examine ways to improve the functioning of housing finance systems to facilitate homeownership. Specifically, we describe the challenges in postcrisis housing markets, examine the structural shifts in demand that will drive housing finance innovation in the future, and pose some underlying policy questions. The next section describes innovative attempts to overcome these challenges.

It is important to realize that many of the financial innovations for housing are similar for both developed and emerging markets. These are as follows:

—Diversifying sources of capital (debt *and* equity)

—Structuring financial products that will promote private capital investment to support construction, maintenance, and sustainable improvement of residential real estate

—Diversifying the types of housing products (single and multiple family)

—Building higher-density, sustainable buildings that increase housing consumers' cash flow and ability to service long-term debt

—Pooling savings and risk management products

—Using credit enhancement products

—Using information technology to monitor and improve efficiency in housing finance.

36. Lea (2010c).

Table 2-7. *Are Housing Prices Considered in Assessing Systemic Risk in the Banking Sector?*

Yes (forty-nine countries)

Armenia	Maldives
Australia	Mauritius
Austria	Morocco
Bahrain	Netherlands
Belgium	New Zealand
Bulgaria	Norway
Canada	Oman
Chile	Palestinian Territory
Cyprus	Philippines
Fiji	Portugal
Finland	Romania
Gibraltar	Russia
Greece	Serbia
Guernsey	Singapore
Iceland	Slovakia
India	Spain
Italy	Sri Lanka
Jamaica	Switzerland
Latvia	Thailand
Lebanon	Tonga
Liechtenstein	United Arab Emirates
Lithuania	United Kingdom
Luxembourg	United States
Macao, China	Zimbabwe
Malawi	

No (ninety-four countries)

Angola	Estonia	Kyrgyz Rep.	Senegal
Argentina	Ethiopia	Lesotho	Seychelles
Bangladesh	France	Madagascar	Sierra Leone
Belarus	Gambia	Malaysia	Slovenia
Belize	Germany	Mali	South Africa
Benin	Ghana	Malta	Suriname
Bhutan	Guatemala	Mexico	Swaziland
Bosnia and Herzegovina	Guinea-Bissau	Moldova	Syria
Botswana	Guyana	Montenegro	Taiwan
Brazil	Honduras	Mozambique	Tajikistan
Burkina Faso	Hong Kong, China	Myanmar	Tanzania
Burundi	Hungary	Namibia	Togo
Cayman Islands	Indonesia	Nepal	Trinidad and Tobago
China	Iraq	Nicaragua	Tunisia
Colombia	Ireland	Niger	Turkey
Cook Islands	Isle of Man	Nigeria	Uganda
Costa Rica	Israel	Pakistan	Ukraine
Côte d'Ivoire	Jersey	Panama	Uruguay
Croatia	Jordan	Paraguay	Vanuatu
Denmark	Kazakhstan	Peru	Venezuela
Dominican Republic	Kenya	Poland	Virgin Islands, British
Ecuador	Korea, South	Puerto Rico	Yemen
Egypt	Kosovo	Qatar	
El Salvador	Kuwait	Samoa (Western)	

Source: World Bank Survey IV, September 2012.

The State of Postcrisis Housing Markets

The record-breaking foreclosures and defaults, decline of homeownership, and surge of "underwater" mortgages overwhelmed aspiring and existing homeowners in recent years. Home prices fell more than 40 percent since their peak in 2006, but have recently appeared to stabilize and even increased somewhat in parts of the countries. At the end of 2011, 23 percent of all residential properties with a mortgage were in negative equity, according to CoreLogic. This is an improvement from a few years ago, when one in seven households with mortgages faced foreclosure or default, and nearly 40 percent of the 48.4 million homes with mortgages were "underwater." Furthermore, sharp falls in property prices contribute to problems for neighborhoods and local and state governments that depend on property taxes to support critical services.

Effectively, most of the costs of housing finance risk have been nationalized due to the recent crisis. As of September 2012, the residential finance system is nearly completely supported by the federal government—a situation that cannot be sustained indefinitely without seriously damaging the prospects for returning to long-term growth. While the management of the financial crisis led the government to recapitalize large financial institutions, the challenge of revitalizing the housing finance system for the long run remains largely unaddressed. Although many parts of the Dodd-Frank Act did focus on perceived problems in housing finance, they did not deal with the problem of government intervention in the mortgage market.

The private sector played a major role in funding residential real estate until the recent financial crisis in the United States. Today, the way that mortgages are originated and sold to the capital markets will have to be reformed before private capital returns to a more normal level. Most lending institutions held mortgages on their balance sheets, and many investors—domestic and international—bought securities backed by those mortgages. Access to housing finance had grown dramatically and steadily over the preceding decade, and homeownership had reached historic highs.

While the financing of the housing sector still needs repair, the demographic drivers that will require the return of financial innovation to support homeownership continue unabated. The developed world and emerging markets continue to serve as laboratories for new financial products. At present, many lending institutions still curtail credit to the real estate sector as they recapitalize their balance sheets and investors cut back on purchases of mortgage-backed securities. The securitization of mortgages by private firms, moreover, collapsed along with the participation of private investors. Most of the funding for home purchases now goes only to the most creditworthy individuals.

This dramatic decline in funding by the private sector poses a major problem that has yet to be addressed: a growing gap in the availability of credit to residential real estate markets in both mature and emerging markets. In the United States, the government has recently focused on stemming the tide of home foreclosures through loan modification efforts, while also providing its own credit to the housing sector. But this crisis management is not designed to get real estate markets functioning normally again.

The resources of government are much smaller than those of the global capital markets that must ultimately return to channel investment into the housing sector. This means that the current reliance on the Federal Reserve system and government-sponsored enterprises (or similar housing finance agencies overseas) to stimulate housing markets is insufficient to promote greater national economic growth and stability. One saying in economics is that trends that cannot go on forever will not. This is one of them.

Structural Shifts in Housing Demand

It is important to step back and examine the structural shifts in the demand for capital in housing that are likely to drive the next wave of financial innovation. By 2011, a major transition occurred as the majority of the world's population came to live in cities—more than 51.4 percent, or 3.6 billion people, now reside in urban areas. Most future population growth will also occur in urban areas.[37] Indeed, by 2030 nearly 60 percent of the world's population will be urban and more than half will be living in slums. In the developing world, 5 million new residents, on average, are absorbed into cities each month. This contributes to high and rising housing shortages. Historically, economic growth fuels demand for new housing units.

In the United States, as in many developed countries, most population growth is driven by immigration. While currently representing 13 percent of the population in the United States, immigrants will account for 70 percent of population growth and thus future demand for housing. Their needs, preferences in housing, and choices of location will be important drivers of housing demand.

Meanwhile, additional age structure and household formation dynamics complicate the demand for capital in housing and the need for financing a mix of types (single or multifamily), forms (ownership and rental), and styles (high and low density) of housing in the market.

Younger people face declining income prospects, with real median household incomes in all age groups under fifty-five not having increased since 2000. For the youngest working cohorts (twenty-five to thirty-four), incomes are continuing to

37. United Nations (2012).

fall. This trend suppresses household formation due to high unemployment and thereby reduces current housing demand, but accelerates it later as the cohort ages.[38]

With stagnant incomes, lost equity in homes, and a declining group of upwardly mobile buyers, housing finance will need to be reinvented. New entrants in the housing market will require a greater variety of housing options and innovations in finance, construction, and sustainability.

What Works? What Doesn't?

Common to all the innovations to be examined are answers to some underlying policy questions: What is the structure or preference of tax or other subsidies? What works best: people- or place-based subsidies and incentives? What are the regulatory supply-side constraints in the provision of land and space for development and associated development rights? How can future construction rights be transferred and ultimately financed? What is the role of information technology in bridging gaps in information about housing credit analysis and risk? How can technology reduce transaction costs and clear the path from savings to investment in housing?

People- versus Place-Based Subsidies

Before we examine new waves of financial innovation in housing, it is important to consider some general principles of the incentives that support housing access and affordability. Tax subsidies, regulatory constraints on the supply of property through zoning and land use planning, and technological advances that can bridge information asymmetries in assessing risk should all be considered as elements in the process.

The mortgage interest rate deduction has been by far the most prominent feature of the tax subsidy for homeownership. From a distributional perspective, the mortgage deduction (like all deductions) disproportionately favors the wealthy. While the ownership subsidy has risen significantly over the past forty years, the rate of homeownership has remained relatively stable. This suggests that the deduction alone has exhausted its ability to increase ownership much further.

While the subsidy has contributed to greater demand for larger dwellings (to maximize tax deductibility), it has done little to increase the total stock of housing and its affordability. Incentives to maximize deductions through increased leverage and housing size undermine housing sustainability, financially and environmentally.

However, there is growing evidence that targeted innovations in public policy and financial innovation can increase housing stock and access. Subsidized housing for lower-income residents in many circumstances complements and does not

38. Joint Center for Housing Studies (2010).

crowd out private investment. Government finance has the potential to increase the total number of units, even with some displacement of privately generated housing. In more populous markets, there is less crowding out.

In terms of innovations, programs that have the greatest effect target individual mobility, rather than specific locations.

Subsidizing brick-and-mortar building through tax preferences rather than individuals' ability to exercise their own housing preferences leads to outcomes opposite of the intended effect of maximizing the quantity, quality, and choice of housing.[39] Project-based programs are least effective at subsidizing housing for those who need it. Tenant-based programs that provide certificates and vouchers maximizing choice are most effective in increasing housing stock.

Supply-Side Housing Innovations

An increasing amount of evidence suggests that zoning and other land use controls work against affordability in housing. Zoning restrictions, which decrease the amount of land available for development, are associated with higher prices. This suggests that such forms of regulation contribute to higher housing costs.

Reducing implied land use taxes on new construction has had considerable impact on housing prices when included in policy innovations. In England, for example, the use of supply-side finance policy demonstrated support for housing affordability through land use planning.

One key element in nearly all programs is the transfer of development rights. These programs increase housing supply by enabling owners to sell development rights, while encouraging denser residential development in city centers. New development can make an important contribution to housing affordability. The transfer of development rights has been used successfully in many developing and transitional markets such as India and Russia.

Technology and Financial Innovation

The nexus between information technology and financial product innovation is a pivotal factor in any housing finance system. The increasing sophistication of risk estimates, assuming data accuracy and the absence of fraud, enables innovation. The ability to evaluate creditworthiness and prepayment risk are examples of quantitative pricing, credit scoring, and risk management systems that are applied to home finance. With lower information processing and communications costs, the activities of back-office mortgage servicers have decreased as service providers extend their geographic scope.

---

39. Rybczynski (2010).

Credit analysis, with data based on debt payments relative to income, enables more precise measurement in the pricing of risk. The ability to assign credit scores and automate centralization of credit information can increase the access to credit and ability to monitor payments and cash flows at the consumer level. All of this enables greater standardization of documentation and financial structures, which again lowers housing costs.[40]

Future Innovations in Financing Housing

The long-established principles that worked in expanding access to capital for the housing industry are the basis for reinventing home finance for the future:

—Aligning interests of private capital funders with policy incentives

—Creating a diversified housing stock by eliminating the bias against subsidies for renters

—Pooling savings to create investment vehicles

—Using credit enhancement and guarantees to manage real estate risks

—Creating flexible capital structures for residential developments through structured finance

—Regulating land use to limit supply constraints.

Restoring the historic partnership of governments with private investors will be central to overcoming housing scarcity. Because government resources are increasingly limited, bringing back private investment is vital to the return of a vibrant housing finance system. However, entrenched biases will have to be overcome. One is the overwhelming preference of subsidies for homeownership over rental housing. This has led to rising homeownership accompanied by decreasing affordability. This situation predictably proved untenable. Loan-to-value ratios of 100 percent and negative amortization mortgages were never a sustainable innovation. Along with nonrecourse mortgages and lax regulation, these practices boosted demand for housing while unintentionally creating hidden incentives to default when prices declined.

Currently, spending programs and tax expenditures (subsidies transferred to consumers or investors through tax reductions) amount to $300 billion annually. The biggest share of these funds supports homeownership (about $230 billion) as compared to rental affordability (about $60 billion).[41] As a result, homeownership increased to 68 percent of all households, while the number of households spending more than 30 percent of their income on housing rose steadily during the past

---

40. Committee on the Global Financial System (2006).
41. Congressional Budget Office (2009).

decade.[42] To improve the housing sector, the gap between shelter and affordability must be bridged. Favorable tax policies and subsidies are needed for rental housing as well as homeownership to promote flexibility and choice in housing markets.

Closing the credit gap and moving beyond crisis management are the only ways to restore the confidence of international investors in mortgage products for residential single-family and multifamily housing. This will require public *and* private capital. The federal government's dominant role in the real estate markets must be phased out to free up its resources for other national priorities. Innovations need to focus on restoring the role of private investors (domestic and international) as drivers of homeownership and financing and on restoring confidence in securitization through mortgage-backed securities and covered bonds. This will require some resolution regarding what to do about Fannie Mae and Freddie Mac.

Rebooting Structured Finance in Housing

Securitizations or structured finance products aimed at spreading risk must return to basics. Important factors in this regard are disclosure transparency, the alignment of interests between mortgage sellers and capital market investors, improvement in collateral quality, and regulatory protections.

Several measures are being discussed that could contribute to solutions. Financial reform after the crisis created some challenges to the resurgence of the mortgage securitization market, including the 5 percent retention of risk by originating financial institutions. Some smaller, private-placement mortgage-backed securitizations have begun to appear recently, including one backed by the FDIC that included the performing loans of twelve failed banks and federal credit enhancement.[43]

More recent transactions have shown that private sector financing can be done with rates that are within 0.5 percent of the rates on mortgages financed through government-sponsored enterprises.[44] Nonetheless, the seemingly unlimited extension of the umbrella of Fannie Mae and Freddie Mac crowds out the private market, given the government's access to a lower cost of funds.

The major debate about how and when private securitization can reemerge revolves around the degree of guarantee provided by the government. One proposal is to create government-chartered issuers of mortgage-backed securities. These issuers would sell some home loans through government-guaranteed securities. The government-chartered firms would have regulated profitability and

---

42. McIlwain (2010) and Barth and others (2009).
43. England (2010).
44. See Adam Tempkin, "IFR-Sequoia Deal Bolsters Case for RMBS Revival," Reuters, March 1, 2011.

fees to cover government guarantees on affordable mortgages and rental housing. This would be an alternative to the almost complete dependence on government-sponsored enterprises.[45]

Alternatively, others recommend eliminating government guarantees and restricting securitization only to the highest-quality mortgages.[46] Issues of affordable housing could then be addressed directly through on-budget social policies rather than by extending off-budget guarantees (that eventually find their way back to the federal budget).

Other alternatives or additions to securitization include covered bonds, which are debt securities backed by the cash flow of mortgages that remain on the balance sheet of the issuing financial institutions. These have been effective in Europe and elsewhere but, to date, lack a statutory framework in the United States. Similar to securitization, the covered bond system creates tradable instruments that increase liquidity.

One feature of the Danish model of covered bonds could be helpful in other countries. The capital structure of these bonds enables borrowers to manage risks and mortgage balances as interest rates change. In this model, when a lender issues a mortgage, it is obligated to sell an equivalent bond with a maturity and cash flow that exactly match the underlying home loan. The issuer of the mortgage bond remains responsible for all payments on the bond, but the mortgage holder can buy back the bond in the market and use it to redeem his or her mortgage and deleverage household balance sheets when interest rates rise and home prices fall.[47] This ability to manage interest rate and credit risks has helped to reduce defaults and foreclosures in other countries and could help to do so in the United States as well.

Working out the Foreclosure Crisis

Usually, as has been the case historically, innovation emerges from new necessities created by crises and scarcity. A good way to see the beginnings of the next wave of financial innovation is to work through the problems created by the overhang of foreclosed properties arising from the mortgage meltdown.[48]

Until recently, the United States averaged more than 70,000 home repossessions a month. The crisis created a demand for ways to buy and rehabilitate

---

45. Mortgage Finance Study Group (2011).
46. Wallison, Pollock, and Pinto (2011).
47. Allen and Yago (2010).
48. This discussion is based largely on a financial innovations lab conducted for the Ford Foundation in 2009. REO Financial Innovations Lab, Milken Institute, February 2009.

properties that had entered foreclosure, had failed to sell at auction, and were owned by mortgage lenders. This real-estate-owned (REO) inventory expanded during the crisis from government-sponsored enterprises as well.

These properties, which remained vacant as supply outstripped demand, represented a resale inventory glut of 13.9 million homes by 2009, roughly 11 percent of all housing units and considerably more than housing vacancies in previous recessions. Housing markets and neighborhoods would benefit if investors were able to buy and rehabilitate these properties and turn them into long-term affordable housing or rental units.

Financing will be needed to address such challenges. The structural demand for capital includes short-term capital to acquire property, mid-term needs to rehabilitate or demolish homes, and exit financing to transfer property to a buyer.

At the same time, operational capacity to handle any surge in foreclosed and defaulted properties is reduced. This demands innovative pricing models that can aggregate capital sources to clear the logjam of foreclosed properties while maintaining ways to make these residences affordable. Let us consider these various dimensions of financial innovation in turn.

Using Innovative Pricing Models

In markets where house values are fluctuating, it is important to find ways to arrive at a fair, affordable price. Two innovative models have emerged from the crisis:

—*Top-down approach.* The National Community Stabilization Trust (NCST) starts with a market price under normal conditions and then derives a current value. It calculates a "net realizable value" by taking the estimated market value and subtracting holding, insurance, and other market-specific costs. Key to this approach is that the final sale price reflects local market conditions and predictions about future home prices.

—*Bottom-up approach.* The Community Asset Preservation Corporation (CAPC) of New Jersey buys pools of nonperforming mortgages and REO properties in low- and moderate-income communities. It then employs a variety of strategies to return these properties to productive use. Its pricing model starts with an estimate of current value and adds the costs necessary to bring the property to market. In March 2009, CAPC was the first nonprofit to complete a bulk purchase of foreclosed properties.

In both of these cases, the focus is on underwriting a borrower (rather than the property) into an affordable mortgage and thereby forcing a write-down of property value to the point where negative equity would be eliminated. By working with private funds that buy marked-down mortgages, the ability to create realistic values emerges.

Clearing the Property Logjam

Another important innovation has been setting up intermediaries between REO servicers and local housing organizations, nonprofits, or governmental agencies seeking to stabilize neighborhoods and alleviate collapsing values. For example, in 2008, some of the country's largest community development organizations— Enterprise Community Partners, Housing Partnership Network, Local Initiatives Support Corporation, and NeighborWorks America—came together to form the NCST. Today, the National Urban League is also part of the effort.

The nonprofit's goal is to act as a bridge between state and local housing providers and the REO departments within financial institutions, which are typically not accustomed to working together. The NCST facilitates the transfer of foreclosed properties to local and community development organizations. In addition, it provides flexible capital to help communities to leverage their Neighborhood Stabilization Program funds and finance state and local acquisition efforts. The trust also builds local capacity by organizing and facilitating collaboration and engagement with the trust's partners and acts as an industry voice for neighborhood stabilization.

Aggregating Capital

After the financial crisis, the Neighborhood Stabilization Program, part of the Housing and Economic Recovery Act, provided down-payment assistance and credit enhancement to leverage private capital by allocating $3.92 billion to state and local governments and nonprofits focused on housing. This amount could obviously only address a small portion of REO properties.

Until housing markets recover more fully, public subsidies and philanthropic capital must leverage private capital in order to have a widespread impact. Creative financing is necessary at each stage, from the acquisition of the properties to disposition.

Some strategies for aggregating capital might include the following:

—*Use program-related investments (PRIs).* PRIs, below-market investments, could be used more widely to subsidize returns for private capital. With public subsidies and dollars from socially motivated investors, PRIs could take the form of subordinated debt as an external credit enhancement.

—*Create credit-enhancement housing funds.* Government dollars could also be used for credit enhancement. Protecting private sector investments from the downside would encourage investors.

—*Create a publicly traded investment vehicle.* A publicly traded tax-advantaged vehicle for foreclosure acquisitions would be able to raise large amounts of private capital to stabilize communities.

—Allow specialized asset managers. New mortgage and securitization paradigms are essential. Creating safe harbors for specialized asset managers would allow them to make decisions on loan modification without fearing litigation from investors and to have more authority in administering the pool of loans. New investors could be brought in to meet stronger underwriting regulatory standards.

—Increase access to takeout financing to retire short-term or long-term debt on terms that are more favorable. Access to responsible takeout financing is essential to put individuals in homes they can afford by retiring and refinancing older mortgages on more favorable and sustainable terms. One example is the model successfully used by Neighborhood Assistance Corporation of America (NACA) in low- and moderate-income communities. NACA developed and uses online software that features a user-friendly application process and stores a borrower's documents. This greatly facilitates the underwriting of mortgages and enables it to offer a thirty-year fixed-rate product at a slightly below-market rate with no down payment and no closing costs. Only 0.0023 percent of homeowners who bought this product defaulted on their mortgages. In addition, the NACA holds free events around the country to restructure unaffordable mortgages.[49]

Preserving Affordability

Innovative financial products can help low- to moderate-income households to achieve the dream of homeownership more safely than the mortgage products that failed in recent years. Excessive leverage without equity sponsorship or equity support created capital structures and financial products that were likely to fail.

Negative equity, nonrecourse loans, and declining markets combine to create an incentive for borrowers to default. The most promising remedy to the problems of inadequate equity is not more but different equity. Financial options have emerged such as lease-purchase mortgages and shared-equity mortgages that provide a middle ground between rental and ownership. They are especially attractive for households that cannot initially qualify for a standard mortgage, but could be a candidate for homeownership several years down the road. Some options are as follows.

Shared-Equity Ownership

Models of shared equity, such as deed-restricted housing, community land trusts, and limited-equity cooperatives, are time-tested in the United States and Europe. A government or nonprofit invests in a property alongside the homebuyer.

---

49. For other interesting financing models, see Boyce, Hubbard, and Mayer (2011) and Shiller and others (2011).

Shared equity enables borrowers to trade some potential upside of a purchase for financing. Hundreds of these programs now operate in the United States.

Lease-to-Purchase Mortgages

The nonprofit Self-Help is piloting this more experimental solution. It buys and rehabilitates properties in Charlotte, North Carolina, and then leases the homes to "tenant purchasers"—renters likely to be able to assume Self-Help's lease-purchase mortgages in one to five years. During the rental period, Self-Help provides credit and homeownership counseling, as well as property management services, to the tenant purchasers. When the tenant qualifies, he or she assumes the lease-purchase mortgage from Self-Help.

Rental Housing

Federal housing policy has largely ignored rented residences. As noted, rental housing represents less than a third of the tax subsidies and expenditures provided for homeownership.[50] This is especially true for low-income rental housing, where the amount spent on assistance declined both as a percentage of nondefense discretionary spending and as a share of GDP. Until recently, rental vacancy rates hovered at their highest levels (8 percent) since 1980, and multifamily starts were down two-thirds from their peak two years ago.

The demand for new rental housing is increasing due to high levels of immigration, lower incomes, and the delayed entry of younger consumers into the workforce and housing markets. At the same time, aside from homeless assistance, all categories of low-income housing assistance for renters have declined in recent years, including Section 8 rental assistance through public-private partnerships, housing-choice vouchers that encouraged tenant mobility, and public housing. Clearly, structured finance products that address this growing demand for rental housing and developers will emerge.

Savings Models

In most rapidly growing Asian economies, some of the most promising models seek to encourage and leverage consumer savings to sustain housing finance. Compulsory and contractual savings schemes to provide a capital base for housing investment have proliferated. In China and Singapore, successful housing finance models have included mandatory "housing provident" funds. Employers and employees contribute a matching percentage of salary for housing-related expenses, including down payments, monthly payments, and building repairs.

50. Rice and Sard (2009).

Borrowings from the housing provident funds can be advanced for homeownership and used to leverage additional bank loans. Funds not used for housing are returned at retirement. China allows for a 5 percent contribution from employees and employers to build the housing fund.[51] In Singapore, the provident fund embeds lifetime earnings for retirement and channels money toward housing by allowing a household to borrow up to 20 percent of its retirement fund. Appreciation can accrue toward repayment of those loans on a deferred basis upon realization.[52]

Australia also has innovative mechanisms matching access to retirement funds with long-term housing assets for households with permanent jobs. Pension funds can provide additional cash that low- and moderate-income families can apply to down payments and mortgages. The use of pension fund savings can lower carrying costs substantially and increase the capacity of homeowners to support mortgage debt.[53]

Land Trusts

Renewable, long-term leaseholds are made available through land trusts that are held by nonprofit housing corporations or cooperatives for development. These land trusts or land banks enable nonprofits or governments to acquire, preserve, convert, and manage foreclosed and other vacant and abandoned properties. By permitting the relevant agency (public or nonprofit) to aggregate and obtain title to these properties, a usable asset is created to reduce blight, generate revenue, and facilitate affordable housing by lowering land acquisition costs and aggregating parcels for development.[54]

Organizational Innovations

Although housing has occupied a relatively small niche of microfinance, some microfinance institutions have expanded into the sector. In South Asia and Latin America, nonprofit microfinance institutions have joined government and private for-profit and nonprofit organizations as co-investors. By linking banks, housing agencies, and individual consumers, intermediaries can provide loans for housing rehabilitation, new homes, resettlement, and infrastructure.[55]

Microfinance institutions (Grameen, Banco Sol, MiBanco), nongovernmental organizations (Acción, FINCA), cooperatives, mutual savings associations,

---

51. Li and Yi (2007).
52. Chiquier and Lea (2009).
53. Ge (2009).
54. Milken Institute (2009).
55. United Nations Human Settlements Program (2008, pp. 13–15).

municipalities, government housing programs, and commercial banks have joined together to downscale lending, create new securities and guarantees, mobilize data technology for tracking credits, and mobilize credit enhancement to reduce lending risks.[56]

Housing Bonds

Mortgage banks have used long-term bonds to finance housing. If the bonds are tax exempt, banks can lower their cost of capital by issuing bonds at below-market interest rates. Housing agencies have issued bonds for mortgages on apartment rentals and owner-occupied housing. The agencies issuing the bonds fund private lending institutions that provide mortgages at a lower cost.[57]

Revolving Loan Funds

Revolving loan funds operate through a variety of organizational forms (government, nongovernmental organizations, and public-private partnerships in conjunction with commercial banks or non-bank lenders). These funds provide long-term, self-sustainable sources of finance to build and upgrade housing based on their initial capitalization (through government and nonprofit foundations) and driven by interest and repayment revenues. Under these funds, deficits are covered by drawdowns from accounts and interest charges. Loans can be disbursed by stages of construction and performance. In many cases, they are available for construction and home improvement and offer flexible conditions and options for repayment.[58]

Credit Enhancement

Credit enhancement, or the ability to cushion or protect against loan losses, has a long history and an important future in housing finance. By spreading the risk of loss, either through internal measures provided by the borrower or through external measures provided by government, philanthropic, or other outside entities, these measures can expand access to credit.

Credit enhancement provides a form of insurance that reduces the risk of loss based on detailed credit analysis. Internal credit enhancement is provided by the mortgage originator within subordinated layers of the capital structure and the structure of loan payments. Reserve accounts to insure against default risk are funded by excess interest rate spread payments (making larger payments

56. Escobar and Merrill (2004).
57. Gyntelberg and Remolona (2006).
58. National Development Council (2008).

than the amount needed for debt servicing), over-collateralization (holding assets of greater value than the debt issued), and additional debt coverage. External measures can be provided by outside parties, bank letters of credit, private or public insurance, additional guarantees or collateral pledged, or subordinated loans from other parties.[59]

In all these cases, loan losses are cushioned by enhancement pools covering a certain portion of the outstanding debt, thereby ensuring extension of additional credit risk. The adaptation of these measures by governments, multilateral organizations, philanthropies, and financial institutions has been increasingly widespread.

Unsecured Home Improvement Loans

When heating and cooling systems fail and must be replaced, homeowners can often obtain unsecured home improvement loans through their contractor. If contractors could refer them to loans offered by different financial institutions (with more choices and made cheaper through subsidies), the consumers' replacement decisions would be more likely to tip toward energy-efficient systems. Capital to support unsecured home improvement loans for greater energy efficiency comes from public and private sources (including Fannie Mae, state and local budgets, and banks). The following are several examples:

—*Public loan programs.* Widely available through partnerships with utilities and local banks, the Fannie Mae energy loan is the largest public source of unsecured loans. After originating a loan, the Fannie Mae–approved lender transfers loan obligations to Fannie Mae but continues to service the loan. It is one of very few loan programs with a functioning secondary market at this time. However, it will be challenging to expand, as the interest rate is high (currently between 12 and 15 percent).

—*Pennsylvania's Keystone Home Energy Loan Program (HELP).* Homeowners receive loans for energy-efficient home improvements at attractive terms in a program provided and subsidized by the state. The state administers the program and acts as a secondary market, buying loans from lenders through its pension funds. By acting as a ready buyer, the state secures the availability of residential home improvement lending and lowers the interest rate offered to borrowers.

While it might be expected that delinquencies and defaults would be a key challenge for these programs, loan-loss rates have been very low and have risen only slightly during the recession. The reason is self-selection by borrowers who are largely homeowners with no plans to move, great credit scores, and high home equity values. EnerBank reports a ten-year loss rate of only 0.8 percent,

---

59. A full discussion of all these measures can be found in Fabozzi and Choudhry (2004).

with a small but manageable rise in 2008 and 2009. There is little need for a secondary-market partner, as so many loans are paid off in the first year.

While funds for unsecured loans are constrained by the current credit crisis, a large and efficient infrastructure for processing and securitization already exists. Contractors sell the loans as part of their offerings, banks originate the loans, and the secondary markets securitize them as part of asset-backed security financings. Infrastructure for originating and distributing these loans and a strong base of expertise are already in place. A tiered interest rate to attract proactive buyers, with the best rates reserved for comprehensive home performance loans, appears to have a good track record. With access to a broader secondary market, these programs could grow.

Property Tax–Based Financing

Municipalities have long used property assessments and taxes to finance public projects. Property tax–based financings could also provide homeowners with funding for energy-efficient improvements and solar installations. The homeowner repays the loan through a voluntary increase in his or her property tax bill. Funds are provided by a local bond mechanism (similar to a municipal bond issued for a specific purpose, but taxable at the federal level). Repayment terms are long (ten to twenty years), and since repayment is tied to the tax bill and carries the same seniority over the mortgage, default rates should be generally low. Any property assessments in arrears have a senior lien in the event of default, which led to a Federal Housing Finance Agency directive not to underwrite mortgages for properties with an energy-related assessment. Current litigation and proposed legislation seek to overcome these concerns through Department of Energy and other certifications to ensure that savings can be supported and will serve the interests of building owners, municipalities, and mortgage lenders.

Because basic efficiency measures can cut energy costs by up to 35 percent annually, energy savings are believed to exceed the cost of the related tax assessment, thereby overcoming the up-front cost barrier by financing over a longer term and improving cash flow for owners.[60] Once regulatory and legal issues are addressed, similar options will almost certainly materialize. The loan obligation moves to the next owner if the home is sold. In theory, the energy savings would be greater than the increase in property tax, generating a positive cash flow to the homeowner.

The pool of loans is not tax exempt at the federal level, so it cannot be sold into the tax-free municipal bond market. This decreases liquidity significantly, as the tax-free segment of the overall market totals $600 billion a year, while the

60. NREL (2010).

taxable segment is $6 billion a year. Additionally, the lack of an active securitization market limits liquidity. Once the secondary markets do open, government agencies and philanthropic funds could provide credit enhancement to pools of loans, enabling purchase at lower risk.

As a voluntary property tax increase, this type of financing is designed to take seniority over an existing mortgage. New mortgages can be issued with this seniority clearly spelled out, but seniority status for existing mortgages has been challenged. It is not a matter of simply getting the mortgage lender to agree to a change in status. Most mortgages are not held by the original lender, but have been placed in securitized loan pools held by a large number of investors. Financial institutions holding large mortgage pools are concerned about losing their senior position. Legal opinions vary on this, and the issue has not been resolved.

Sixteen states have passed legislation for these property tax–based programs, allowing municipalities to create financing districts. Pilots have been launched in California (Sonoma County, Berkeley, and Palm Desert); Babylon, New York; and Boulder, Colorado. In these programs, home loans have been financed out of general obligation funds, so the market's acceptance of these new financial products has not been tested. Homeowner acceptance has been good, but project scale to date has been small in each locale. The White House included property-based finance as a major component of the Recovery through Retrofit Plan.[61] The California Energy Commission has funded expansion of the Property Assessed Clean Energy Program throughout California with its allocation of the American Recovery and Reinvestment Act of 2009 funds for energy efficiency.

Whether programs are administered by local government or by an outsourced administrative partner (such as the start-up company Renewable Funding), the key bottleneck is the transfer of loans from the originator to the secondary markets. An early aggregator and buyer of bonds would resolve a key risk. Credit enhancement by the federal government, or possibly state and local government, is needed for property-backed bonds to be placed in the secondary market. Private markets are not in a position to provide this insurance, but such bonds may have strong appeal to new lenders since they are secured by tax liens and have seniority to mortgage debt, pending expected legislative resolution of the issues surrounding these innovations. In any case, the attempt to link long-term asset development to improved energy and environmental efficiency will continue.

One large investment required by Clean Energy Works Portland was a unified software platform for loan origination and processing. This platform works for three utilities. It is hoped that access to loan payment history, the best predictor of

61. White House Council on Environmental Quality (2009).

default risk, will help with underwriting and servicing. The platform is intended to become a regional demonstration project.

Lessons Learned: Back to the Future

Financial innovation is an imperative for promoting well-functioning housing markets. Changes in the structural demand for capital in housing are demographically driven and shape market structure and performance. Urbanization and household formation have fueled financial innovation in housing markets throughout history—from the very first mortgages to covered bonds, guarantees, insurance, tax credits and subsidies, and secondary-market development. Regardless of geography, using cash alone to buy or build housing has long proven infeasible for the vast majority of people. In earlier historical periods, specialized lenders charged relatively high interest rates that limited access to capital and impeded the entry of new participants, such as developers, consumers, and financial intermediaries. Financial innovations, however, enabled private investors to enter the market, fund development, and create long-term, low-cost sources of capital. All of these innovations required reporting, regulation, and oversight.

Securitization contributed to the housing bubble. Originators ignored credit risk, underwriting standards were excessively loosened, and investors in such securities failed to exercise proper diligence. However, securitization—directly and through covered bonds and other structured products—lowered funding costs, created sources of capital for borrowers, and expanded opportunities for institutional investors around the world. Innovative loan products can reduce the costs to creditworthy borrowers (either homeowners or developers of rental housing), while other products enable financial institutions to manage risk and free up capital that can be used to fund housing.[62]

From the Homestead Act and other nineteenth-century land reforms to the emergence of secondary mortgage markets and securitization, innovation has been a vital element of housing finance. Market-based finance emerged over the past century and became important throughout the world. It has varied widely in form, mix of instruments, government support, market structure, and types of housing. There is no "one size fits all" version.

Highly regulated and noncompetitive financial systems have been curtailed as the importance of property rights has become more widely recognized through land reform, land registries, and collateralization.

---

62. Phelps and Tilman (2010).

With greater access to capital, the cost of financing has fallen, making home-ownership and rental housing more affordable over the past century. The increased availability and range of mortgage products for homebuyers and developers, combined with structured finance, has created greater liquidity in real estate markets and driven trillions of dollars of investment into this sector. Moreover, mortgage-equity withdrawals have contributed greatly to credit availability and hence aggregate consumption.[63]

During the recent housing bubble, however, home prices went far above what average families could afford. Public and business policies that eased lending requirements and led to laxer and less transparent underwriting standards seriously slanted debt-to-equity ratios. As ever more mortgage defaults and foreclosures ensued, liquidity constraints in markets collapsed when the housing price bubble burst. As credit markets froze and contagion spread throughout the financial sector, the macroeconomic conditions that had encouraged growth and access disappeared.

Housing markets, structured finance, and mortgage-backed securities function properly when transparent information, independent analysis, and standardized reporting are available. But, as transparency is replaced by conformity and opaque reporting—and as mortgage originators become detached from the consequences of excessive lending due to perverse incentives—problems arise. The wisdom of crowds is replaced by the madness of mobs in the mortgage marketplace and, as investors flee, markets spiral downward.

In all the banking and financial crises we have studied, periods of initial financial liberalization and prosperity in real estate markets drove demand to peaks that led to regulatory failures, overpricing, and shoddy risk analysis.[64] Our review of the long sweep of housing finance history yields the following lessons, which are consistent across time in developed and emerging markets alike.

Lesson 1: Do Not Compromise on Credit Analysis

As demand for mortgage-backed securities outstripped supply and inflated home values, guidelines designed to ease credit failed. Lenders neglected fundamental analysis, thereby increasing information asymmetries between all parties in the housing market (largely through principal-agent conflicts that drove moral hazard and adverse selection).

Nearly $20 trillion in mortgages originated during the period of easy credit from 2003 to 2008. Before 2007, when housing prices began to decline,

---

63. Ducka, Muellbauer, and Murphy (2011).
64. Barth and others (2003).

residential real estate was estimated at $60 trillion. By 2011, it had declined to $50 trillion with a lot of wealth destroyed in Ireland, Spain, and other European countries, as well as the United States.

Whether attempting to fund new housing in emerging countries or to understand the complexities of CDOs, clear and reliable information is essential. Investors need to know about titles, financial accounts, deeds, and contracts. This information makes it possible to determine values, assess risks, and track performance. As Hernando de Soto states, "Without standardization, the values of assets and relationships are so variable that they can't be used to guarantee credit, to generate mortgages and bundle them into securities, to represent them in shares to raise capital."[65]

Clear property rights are vital in order to expand access to affordable housing—whether owned or rented—in emerging or developed markets. Property rights facilitate housing credit by establishing clear collateral and legal claims. Transparent real estate laws are also critical for effective credit analysis and allocation.

Weakly underwritten instruments and private securitizations (which were later replaced by government agencies during the crisis) increased borrowers' incentives to default due to their limited equity at stake and lack of adequate recourse by lenders. The proliferation of new and flexible mortgage products alone was not the primary cause of the market failure. Instead the abbreviated loan process and abandonment of long-proven underwriting standards led many of those products to fail.

Underwriters ignored transaction costs (such as escrow taxes and insurance), enabled loan-to-value ratios above historically proven safe limits, and allowed automated and unverified valuation models. A large part of the problem was that mortgage brokers that originated the loans passed on the risk and were paid by volume. The resulting layering of risk—based on deceptive credit terms, financial illiteracy, or fraud by borrowers—led to a flood of credit on inappropriate terms.

These failings led to the explosion of moral hazard, which ultimately pushed the costs of excessive risk onto taxpayers. Foreclosures, delinquencies, and negative equity left an unprecedented number of vacant homes, increasing downward pressure on values in struggling neighborhoods.

Lesson 2: Flexible Capital Structure Matters

Financially sustainable capital structures for the housing market require a balance of debt *and* equity. Early innovations in funding for housing, such as savings and loans, developed a method for collectively accumulating equity to support

---

65. Hernando de Soto, "The Destruction of Economic Facts," *Bloomberg BusinessWeek*, April 28, 2011.

long-term lending. These pioneering principles were later embedded in government entities, nonprofit organizations, formal financial institutions, and home-
savings products. Lessons from these earliest models of peer-to-peer lending
could be applied to recent problems in developed economies and help to satisfy
the growing demand in emerging and frontier markets. New investment vehicles
can arise from old innovations.[66]

Since the Great Depression, long-term (twenty- to thirty-year), fixed-rate mortgages have financed homeownership and enabled developers to provide affordable
rental housing. This innovation sprang from the failure of earlier capital structures
in housing and the absence of long-term, low-cost loans. After the saturation of
the housing market in the United States in 1925, lending standards were loosened as property values rose. Homes were bought with short-term loans (three
to five years) requiring 50 percent equity payments. Many buyers would take out
secondary loans to pay for the primary loan and purchase price. The classic mistake of financing long-term housing assets with short-term loans, coupled with
inadequate equity, led to massive defaults and delinquencies as values declined.

When the housing market collapsed in the Great Depression, the federal government offered refinancing through creation of the Home Owners' Loan Corporation. Later the Federal Housing Administration provided broader mortgage
insurance, which enabled the absorption of excess inventory and restored the
flow of credit. Extended loan maturities became the new standard in real estate
markets in the United States and abroad.

With proper underwriting, the thirty-year, fixed-rate mortgage increased the
supply of sustainable credit. The alignment of interests between homebuyers,
developers, and lenders continued under conditions that enabled liquidity, standardization, and transparency. Rebooting securitization with retained-interest
transactions by originators, introducing covered bonds, and dealing with other
gaps in the market's capital structure are vital to reinventing housing finance.
Loan modification programs, debt-for-equity swaps that allow rent-to-own as
an alternative to foreclosure, and encouragement of investor finance could also
be helpful.[67] All of these measures could improve liquidity over the longer run.

New policies and programs that enable shared equity, flexibility in mortgage
refinancing, and lower transaction costs in finance for homeownership and rental
housing can overcome the frictions that have hampered monetary policy, inflated
foreclosures, and slowed economic recovery.[68]

66. Tufano and Schneider (2007, 2008).
67. Ranieri and others (2011).
68. Miles and Pillonca (2008).

Lesson 3: Size Matters

Supersized mortgages and houses contributed to much of the overleveraging and sprawling developments that made housing unaffordable. According to the Census Bureau, the average new home sold in the United States ballooned in size over the last three decades from 1,700 square feet to 2,422. That's a 42 percent increase, with the trend intensifying since the late 1990s. "McMansions" had nothing to do with making room for more kids. (The average size of the American household fell from 2.76 people in 1980 to 2.57 in 2009.) Instead, rising home prices lured some consumers into an excessive reliance on housing as an investment—building homes that were larger than needed and harder to maintain, with the anticipation that they would serve as a giant savings account and the added benefit of appreciation.[69] Taste may also have been a factor in the shift to larger homes.

What if houses shrank back to the size expected by the typical U.S. homebuyer thirty years ago? The average new home would have been 722 square feet smaller in 2009. If you consider the average cost per square foot, returning to the expectations of our parents' generation would have produced a savings of $80,000 per home in 2009 alone. America's total expenditures on all new homes sold over the past thirty years would have been $1.2 trillion less in today's dollars, and those savings would continue to accrue in the future—that is, before taking into account the cost of furnishing, heating, cooling, and cleaning all that extra space.

Today, Americans devote 34 percent of their household expenditures to their homes. But if Americans are willing to rethink their assumptions about what size their houses should be, they could radically improve the lives of those who live in those homes.

The relationship between housing size, suburbanization, and exurbanization and the demand for increased energy inputs have created costs that should be factored into twenty-first-century credit analysis. Factors such as neighborhood compactness, access to public transit, and rates of vehicle ownership affect mortgage performance. There is a direct, statistically significant link between longer, costlier commuting and a higher risk of default.[70] Transportation and energy costs take a growing toll on disposable income as urban settlement patterns are increasingly dispersed. Since roughly 17 percent of an average U.S. household income goes to transportation costs, mortgage underwriting procedures should consider this factor as it relates to financial risk.

Mixed use and diversification that accompany location efficiency are also key factors in stabilizing housing markets. Diversification by income levels, use (retail

---

69. See James R. Barth, Tong Li, and Rick Palacios, "McMansion Economics," *Los Angeles Times*, November 21, 2010.

70. Rauterkus, Thrall, and Hangen (2010).

and residential), and tenure (rental and ownership) attract different elements of demand that result in more sustainable communities. Reduced isolation, labor market access, and other elements that strengthen social capital in communities appear to bolster financial and environmental sustainability as well.[71]

Lesson 4: Structured Products and Secondary Markets Work

If lenders and investors monitor credit quality and if timely, adequate information is provided, securitization works well. Beyond the product, market, and regulatory failures previously noted, the ability to securitize (with proper risk retention by originators to align interests) is central to housing finance. The linkage of risk management and capital access for housing has been historically demonstrated.

Secondary markets expand liquidity and help to balance the broader costs and risks of housing finance. They provide access to capital across market segments (including low- and moderate-income borrowers), types (owner-occupied and rental housing), geographies (urban and rural), and originators (including credit unions, micro lenders in developing countries, and community-based lenders). The link between housing finance and macroeconomic growth policy can be achieved by providing borrowers with a wide choice of products.

As information technology, data reporting, and regulatory transparency become more widespread, the transitions to recovering secondary markets and securitization will succeed without sacrificing stability.

For housing to be affordable and sustainable, securitization, covered bonds, and other hybrid products are required. Long-term, fixed-rate mortgages require liquidity in real estate financing. Capital markets have proven fundamental to this process insofar as they enable the diversification of risk for investors while avoiding its re-concentration on financial institution balance sheets, as occurred in the most recent crisis.

Regulatory measures, when successful, ensure benefits to renters, owners, and developers in single-family and multifamily housing. Government guarantees and subsidies could enable sustainable financial innovation by private, nonprofit, and public investors. New products and delivery modes for housing construction, access, and retrofitting are important.

Final Remarks

Beyond the economic characteristics of housing as a physical structure providing shelter and investment value to consumers lies the broader meaning of homes and the hopes and dreams tied to them. As the housing crisis in the developing world and the major disruptions in developed markets prove, there

71. Lees (2008).

are no quick fixes or applications that can be cut and pasted into vastly different demographics, economic environments, and capital markets. Nonetheless, the principles of housing finance remain consistent, achievable, and available to guide the creation of affordable homes and sustainable communities to better serve society's interests.

References

Allen, Franklin, and Glenn Yago. 2010. *Financing the Future.* New York: Pearson.

Allen, Franklin, James R. Barth, and Glenn Yago. 2012. *Fixing the Housing Market: Financial Innovations for the Future.* New York: Pearson.

Bardhan, Ashok, and Robert H. Edelstein. 2009. "Housing Finance in Emerging Economies: Applying a Benchmark from Developed Countries." In *Mortgage Markets Worldwide,* edited by Danny-Shahar, Seow Eng Ong, and Charles Leung. Oxford, U.K.: Blackwell Publishing.

Barth, James R., with Tong Li, Wenling Lu, Tripon Phumiwasana, and Glenn Yago. 2009. *The Rise and Fall of the U.S. Mortgage and Credit Markets: A Comprehensive Analysis of the Meltdown.* Hoboken, N.J.: John Wiley and Sons.

Barth, James R., Daniel E. Nolle, Triphon Phumiwasana, and Glenn Yago. 2003. "A Cross-Country Analysis of the Bank Supervisory Framework and Bank Performance." *Financial Markets, Institutions, and Instruments* 12, no. 2 (May): 67–120.

Bernanke, Ben S. 2009. "The Future of Mortgage Finance in the United States." *B.E. Journal of Economic Analysis and Policy* 9, no. 3: 1–10.

Bodfish, Morton. 1931. "History of Building and Loans in the United States." Chicago: U.S. Building and Loan League.

———. 1935. "The Depression Experience of Savings and Loan Associations in the United States." Address delivered in Salzburg, Austria, September.

Boyce, Alan, Glenn Hubbard, and Chris Mayer. 2011. "Streamlined Refinancings for up to 30 Million Borrowers." Columbia University, September 1. (www4.gsb.columbia.edu/filemgr?file_id=739308).

Census Bureau. 1961. *Historical Statistics of the United States, Colonial Times to 1957: A Statistical Abstract Supplement.* Washington: Government Printing Office.

Chiquier, Loic, and Michael Lea. 2009. *Housing Finance Policy in Emerging Markets.* Washington: World Bank.

Cohen, Jeffrey P., Cletus C. Coughlin, and David A. Lopez. 2012. "The Boom and Bust of U.S. Housing Prices from Various Geographic Perspectives." *Federal Reserve Bank of St. Louis Review* 94, no. 5 (September-October): 341–68.

Collins, Williams J., and Robert A. Margo. 1999. "Race and Home Ownership." NBER Working Paper 7277. Cambridge, Mass.: National Bureau of Economic Research, August.

———. 2011. "Race and Home Ownership from the Civil War to the Present." NBER Working Paper 16665. Cambridge, Mass.: National Bureau of Economic Research, January.

Committee on the Global Financial System. 2006. "Housing Finance in the Global Financial Market." Working Paper 26. Geneva: Bank for International Settlements, January.

Congressional Budget Office. 2009. "An Overview of Federal Support for Housing." Washington, November 3.

Ducka, John V., John Muellbauer, and Anthony Murphy. 2011. "How Financial Innovations and Accelerators Drive Booms and Busts in U.S. Consumption." Working Paper. Federal Reserve Bank of Dallas, May.

Ellis, Luci. 2008. "The Housing Meltdown: Why Did It Happen in the United States?" BIS Working Papers 259. Geneva: Bank for International Settlements, September.

EMF (European Mortgage Federation). 2009. *Hypostat 2009*. Brussels.

———. 2010. *Hypostat 2010*. Brussels.

England, Robert Stowe. 2010. "Rebooting the Private MBS Market." *Mortgage Banking*, October 1.

Ergungor, O. Emre. 2011. "Homeowner Subsidies." *Economic Commentary*. Federal Reserve Bank of Cleveland, February 23.

Escobar, Alejandro, and Sally R. Merrill. 2004. "Housing Microfinance: The State of Practice." In *Housing Microfinance: A Guide to Practice*, edited by F. Daphnis and B. Ferguson. Bloomfield: Kumarian Press.

Fabozzi, Frank J., and Moorad Choudhry, eds. 2004. *The Handbook of European Structured Financial Products*. Hoboken, N.J.: John Wiley and Sons.

Fine, John V. A. 1951. *Horoi: Studies in Mortgage, Real Security, and Land Tenure in Ancient Athens*. Hesperia, Supplement IX. Athens: American School of Classical Studies in Athens.

Fisher, Lynn M., and Austin J. Jaffe. 2003. "Determinants of International Homeownership Rates." *Housing Finance International* (September): 37.

Frederiksen, D. M. 1894. "Mortgage Banking in America." *Journal of Political Economy* 2, no. 2 (March): 203–34.

Ge, Janet Xin. 2009. "An Alternative Financing Method for Affordable Housing." *Housing Finance International* 24, no. 3 (December): 34–38.

Global Property Guide. 2011. "Global Housing Markets under Pressure, Says Global Property Guide." *Investment Analysis*, August 26 (www.globalpropertyguide.com/investment-analysis/Global-housing-markets-under-pressure-says-Global-Property-Guide).

Green, Richard K., and Susan M. Wachter. 2005. "The American Mortgage in Historical and International Context." *Journal of Economic Perspectives* 19, no. 4 (Fall): 93–114.

Gyntelberg, J., and E. Remolona. 2006. "Securitization in Asia and the Pacific: Implications for Liquidity and Credit Risks." *Bank for International Settlements Quarterly Review* (June).

Haines, Michael R., and Allen C. Goodman. 1991. "A Home of One's Own: Aging and Homeownership in the United States in the Late Nineteenth and Early Twentieth Centuries." NBER Working Paper 21. Cambridge, Mass.: National Bureau of Economic Research, January.

Joint Center for Housing Studies. 2010. "2009 State of Nation's Housing." Harvard University.

Lea, Michael. 2010a. "Alternative Forms of Mortgage Finance: What Can We Learn from Other Countries?" Paper prepared for Joint Center for Housing Studies National Symposium, Moving Forward: The Future of Consumer Credit and Mortgage Finance, Harvard Business School, February 18.

———. 2010b. "International Comparison of Mortgage Product Offerings." Special Report. Research Institute for Housing America, Mortgage Bankers Association, September.

———. 2010c. Testimony to Subcommittee on Security and International Trade and Finance, Committee on Banking, Housing and Urban Affairs, United States Senate, September 29.

Lees, Loretta. 2008. "Gentrification and Social Mixing: Towards an Inclusive Urban Renaissance." *Urban Studies* 45, no. 12 (November): 2449–76.

Li, Si-Ming, and Zheng Yi. 2007. "Financing Home Purchase in China, with Special Reference to Guangzhou." *Housing Studies* 22, no. 3: 409–25.

McIlwain, John. 2010. "Housing in America: The Next Decade." Trustees Meeting, Urban Land Institute, January 26.

McKinsey & Company. 2009. "Global Capital Markets: Entering a New Era." September.

Miles, David, and Vladimir Pillonca. 2008. "Financial Innovation and European Housing and Mortgage Markets." *Oxford Review of Economic Policy* 24, no. 1: 176–79.

Milken Institute. 2009. "Financial Innovations for Housing: After the Meltdown." Financial Innovations Lab Report 12. Santa Monica, Calif., November.

Mortgage Finance Study Group. 2011. "A Responsible Market for Housing Finance: A Progressive Plan to Reform the U.S. Secondary Market for Residential Mortgages." Washington: Center for American Progress, January.

National Archives and Records Administration. 2010. "The Homestead Act of 1862." Washington, June 30.

National Development Council. 2008. "Revolving Loan Fund Handbook." California Department of Housing and Community Development.

NREL (National Renewal Energy Laboratory). 2010. "Property-Assessed Clean Energy (PACE) Financing of Renewables and Efficiency." Fact Sheet Series on Financing Energy Renewable Projects. Golden, Colo.: NREL Energy Analysis, July (www.nrel.gov/docs/fy10osti/47097.pdf).

Odaira, Noritsugu, and Shuichiro Takado. 2008. "Update on Japan's Securitization Market Initiatives to Enhance the Transparency and Traceability of Information." *CMBS World* 10, no. 3 (Fall): 14–56.

Office of Thrift Supervision. 2011. "2010 Fact Book: A Statistical Profile of the Thrift Industry." Washington, June.

Paulson, Henry. 2008. "Best Practices for Residential Covered Bonds." Washington: U.S. Treasury Department, July.

Peterson Institute for International Economics. 2012. "Household Wealth and the Housing Market." March 6.

Phelps, Edmund S., and Leo M. Tilman. 2010. "Wanted: A First National Bank of Innovation." *Harvard Business Review* (January): 6–13.

Pollock, Alex. 2010. Testimony to Subcommittee on Security and International Trade and Finance, Committee on Banking, Housing, and Urban Affairs, U.S. Senate, September 29.

Rabinowitz, Harvey. 2002. "The Woods at Bath: Pioneers of Real Estate Development." *Wharton Real Estate Review* (Fall): 65–71.

Ranieri, Lewis S., Kenneth T. Rosen, Andrea Lepcio, and Buck Collins. 2011. "Plan B: A Comprehensive Approach to Moving Housing, Households, and the Economy Forward." Ranieri Partners Management and Rosen Consulting, April 4.

Rauterkus, Stephanie Yates, Grant Thrall, and Eric Hangen. 2010. "Location Efficiency and Mortgage Default." *Journal of Sustainable Real Estate* 2, no. 1: 117–41.

Rice, Douglas, and Barbara Sard. 2009. "Decade of Neglect Has Weakened Federal Low-Income Housing Programs." Washington: Center for Budget and Policy Priorities, February 24.

Rybczynski, Witold. 2010. "How Affordable Is Affordable Housing?" Working Paper 497. Philadelphia: Zell-Lurie Real Estate Center, December.

Shiller, Robert J. 2007. "Understanding Recent Trends in House Prices and Home Ownership." Economics Department Working Paper 28. Yale University, October.

Shiller, Robert J., Rafal M. Wojakowski, M. Shahid Ebrahim, and Mark B. Shackleton. 2011. "Continuous Workout Mortgages." Discussion Paper 1794. Yale University, Cowles Foundation for Research in Economics, April.

Summers, Lawrence. 2007. "Recent Financial Market Disruptions: Implications for the Economy and American Families." Panel discussion, Brookings Institution, Washington, September 26.

Traclet, Virginie. 2010. "An Overview of the Canadian Housing Finance System." *Housing Finance International* (Autumn): 6–13.

Tufano, Peter, and Daniel Schneider. 2007. "New Savings from Old Innovations: Asset Building for the Less Affluent." In *Financing Low-Income Communities*, edited by Julia S. Rubin. New York: Russell Sage Foundation Publications.

———. 2008. "Using Financial Innovation to Support Savers: From Coercion to Excitement." In *Insufficient Funds: Savings, Assets, Credit, and Banking among Low-Income Households,* edited by Rebecca Blank and Michael Barr. New York: Russell Sage Foundation Publications.

United Nations. 2012. "2011 Revision of World Urbanization Prospects." New York, March.

United Nations Human Settlements Program. 2008. "Housing for All: The Challenges of Affordability, Accessibility, and Sustainability: A Synthesis Report." Nairobi, Kenya.

Wallison, Peter J., Alex J. Pollock, and Edward J. Pinto. 2011. "Taking the Government Out of Housing Finance: Principles for Reforming the Housing Finance Market." Washington: American Enterprise Institute, March 24.

Warnock, Veronica C., and Frank Warnock. 2008. "Markets and Housing Finance." *Journal of Housing Economics* 17, no. 3: 239–51.

White House Council on Environmental Quality. 2009. "Recovery through Retrofit: Saving Homeowners Money and Creating Jobs." Middle Class Task Force, October (www.white house.gov/assets/documents/Recovery_Through_Retrofit_Final_Report.pdf).

THOMAS JACKSON
DAVID SKEEL

3

Bankruptcy and Economic Recovery

T O MEASURE ECONOMIC growth or recovery, one traditionally looks to metrics such as the unemployment rate and the growth in gross domestic product (GDP). To devise institutional policies that will stimulate economic growth,
the focus most often is on policies that encourage investment and entrepreneurial
enterprises and reward risk taking with appropriate returns. As bankruptcy academics, we tend to add our own area of expertise to this stable—with the firm
belief that thinking critically about bankruptcy policy is an important element of
any set of institutions designed to speed economic recovery. In this paper, we outline the crucial role that bankruptcy plays in advancing a robust economy, while
also identifying several areas in which bankruptcy law—and practice—could be
improved so as to enhance bankruptcy's role in economic growth, including its
recovery from periods of recession. Along the way, we suggest that a standard
(and appropriate) baseline metric for successful economic policies—namely, employment—if carried outside its macro focus so as to become an independent
bankruptcy policy (as it often is), carries with it, often inadvertently, the potential
to undermine bankruptcy's key role in facilitating economic growth.

Bankruptcy and Economic Growth

We start by outlining our underlying proposition: an effective free-market,
entrepreneurial economy depends on the existence of an effective bankruptcy

process. This is so because, while entrepreneurial innovation is usually conceived in terms of its successes—encouraging the flow of funds to new businesses and ideas driven by the prospect of riches—the reality is that the prospect of large returns for risk taking also means the necessary potential for failure and loss. The correlation between risk and return has a downside as well as an upside; thus in anything resembling a free-market, entrepreneurial economy, rewarding successful risk taking requires consequences to unsuccessful risk taking. Only in Lake Wobegon—or a society where government bailouts are the norm—can all ventures succeed. The natural opposition to bailout by those who have faith in the reward and punishment nature of markets, whether of financial firms or industrial firms—or, indeed, categories of creditors—is born from the realization that bailouts distort incentives and interfere with important market mechanisms for monitoring and disciplining firms.

Modern bankruptcy law primarily exists[1] to reduce the frictions that otherwise would impede assets from moving to their highest-and-best use. Even those who think this is too narrow a description of the purposes of bankruptcy law would almost certainly agree that it is a, if not the, *primary* purpose. When a firm is insolvent—when its liabilities exceed its assets at fair valuation—and the creditors realize that not all of them will be paid in full, the creditors have incentives to demand payment or to use available judicial procedures to seize assets sooner rather than later. "First-come, first-served" is a sensible policy for solvent firms, but it creates externalities—a common pool problem—for insolvent firms.[2] This use of individual creditor remedies will result in the assets of a firm being pulled apart and the firm being dismantled. But not all insolvent firms should be liquidated; there is a recognized distinction between economic failure (a firm should be shuttered) and financial failure (liabilities exceed assets). Sometimes, the assets are being used for their highest-and-best use, and it would be inefficient to have creditors, lacking a coordination mechanism, pull the firm apart, "saving" some creditors but imposing costs on the creditors as a group—and on society.

A simple example of the distinction between insolvency and financial failure is perhaps helpful. When Johns Manville filed for bankruptcy in the early 1980s, the firm appeared to be solidly solvent but, in fact, was hopelessly insolvent. The insolvency was due, in significant part, to crushing liability in tort for its manufacture of asbestos, generally twenty to forty years earlier—the time

---

1. Here we speak of its role for firms and other commercial ventures. We set aside the separate policy, applicable to human beings, of a "fresh start."

2. This was first explored in a systematic fashion in Jackson (1982). While the author may regret the phrase "creditors' bargain," which has taken on a life of its own (often as used by critics), the central point of bankruptcy as a response to externalities remains core.

frame for asbestosis to reveal itself. It would take time for the tort creditors to manifest themselves, but it was clear in 1982 when it filed that—over time—Johns Manville simply could not pay bank, trade, and tort creditors alike. By the 1980s, Johns Manville was no longer manufacturing asbestos; it was a diversified building-supply company. If it did not have the crushing tort liability based on products it produced in its past, there was every reason to believe that one would want Johns Manville to continue doing just what it was doing—producing (non-asbestos-based) building supplies. But as the realization of this massive tort liability "overhang" spread, it would have been impossible for Johns Manville to continue in business without a collectivizing process such as bankruptcy: its consensual creditors would have demanded payment, so as to finish ahead of the tort creditors (whose claims were often still latent or disputed), and new lenders and suppliers would have become increasingly leery of Johns Manville. By collectivizing the creditors, stopping the use of individual creditor remedies, and giving priority to post-bankruptcy creditors who dealt with Johns Manville, bankruptcy allowed the thorny issues of "who got what" to be separated from the simpler issue of the "highest-and-best" use of the assets—that is, continuing the business Johns Manville was in.[3]

There is a second frictional problem that bankruptcy is designed to address—although, as we discuss, we believe it is less effective in reaching this goal. And that is to shift control (and ownership) from the old equity owners to the creditors. In an insolvent firm, the old equity owners are the wrong decisionmakers. They have every incentive to take extravagant risks, since the (small) possibility of enormous returns becomes the only way in which the equity owners will see their interests return "to the money."[4] In effect, at this time, they are playing with "other people's money" for their own potential benefit. Equity owners of an insolvent business have incentives not only to string things along for as long as possible, but also to increase the riskiness of the firm's business. Bankruptcy responds to this concern by allowing the creditors to commence—or force—a proceeding in which residual ownership claims pass from the equity owners to the creditors.[5]

---

3. This is not to say that accomplishing this was "simple." Many of the asbestosis claimants were unknown and awkwardly fit within the definition of a "claim" under Bankruptcy Code § 105. See, generally, Roe (1984, p. 846), Jackson (1986, pp. 47–54), and Skeel (2001, pp. 217–21).

4. This is different from "retain *any* value," as—absent a control-shift mechanism that wipes equity out—equity *always* has a positive value. This is a consequence of limited liability, which prevents equity from ever being worth less than nothing. Thus even the remotest upside possibility creates positive value for equity.

5. As with collectivization, this is almost impossible to "write" as a contract term—as a form of an "option" contract giving creditors equity control rights upon insolvency—although it might be more plausible as a nonbankruptcy legal rule, as indeed it is possible to see state-law fiduciary duty obligations imposed on boards when a firm is insolvent. See note 15.

Thus bankruptcy plays a crucial role in undergirding the mobility of assets to their highest-and-best use; it is an essential component of any market-based economic system and hence an important element to enhance policies for economic growth and economic recovery. The question, which we turn to next, is whether bankruptcy's policies and practices are, by and large, sufficient, or whether consideration should be given to tweaking bankruptcy, so as to strengthen its important role in facilitating economic growth.[6] Although we suggest a variety of possible adjustments, overall U.S. bankruptcy law works quite well.

Bankruptcy Law and Practice: Two Problems and Some Suggested Remedial Steps

At the start of the twenty-first century, American bankruptcy law is probably the best in the world at separating the consequences of insolvency from impeding the placement of assets in their most productive use.[7] Part of this is due to long experience with bankruptcy law and the American system of adhering to the "rule of law," meaning that bankruptcy's rules are known in advance and usually adhered to in reality. And part of it is the consequence of a history of remarkable innovation—such as the equity receivership for railroad reorganizations in the late nineteenth and early twentieth century—that led us to use bankruptcy as a utilitarian tool rather than as a device of shame and punishment. What has emerged is a set of rules such as the automatic stay provisions that impose an across-the-board standstill the moment a company files for bankruptcy; provisions permitting the debtor to assume executory contracts—contracts with material performance left on both sides—even if they are in default; reach-back rules that permit the debtor to retrieve transfers that were made shortly before bankruptcy; and priority rules that generally fit within the broader notion that bankruptcy law has something important to say about the separation of financial failure from economic failure. Perhaps less obvious, but no less important, for bankruptcy's effectiveness are its rules permitting a company's existing managers to continue running the business

---

6. Our focus here is on larger firms—without defining precisely what we mean by that. Our focus is not on sole proprietorships, or "mom and pop" stores, or the numerous restaurants that come and go, although some of our ideas may be relevant to them as well. While we do not propose reinstating the old, pre-1978 bankruptcy laws, which include separate frameworks for small and publicly held firms (Chapter XI for the former, Chapter X for the latter), there are ways in which large, publicly regulated (and often publicly traded) companies should be thought of differently from the very small businesses that line Main Street.

7. As Skeel (2001, p. 1) has noted, "Bankruptcy law in the United States is unique in the world. Perhaps most startling to outsiders is that individuals and businesses in the United States do not seem to view bankruptcy as the absolute last resort, as an outcome to be avoided at all costs."

in bankruptcy[8]—an outgrowth of the same long-standing, nonpunitive notion that bankruptcy exists to rehabilitate (where it makes sense) rather than punish; its generous terms for new financing (thus ensuring that businesses that should continue can continue);[9] and its growing facilitation of market-based interventions and valuations.[10]

But, as good as it is—and despite significant improvements in bankruptcy's facilitation of the highest-and-best use of assets by largely separating the question of what to do with assets from the question of who gets the value of those assets—bankruptcy law, and the shift of control that it brings, continues to suffer from at least two structural problems. First, as a general matter, bankruptcy is likely to occur too late; earlier interventions would facilitate better achievement of its goals. Second, bankruptcy law and practice have always faced a conflict—or at least a tension—between making efficient asset decisions and preserving jobs (the latter being, perhaps ironically, one of the key metrics of an economic recovery). We would like to explore each problem and offer some ways in which changes could be made to reduce, although almost certainly not eliminate, both.

The Delayed Commencement of a Bankruptcy Case— and What to Do about It

While bankruptcy permits both voluntary petitions (cases commenced by the debtor) and involuntary petitions (cases commenced by three or more unsecured creditors),[11] the vast majority of reorganization cases for firms are, in fact, commenced by the debtor with the voluntary filing of a petition under Section 301.[12] But this statistic almost certainly obscures the underlying dynamics. This is a consequence of the layering of ownership rights to a firm and the reality that decisions about what to do with the assets of the firm are normally made by the equity owners, through their agents, the managers. For the typically solvent firm, this location of decisionmaking rights is not particularly problematic. Equity is, at least for a large range of actions, "playing with its own money," in the sense that it reaps the benefits of good decisions (as equity is entitled, in an unlimited fashion, to the upside value of a firm) and—at least for a while—pays the price of bad decisions (as equity is the first to have its value stripped as a firm declines in value). While imperfect, it is enormously practical and comes closest to repli-

8. Bankruptcy Code §§ 1104, 1107.
9. Bankruptcy Code § 364.
10. See Skeel (2001, p. 213).
11. Bankruptcy Code §§ 301, 303.
12. Block-Lieb (1991).

cating the decisions that an owner of the assets without competing demands on them would make.[13]

This, however, changes as a firm begins a slide toward insolvency—toward a world in which its assets are insufficient to pay all of the fixed (creditor) claims against it. By the time of insolvency, equity is, in a very real sense, playing not with its own money, but with the money of the creditors. At the moment of insolvency, the creditors pay the price for bad decisions (any diminution in the value of the firm will fall directly on them), while the benefit of good decisions redounds to the equity owners (any increase in the value of the firm goes directly to them). This changes the incentives of decisionmaking in a major way.[14] Rather than making decisions that have the highest expected value (within the risk tolerance of a typical investor), equity owners are likely to increase the risk in their investment decisions and make risky decisions even if they do not have a similar expected value, risk aside. This is the natural incentive of a group that, at this point, gains all the upside value of such decisions (as the residual owner) but pays none of the price of declining values (as limited liability leaves equity owners in a situation in which they can do no worse than lose the investment they have made), but it is increasingly the wrong incentive for the owners of the firm as a group. It distorts decisionmaking away from the kind of decisions that would be made by a firm with a single class of owners.

Even outside of bankruptcy, courts have recognized and wrestled with this problem. Although directors of a corporation ordinarily owe fiduciary duties to shareholders and the corporation, but not to creditors, their duties expand to include creditors when a firm is insolvent.[15] The precise contours of this duty and the point at which it is triggered, however, are unclear—courts speak of the "zone of insolvency" or "vicinity of insolvency." Courts in Delaware, the most important jurisdiction for corporate law, have been reluctant to give creditors broad powers to enforce these duties.[16]

13. Sometimes referred to as a "sole owner." See Baird and Jackson (1984, pp. 104–09).

14. The incentives begin to change before the actual point of insolvency. As a firm slides toward insolvency, it is more and more the case that the benefits go to equity, while the burdens increasingly fall on creditors. There is no momentary "light switch": identifying the appropriate moment to switch control prior to insolvency is itself complicated. Precisely the ease of using "insolvency" as the moment to switch control is at least a part of the problem of delay that we are examining in this section of the paper.

15. A Delaware court signaled that the directors of an insolvent or nearly insolvent corporation may owe duties to creditors in *Credit Lyonnais Bank Nederland* v. *Pathe Communications Corp.*, 1991 Del. Ch. LEXIS 215 (Del. Ch. Dec. 30, 1991). The *Credit Lyonnais* case prompted a flurry of commentary on the nature and scope of the duty.

16. Most recently, the Delaware Supreme Court ruled that creditors can sue derivatively—that is, on behalf of the corporation—to enforce directors' duties when a corporation is insolvent, but that they cannot enforce the duties directly. *North American Catholic Educational Programming Foundation, Inc.* v. *Gheewalla*, 930 A.2d 92 (Del. 2007).

One can see in bankruptcy a more decisive solution to this concern. Even though the debtor (for example, managers) may remain "in possession" in a Chapter 11 reorganization,[17] two things change. First, the decisions of the debtor fall under judicial scrutiny during the time of the bankruptcy proceeding itself. And, second, the end point of the bankruptcy proceeding results in a reshuffling of the ownership claims against the debtor's assets. Under the absolute priority rule,[18] the equity will lose its interest in an insolvent company, and the creditors will become the new equity owners of the firm.[19] The faster the bankruptcy proceeding occurs, the less time there is for strategic decisionmaking during the bankruptcy proceeding.[20] Thus bankruptcy can be seen as a legal rule—or mechanism—for converting ownership from the old residual owners (the equity owners) to a new class of residual owners (the creditors).

The reason for a legal rule to accomplish this change of ownership is integrally related to the other, well-recognized, major purpose behind bankruptcy law—the substitution of a collective creditor collection mechanism for the nonbankruptcy "first-come, first-served" individualistic creditor collection mechanism. The same concerns that are seen in the individualistic creditor collection "race" upon insolvency—"I need to collect sooner rather than later, because someone is going to be left holding the bag, and I don't want it to be me" and the potential destruction

17. Thus allowing those with the most knowledge about the debtor to continue (presumptively at least) to run the ship. In this respect, this sharply differentiates U.S. bankruptcy law from that of many other nations—and, indeed, from the "orderly liquidation authority" of Dodd-Frank for financial institutions.

18. In general, the absolute priority rule provides that each senior class of claimants—starting with secured creditors—gets paid in full before any value can be distributed to the next junior class of creditors. It is embodied in Bankruptcy Code §§ 725, 726, 1129(b)(2). There has recently been a challenge to the absolute priority rule's allocation of value between secured creditors and unsecured creditors, arguing that it does not replicate the nonbankruptcy priority rights of these classes of creditors. See Casey (2011). The merits of that challenge are a story for another day. For the present purposes, the challenge acknowledges that it is proposing a change to existing practices and tradition, and our sense is that the case against the current understanding of the operation of the absolute priority rule is not beyond challenge.

19. This vastly simplifies what can become a complex process—in terms of new sources of investment, valuation issues, class-wide voting rights, and the like. These complications can shift value, although—as we discuss in a bit—increasingly shortened bankruptcy proceedings and reliance on market valuations push in the direction of a shift in ownership and a distribution based on the absolute priority rule.

20. Management, once a bankruptcy proceeding has commenced, may have strong incentives to begin to please the likely new equity owners of the firm—the old creditors. Moreover, the Bankruptcy Code has procedures for ousting the "debtor in possession" upon creditor petition. Bankruptcy Code § 1104. Even so, the period "during" a bankruptcy proceeding almost certainly continues a conflict in purposes between the prior equity owners and the creditors that appears in several ways. While it may no longer have the same control that it did outside of bankruptcy, equity still has incentives to use whatever mechanisms it has to delay the final day of reckoning and to push for riskier asset-deployment decisions. Recent changes in reorganization practice suggest that, at least since enactment of the Bankruptcy Code in 1978, the balance of power has shifted toward creditors, even within a debtor-in-possession model. For discussion of the shift and its significance, see Baird and Rasmussen (2002) and Skeel (2003).

of going-concern value that can result—exist with respect to the shift in control as well. While equity can act collectively, unsecured creditors generally cannot. If there were a single unsecured creditor, there would be no need for bankruptcy. But unsecured creditors are an amalgamation of commercial lenders, trade creditors, tort claimants, workers (and retirees) with health care claims, and other dispersed and uncoordinated individuals and firms. Given that dispersion, there is no effective way to write, or implement, a set of contractual provisions that either "collectivize" or "change ownership." An option—or legal requirement—to convert from a creditor claim to an equity ownership right (and eliminate the old equity interests) is possible, but tricky. Without implementing a bankruptcy-like judicial proceeding, it requires clear valuations, not just of assets but also of claims (many of which may be disputed, contingent, or unliquidated). Having the rule but then requiring these issues to be sorted out in court does not sound much different to us than current bankruptcy practice.[21]

Thus bankruptcy supplies the "rule" (or rules) that the uncoordinated creditors could not otherwise easily achieve—"collectivization" in terms of asset distribution to the creditors and "ownership shift" from equity to creditors in terms of asset determination. Both exist for what can be seen as a single goal: effective decisionmaking over the firm's assets and future.[22]

But, as with the physics concept that the observation will affect the thing being observed, this bankruptcy rule (or rules) itself changes behavior. While three or more individual creditors have the right, under certain circumstances, to commence a bankruptcy proceeding,[23] there is the immediate question of whether individual creditors perceive it as preferable to commence a case—in which they share in the assets collectively—or to pursue their individual creditor remedies, get paid in full, and depart. The realization that oftentimes the

21. This is not to say that this alternative has not been vigorously supported as an alternative to bankruptcy. The foundational work here is by Bradley and Rosenzweig (1992) and Adler (1993). Concerns about this approach were early sounded by Skeel (1993). This debate has been "dusted off" in modern garb as proposals for "opt-in" solutions for significant financial institutions post-2009 abound. See Coffee (2011). Our preliminary concerns with this new garb are expressed in Jackson and Skeel (2012).

22. Ayotte and Skeel (forthcoming) argue that bankruptcy also has a liquidity-providing role. We put this issue aside for the purposes of the current discussion.

23. Bankruptcy Code § 303(b)(1). Since 1978, the standard for an involuntary petition has been demonstrating, upon challenge, that "the debtor is generally not paying such debtor's debts as such debts become due," Bankruptcy Code § 303(h)(1). The prior "balance sheet" insolvency test was eliminated (as were "acts of bankruptcy"), on the ground that it was too ambiguous. The "generally not paying" debts test, while perhaps more easily shown, itself exacerbates the problem, and an insolvent debtor, by liquidating assets, can—in theory—pay debts well into insolvency. (The same was true in the case of Johns Manville, discussed earlier.) In many cases, the need to borrow money to continue to pay off creditors becomes the device that tends to collapse the two standards.

incentives are clearly to "exit" rather than to commence an involuntary bankruptcy proceeding leads to a well-known second-level bankruptcy response, known as preference law. Pursuant to it, such actions by creditors are subject to being unwound if done within ninety days of bankruptcy.[24] This reduces, but does not necessarily eliminate, a creditor's incentive to attempt to exit rather than commence an involuntary case, as the creditor still "wins" if it collects its payment (or security interest) and ninety days pass without a bankruptcy petition being filed. All preference law does is return the debtor and the creditor to the status quo. It is like saying, "If you cut in line, and we catch you, we will return you to where you would have been had you not cut in line." It does not, itself, eliminate the incentive for creditors to prefer an asset grab over the commencement of a bankruptcy case.[25]

And involuntary petitions against firms seem to be the exception rather than the rule.[26] This leaves voluntary petitions and the concern we have already noted that equity owners have every reason not to pull the bankruptcy trigger, as doing so becomes the triggering mechanism for them to lose their right to the upside value of the firm. So, creditors do not seem to have an incentive to start a bankruptcy proceeding. And equity does not seem to have an incentive to start a bankruptcy proceeding.

Given this state of affairs, then, why do we observe bankruptcy proceedings at all? We suspect that the usual scenario, at least with large firms, is the insistence of *new* creditors that equity (and management) file for bankruptcy as a condition of receiving new credit. Because of the sharp division between pre-petition creditors and post-petition creditors, a firm needing liquidity that is also facing insolvency (even if there is a solid going-concern underneath) is likely to be met with an insistence by new lenders that it file for bankruptcy, as a condition of receiving the new funds (which, in bankruptcy, would be entitled to "administrative expense" priority—that is, priority senior to all pre-petition unsecured claimants).[27] The question is whether this mechanism is timely enough to get bankruptcy cases to commence at about the right time, rather than too late— since, as we have shown, none of the other incentives is likely to lead to timely bankruptcy proceedings.

---

24. Bankruptcy Code § 547. The reach-back period is one year if the creditor is an "insider" within the meaning of Bankruptcy Code § 101(31).

25. This is complicated by the introduction of real-world costs—both in terms of collecting in the first instance and in terms of litigation expenses if the creditor wants to contest a preference assertion by the debtor once a bankruptcy case commences.

26. See Baird and Jackson (1984, p. 104).

27. Bankruptcy Code § 364.

We are skeptical that this triggering mechanism is effective in getting bank-ruptcy cases generally to start on time. In part that is because the optimal time for bankruptcy probably is not the moment of insolvency, but somewhat earlier—when equity's incentives begin to get distorted from those of a solvent residual owner in the slide toward insolvency. In part that is because information flows from the debtor tend to lag reality. By the time a potential new lender realizes that it should insist on a bankruptcy filing as a condition of making a loan, it is likely that the firm already should have been in bankruptcy.[28]

If this is so, then bankruptcy's goals could be better realized by getting cases to start even earlier. The trick, as always, is how to accomplish this without making the cure worse than the disease. There is no silver bullet, but a series of steps are worth exploring.

The first is to expand upon one of the (few) good ideas that emerged out of the Dodd-Frank Act's regulations for significantly important financial institutions: living wills.[29] At least for firms over a certain size, a requirement that the firm have, on file and subject to review and challenge, a document, regularly updated, specifying how a bankruptcy proceeding would unfold would have important benefits. Most significant, these procedures, spelled out in advance and known to creditors and regulators, would remove some of the uncertainty about what would occur if and when a bankruptcy case commences. The most obvious objection to the living will approach is the added cost of creating and updating the resolution plan. Although this is a legitimate concern, it is important to recognize that, even for a very large corporation, preparing a living will would not be nearly as complex as for the systemically important financial institutions that have recently prepared resolution plans as required by the Dodd-Frank Act. A living will requirement for some subset of the largest firms not only could facilitate the bankruptcy case itself, but the reduction in uncertainty conceivably would make the case more palatable to creditors, if not to the debtor itself. It would also facilitate a potential role for the Securities and Exchange Commission (SEC) or other regulators in terms of the commencement of the case, an idea we introduce shortly.

The second, we believe, is to reintroduce the possibility of filing an involun-tary petition based on the debtor's balance sheet insolvency or unreasonably small capital. That is, add to the existing "cash flow" test for involuntary bankruptcy a provision permitting the filing of an involuntary petition that can withstand

28. There is a robust legal debate about this. See Schwartz (2005), Rasmussen (1994), Adler (1992, 1995).

29. The Dodd-Frank Act requires that every systemically important financial institution file a rapid resolution plan indicating how it would respond to financial distress, including the steps it would take to minimize the risk of systemic spillover effects. Dodd-Frank Act, Section 167(d).

challenge based on "balance sheet" insolvency. The reasons for its removal—that balance sheet insolvency is difficult to ascertain; that creditors will abuse their ability to file based on such a test—seem not to have passed the test of time. While balance sheet insolvency may be difficult to ascertain, so, too, may be a standard of generally not paying debts as they become due, particularly when the debtor may be selectively paying some (favored) creditors while ignoring others.[30] Moreover, at least for larger firms, the true problem does not appear to be the possibility of abusive filings, but delayed filings. While reintroduction of a balance sheet insolvency test will not, itself, significantly solve the problem, it is a step in the right direction.[31]

The third, and related to the first two, is to permit the SEC, or other identified primary government regulator, to file an involuntary petition on the same basis as creditors—and subject to the same right of the debtor to challenge the filing—at least for publicly traded firms over a certain size.[32] This idea has been floated as a part of a proposed Chapter 14 for the nation's largest financial institutions, giving the Federal Deposit Insurance Corporation (FDIC) the right to file involuntary petitions under a balance sheet insolvency test.[33] We believe it deserves broader consideration, precisely because the concerns identified in Chapter 14 are not themselves limited solely to *financial* institutions. Moreover, involving the SEC (or primary regulator) at the commencement of the bankruptcy case may provide it with a role within the court-supervised process that will mitigate "side door" efforts by government to intervene to bail out the firm or to save jobs later down the line—issues that we take up in the next part of this paper.

Moving to somewhat more radical, or at least controversial, suggestions, we believe it is worth considering—albeit with caution—a modest series of incentives and penalties to nudge the primary players to commence a more timely bankruptcy proceeding. Let us suggest three, although there are surely others.

30. To continue with the Johns Manville example: When there are latent tort creditors, it would be possible to "generally pay debts as they become due" to existing, liquidated, creditors for quite some time, even though the firm was hopelessly insolvent in a balance sheet sense.

31. If one wanted to proceed cautiously, one could limit invocation of this balance sheet insolvency test to creditors holding, in the aggregate, more than 5 percent or $1 million in claims (or some such similar numbers).

32. There may be a certain irony in this suggestion. The great innovation of 1938's Chandler Act was the prominent role of the SEC in reorganizations under Chapter X—a role that was largely repudiated in the Bankruptcy Code of 1978. Skeel (2001, pp. 119–23, 160–83). We do not anticipate the SEC having the same power to dictate the reorganization process that it had under Chapter X; and unlike with Chapter X, the parties would retain principal decisionmaking authority.

33. "Bankruptcy Code Chapter 14: A Proposal," February 2012 (Resolution Project Subgroup of the Working Group on Economic Policy at the Hoover Institution). In the interest of disclosure, both of us are members of the Resolution Project and played a role in drafting the Chapter 14 proposal.

First, consider adding an incentive (a bounty) for the debtor—through its equity decisionmakers—to file a bankruptcy proceeding rather than delay in the hopes of striking gold. We are thinking of something that would preserve, in a successful reorganization, a small portion of value—and hence upside—for the old equity holders. For example, consider a regime in which the equity owners would retain a percentage of the difference in value between the going-concern value of the assets (as determined by a market-driven valuation process) and the piecemeal liquidation value of the assets, with the size of the percentage determined inversely with respect to how insolvent the firm was.[34] Thus, for example, a firm that files at the tipping point of insolvency—when assets and liabilities are in equipoise—and successfully reorganizes might allocate 10 percent of the difference between going-concern and liquidation value to equity,[35] whereas a firm that files at a point when liabilities exceed assets by a significant amount would not allocate any value to equity. This idea is, admittedly, somewhat crude[36] and subject to considerable measurement problems.[37] But to the extent that there is a cost to the current system—late commencement of bankruptcy cases—that causes a destruction in value, the question is whether such a bounty would produce benefits that exceed its easy-to-imagine costs.[38] We think that, sensibly designed, there is a plausible case that the answer to this is "yes."

Second, one could, in parallel fashion, consider a bounty for the actual creditors who file an involuntary petition that is either unchallenged or withstands the challenge. Again, to avoid perverse incentives, the bounty would need to be modest, but large enough to encourage at least some offset to the natural inclination of creditors to see little reason to do anything other than seek payment (or security) rather than commence a bankruptcy proceeding. For illustrative purposes, we are

34. Skeel (1998) proposed a similar strategy for encouraging timely initiation of bank insolvency proceedings some years ago.

35. The reason for the allocation is pragmatic, not principled. It is not based on any underlying sense that the nonbankruptcy world should, for example, limit creditors to their liquidation values in any form of reorganization.

36. For one example, to again pick on Johns Manville, the past tort liability, by the time it became known, may have put Johns Manville completely under water. Even so, as the magnitude of the emerging liability unfolded, a rule such as we discuss in the text conceivably could have led to a somewhat earlier bankruptcy filing.

37. Even with a going-concern sale of the business, which determines the going-concern value, who determines the hypothetical liquidation value? We would lean toward a court-determined liquidation value, led by a court-appointed valuation expert, but this admittedly reintroduces some of the court-determined valuation issues that (intentionally) dominated early reorganizations under the 1978 Bankruptcy Code and that recent practices have tended to deviate from.

38. See, for example, Adler (1992), arguing that permitting shareholders to recover in bankruptcy increases ex ante risk-taking incentives.

thinking of something along the following lines: a payment of 105 percent of the payment ultimately received by other unsecured creditors would go to the creditors who file an involuntary petition, but in no case more than 2 percent of the aggregate payments going to the class of unsecured creditors.[39] This alternative has the added advantage of avoiding the need to rely on a valuation made by the court.

Third, as noted, other than the transaction costs of receiving a preferential payment and the associated costs of needing to return the payment, preference law's deterrent effect is limited—or, at least, incomplete. It seems to be commonplace that a bankruptcy case is commenced shortly after the preference period on a large payment ends and that this is more than a coincidence.[40] The creditor's interests—particularly a creditor with influence over the debtor—are (a) to receive payment and (b) to delay bankruptcy until ninety days have passed. While it makes no sense to penalize all preferences—too many are innocent or inadvertent (well beyond the safe-harbor rules of Section 547)—it would be possible to create a deterrent rule that attempts to separate the advertent from the inadvertent preference. It would make considerable sense, we believe, to consider adding a modest penalty—perhaps 5 or 10 percent of the amount of the preference received—for any creditor who receives a preference with "actual intent to avoid an imminent bankruptcy proceeding."[41] While bright-line rules have a great deal of virtue, particularly in terms of administrative simplicity and avoidance of wasted litigation costs, the "actual intent" test appears elsewhere,[42] while the incremental penalty is small enough to make its invocation unusual except in the case of either large—or flagrant—violations. In addition, its presence is perhaps as valuable for its "in terrorem" effects as for its actual ex post impact.

Finally—and before leaving the topic of improving bankruptcy's role in facilitating economic recovery and growth by ensuring that a bankruptcy proceeding does not commence too late—we should note a more general issue. Both of us have written, together and separately, about our concerns with the wholesale

39. To ensure that creditors filing an involuntary petition do not first receive partial payments, wait out the preference period, and then commence an involuntary case, it would be possible to limit the bounty payments to creditors who had not received a preferential payment within six months of the commencement of the bankruptcy case. We tend to think that this unnecessarily complicates things and that the complementary adoption of our next proposal—placing a penalty on intentionally opt-out preferences—would be sufficient.

40. Adler, Baird, and Jackson (2007, p. 353).

41. This might be coupled with an extended preference period for significant lenders—or significant preferences—to get at the "big creditor [who] can twist the debtor's arm, bleed the debtor dry, and then prop it up for ninety-one days" (Adler, Baird, and Jackson 2007, p. 308), even though the creditor is not formally an insider under Bankruptcy Code § 101(31).

42. For example, Bankruptcy Code § 548(a)(1)(A); see also Bankruptcy Code § 550(b).

exception of qualified financial contracts from bankruptcy's automatic stay and preference provisions.[43] Among our objections is a belief that, by attempting to insulate counterparties—often the most sophisticated of entities involved with a debtor—from the consequences of bankruptcy, these safe harbors have weakened the incentives of some of the most effective monitors of the firm from doing precisely that monitoring. Good monitoring carries positive externalities. It protects not just the creditors doing the monitoring, but the broader group of creditors as well. And the signal sent by a counterparty who bears costs in bankruptcy of efforts to withdraw from the debtor or shore up its position may be one of the most effective ways for other creditors to realize that a bankruptcy proceeding is inevitable and should be started sooner rather than later.

Our point in mentioning this here is that the lesson is not just about counterparties to qualified financial contracts or the effects on monitoring of protecting them from the consequences of bankruptcy. The point may be generalized. Rules that interfere with effective creditor monitoring or the free flow of visible information interfere with a positive externality that is one of the better ways to have creditors understand what might be occurring as a firm slides toward insolvency. Keeping those mechanisms—and channels of information—open is, itself, one of the most effective ways we know of to ensure that knowledge is disseminated and bankruptcy proceedings commence (at least closer to) on time. One needs to think twice about ex ante rules that protect particular creditors from bankruptcy's impact as well as from any sense that there will be ex post bailouts or protections of particular creditors, which have similar impacts on monitoring and the consequent dissemination of information to the creditors as a group.

A Conflict of Goals: The Efficient Use of Assets versus "Saving Jobs"

In our view, effectively addressing the two structural issues we have discussed—the common pool problem and the optimal decisionmaker problem—is the most important reinforcement of the contribution that bankruptcy can make to economic recovery, the focus of this book. But it is also almost certainly the case that most people, looking at measures of economic recovery, will pay particular—although, obviously, not exclusive—attention to issues of job creation and employment levels. Appropriately so.

Why, then, have we not focused on issues of jobs and employment? There is a specific reason for that. Throwing into bankruptcy an explicit focus on jobs, at least as an independent policy (or one that takes on a life of its own), we believe, more often than not, causes an unintended conflict with the issue of asset deployment

---

43. These exclusions generally appear in Bankruptcy Code §§ 362(b)(7), (17), (27); 546(e)–(g), (j); 559–62. Our concerns can be found in Duffie and Skeel (2012) and Skeel and Jackson (2012).

that, at least for firms, bankruptcy is so uniquely suited to address. While we believe the concern about jobs—and job preservation—is pervasive and almost impossible to keep out of bankruptcy at one level or another as an independent focus or policy, we also think that paying heightened attention to its disruptive effects when used as an independent focus of bankruptcy is at least a worthwhile, albeit partial, palliative. To be sure, in the case of a successful reorganization, the two policies—economic efficiency and job preservation (if not growth)—tend to merge. But where the economic decision about what to do with a firm's assets points to a possible liquidation, the two policies tend to come into conflict.

We take seriously the issue of job creation—and the dislocations caused by job termination—but think that pressing this into bankruptcy as an independent policy along with asset deployment asks too much of bankruptcy. The issue of jobs, if inconsistent with the issue of asset deployment, should generally be addressed transparently and humanely through other vehicles. Bankruptcy's solutions for the use of assets are necessarily "micro," whereas too often the focus on "jobs" in bankruptcy has unintended, and indeed perverse, "macro" implications. In this part of the paper, we attempt to explain why this is so—but only after a short primer on the history of bankruptcy reorganization and a concern about jobs.

Bankruptcy and Jobs: A Brief Primer

Bankruptcy's core statutory rules—again, when the focus is on firms—are concerned with requiring creditors to work for the collective benefit of all, rather than simply saving their own hides, and then distributing the results according to the principle of absolute priority, which means that senior creditors get paid in full out of assets to which they have senior claims prior to junior classes receiving anything on account of their claims or interests.[44] The basic priority hierarchy can be found in the distribution rules in Chapter 7, the so-called "liquidation" chapter. Rules that apply to all bankruptcy proceedings—reorganizations and liquidations alike—include basic "collectivizing" rules. Thus the automatic stay stops individual creditor collection efforts.[45] Incomplete—executory—contracts that potentially have a net value to the debtor are treated like assets, and thus counterparties are prohibited from terminating the contract.[46] Preferences—eve-of-bankruptcy payments to (particularly) unsecured creditors are treated as efforts to opt out of bankruptcy, in conflict with the collectivization rule, and are thus unwound if done within ninety days of bankruptcy (or one year if the recipient is

---

44. Related to this is a shift in decisionmaking from equity to creditors. For present purposes, we can safely set this related policy aside.

45. Bankruptcy Code § 362.

46. Bankruptcy Code § 365.

an "insider" with presumably better knowledge of a forthcoming bankruptcy).[47] The assets that have been "collectivized" are then sold (prototypically, in piece-meal fashion), and the proceeds are distributed to the claimants according to the absolute priority rule.[48]

But the genius of bankruptcy's rules does not shine in the prototypical liqui-dation under Chapter 7. The assets are liquidated—which would have occurred outside of bankruptcy as well. The value of those assets—in keeping with the now almost timeless phrase "equality is equity"—is distributed more evenly among creditors than would have occurred outside of bankruptcy, but the sys-temic economic benefits of doing so are not particularly clear.

Where bankruptcy proves its weight in gold is in the reorganization arena. Here, the "collectivizing" rules have real consequence. If the assets are worth more together, they can be kept together. Unlike the prototypical Chapter 7, where the issue is interclass distribution, but the asset use inside and outside of bankruptcy is more or less the same, Chapter 11 rather dramatically changes the asset use outcome from outside of bankruptcy to inside of bankruptcy. It is the ability (but not the requirement) to keep the assets together that makes bankruptcy an essential tool in a free-market, entrepreneurial economy, concerned with moving assets to their highest-and-best use. In theory, these assets (kept together) could be allocated exactly the same way as they were in Chapter 7, strictly according to the principles of the absolute priority rule.

When the economic decision is to keep the firm together as a going concern, there is at most a muted conflict with the interests of workers (or the surrounding community). The (existing) workers get what they want—or, at least, as much as they could reasonably hope for under the circumstances. When reorganiza-tion "works" because it keeps assets from being ripped apart, there is likely to be a large congruence between the decision about what to do with assets and the spillover effects on workers and others. But when a firm faces not only financial but also economic failure—meaning that its assets would be better deployed else-where than in the continuation of the firm—the interests of creditors and the interests of (existing) workers almost certainly diverge. It is here where the legal landscape created by the Bankruptcy Code matters in terms of how it addresses this divergence in interests.

The framework of the 1978 Bankruptcy Code, as originally conceived, assumed that assets would be sold in Chapter 7, the liquidation chapter, but pre-sumptively reorganized pursuant to a negotiated plan rather than sold in Chapter

47. Bankruptcy Code §§ 547 (preferences); 101(31) (insider).
48. Bankruptcy Code §§ 725, 726.

11, the reorganization chapter.[49] If it was obvious that assets truly needed to be liquidated, the procedures of Chapter 7 were optimal, and the plight of workers (or communities) got little, if any, attention. But the incentives were strong to use Chapter 11 and its negotiation framework even for firms that were unlikely to reorganize. As we have already seen, almost all bankruptcies are (so-called) "voluntary," and debtors have enormous incentives to try to keep things going, if not outside of bankruptcy, then inside of it.

Without a premise that assets would be sold, the structure of Chapter 11 necessarily built itself around issues of valuation, conflicts over valuation, and their resolution. The solution written into the Bankruptcy Code of 1978 was an extended period for the debtor (in possession, usually) to have to formulate and file a plan of reorganization; during such time no other party in interest could file a competing plan.[50] There was then an additional period in which to solicit acceptances and a vote on the plan.[51] Valuation disputes would be resolved by the bankruptcy judge.[52] Individual creditors would be protected by a "liquidation" standard;[53] only a class of creditors could invoke the absolute priority rule by voting against the plan.[54] And, even then, the resolution would turn on valuation issues (over the firm as a whole and over the claims against the firm being issued) that were being resolved by a bankruptcy judge, not by the market.

In the early years after the adoption of the Bankruptcy Code of 1978, reorganization proceedings under Chapter 11, following these procedures and instincts, were likely to be lengthy and driven by valuation disputes. The "exclusivity period"—the period in which the debtor (in possession) had to file a plan of reorganization—was routinely extended beyond 120 days, often to a period exceeding (sometimes greatly exceeding) a year. Not only did delay—potentially advantageous to equity owners, just as it was outside of bankruptcy[55]—continue, but the lack of resort to, or reliance on, market valuations meant that the bankruptcy judge was making the "live or die" valuation decisions about whether a firm should continue or be liquidated and whether the firm's valuation included enough for a greater participation by creditors or even by equity.

---

49. Enough so that if a reorganization looked to be infeasible, the structure seemed to assume that the case would be converted to Chapter 7. See Bankruptcy Code § 1112(b).

50. Bankruptcy Code § 1121(b) (120 days). The period may be reduced or extended (up to a total of eighteen months). Bankruptcy Code § 1121(d). That limit on extensions was added in 2005; prior to that time, there was no limit on possible extensions.

51. Bankruptcy Code § 1121(c)(3) (initial total of 180 days).

52. Bankruptcy Code §§ 1128, 1129.

53. Bankruptcy Code § 1129(a)(7)(A)(ii).

54. Bankruptcy Code § 1129(b).

55. Although the decisions of the debtor in possession were now subject to judicial oversight.

Faced with the role of potential executioner, bankruptcy judges were inclined to be optimistic about going-concern possibilities and thus about valuations. Doing so had two salutary—from the perspective of the bankruptcy judge— benefits. Participation rights could be extended so that more could be around to share in a potential upside than otherwise, and the firm was "kept alive," which clearly reduced the (visible) stress on the workers, the suppliers, and the community that often surrounded the bankruptcy judge. And these instincts were fueled by a long-standing notion that a goal of a bankruptcy reorganization was to "preserve jobs" (rather than—or at least in addition to—finding the highest-and-best use of assets).[56] Optimistic, non-market-driven valuations allowed this to occur, which often meant that the firm ultimately failed to survive (although, of course, fortunes can change—it is a part of the fundamental idea that valuations have upsides and downsides alike), but it meant that the bankruptcy judge was not perceived as the executioner.

Moreover, when prominent bankruptcy decisions were perceived to be destructive of jobs or the rights of workers, Congress often stepped in with a fix, to ensure that the rights of workers and the focus on jobs were *not* lost in bankruptcy. Prominent examples of this include Section 1113, constraining the ability to reject collective bargaining agreements in bankruptcy,[57] and Section 1114, constraining the ability to reduce retiree health care benefits in bankruptcy.[58] In these cases, it would be hard to argue with the perception that decisions that

---

56. This is an important part of the disagreement in the now-classic "debate" between Elizabeth Warren and Douglas Baird in 1987 over the purposes of bankruptcy law, primarily in terms of its role in deviating from nonbankruptcy priorities and entitlements. See Warren (1987) and Baird (1987). And it reflects, as well, the reality that bankruptcy law has never been the pure product of academic analysis, but has always reflected the tugs and pulls of various political perspectives and groups. See Skeel (2001, pp. 14–20).

57. Enacted in 1986, in response (primarily) to *NLRB* v. *Bildisco & Bildisco*, 465 U.S. 513 (1984) (unilateral rejection under Bankruptcy Code § 365 of a collective bargaining agreement did not violate the National Labor Relations Act).

58. Added in 1988 as a part of the Retiree Benefits Bankruptcy Protection Act of 1988, in response to LTV Corporation's termination of the health and life insurance benefits of 78,000 retirees during its 1986 bankruptcy. See generally *In re Visteon Corp.*, 612 F.3rd 216 (3rd Cir. 2010). The actions (or decisions) that prompted these congressional responses were not necessarily correct as a matter of bankruptcy policy. There is a strong case to be made that the "attributes" of workers under a collective bargaining agreement, in particular, are such that neither the firm, nor its creditors, can unilaterally change the terms of those agreements during its life outside of bankruptcy. And, under the principle that "attributes, not labels" control, first prominently given recognition in *Chicago Board of Trade* v. *Johnson*, 264 U.S. 1 (1924), the rejection of collective bargaining agreements in bankruptcy may have been mistaken—just as the rejection of auto franchise agreements may have been incorrect, given the nature of state franchise laws, in the recent bankruptcies of Chrysler and General Motors. But our point is not the abstract "correctness" of the decisions, as a matter of bankruptcy law and policy, but the obvious congressional response to decisions that were perceived to be "worker unfriendly."

focused solely on the highest-and-best use of assets were running headlong into other political and policy considerations.

At almost the same time, efficiency considerations about the best use of assets began to erode some of the formal structure and rules of Chapter 11, particularly its reliance on exclusivity periods, negotiation, and judicial "umpiring" over valuation. Whether in response to creative lawyering, academic criticism, or judicial awareness—or, very probably, all three—while the formal structure of the Bankruptcy Code of 1978 as it applied to reorganizations did not change in significant respects, practices pursuant to it did.[59] Creditors began to push for "going-concern sales" of the firm—and hence for market-based valuations of the assets of the firm. A general bankruptcy provision, almost certainly originally thought to apply generally in Chapter 7 and to the sale of stray, unwanted, assets in Chapter 11, began to be used in Chapter 11 as a vehicle for the sale of the firm as a whole.[60] Almost simultaneously—and indeed, in a practical sense, related— lenders began to exert increasing control over the case by including stringent covenants in their loan agreements with the debtor. Indirectly and at times directly, these covenants effectively cut back on a debtor's exclusivity period.

Together, these two changes had several dramatic effects. First and foremost, they severed the decision about what to do with the assets from the fights over how to distribute the value of those assets. The assets could now be sold early in a bankruptcy process, even while some fights over the validity of claims or priorities had not yet been resolved.[61] Second, and equally important, they substituted judicial valuations of the assets with market valuations. If the assets were worth more alive than dead, it was expected that the market bids would reflect this.[62] And, finally, without asset valuations to fight about, there was no longer much room to argue about the impact of the decision concerning what to do with assets or workers or the community. A shift in practice had accomplished what hard-edged legal rules had been unable to accomplish.

59. See Skeel (2001, p. 213): "Law-and-economics scholars and their insights had remarkably little influence on the 1994 commission . . . but actual bankruptcy practice has taken on many of the market-oriented characteristics that these scholars have advocated."

60. The provision is Bankruptcy Code § 363, providing for the "use, sale, or lease of property" of the estate. The major cases heralding the new era were *In re Lionel Corp.*, 722 F.2d 1063 (2nd Cir. 1983) and *In re Braniff Airways*, 700 F.2d 935 (5th Cir. 1983). See, generally, Baird (2004) and Baird and Rasmussen (2002).

61. The Bankruptcy Code explicitly allows the assets to be sold "free and clear" of many, if not most, claims; Bankruptcy Code § 363(f). For an argument that overriding doctrines of successor liability may make sense under certain circumstances, see Jackson (1985, pp. 94–97).

62. Although we generally applaud the increased use of sales, there may be grounds for concern when the debtor's lender is also a potential buyer or insiders of the debtor will move to the acquiring firm. See Ayotte and Skeel (2006, pp. 465–67).

The Lessons of Chrysler

But the story was not finished, as the dramatic example of the 2009 Chrysler bankruptcy reveals. For whatever reasons—natural political instincts to protect visible and numerous jobs is probably reason enough to have prompted the bailout without needing to get into more union-support-buying notions—the federal government had a keen interest in preserving the jobs of Chrysler's workers. We would assert that the resulting sale and reorganization of Chrysler "saved jobs," but only in a very perverse understanding of when, how, and why jobs are, or should be, preserved.

To understand our perspective, it is worth dropping back to the *first* Chrysler bailout by the federal government in 1980, as the dynamics are clearer—although they apply equally well to the Chrysler reorganization of 2009.[63] In the first Chrysler bailout, we were at a period in America where, through agreements brought about by political pressure, Japanese automotive companies—virtually none of which at that time had U.S.-based plants—agreed by 1981 to "voluntarily" limit imports to the American car market[64] and probably had begun to do so even earlier, in fear of the political reaction in Washington. Demand for those Japanese cars was well-nigh universally conceded to exceed that "voluntary" quota, which thus performed as an artificial constraint on foreign supply. Given that, whether Chrysler lived or died in the early 1980s, as a first approximation, affected not *the number* of domestic cars that would be sold—something that was largely demand driven—but *which entity* would sell them.[65] In a fixed-demand world, the more cars were being sold by Chrysler, the fewer cars were being sold by General Motors and Ford—the other two domestic automobile producers of any consequence.[66]

---

63. The foundation for the 1980 Chrysler bailout was passage of the Chrysler Loan Guarantee Act that gave a U.S. government guarantee to $1.5 billion in private loans to Chrysler. The loans carried an interest rate of around 10 percent, which was approximately 4 percentage points below market at the time, and the U.S. government received warrants for 14.4 million shares of Chrysler stock. In addition, the loan guarantee statute required $2 billion in commitments or concessions from "owners, stockholders, administrators, employees, dealers, suppliers, foreign and domestic financial institutions, and by State and local governments." Pursuant to pressure from the Treasury Department, most of the concessions came from lenders. Chrysler was able to pay off nearly $600 million of debts at 30 cents on the dollar, and it converted nearly $700 million of debts into a special class of preferred stock. The essential public justification for the bailout was that keeping Chrysler afloat would save as many as 200,000 U.S. jobs. See, generally, Ritholtz (2009) and Hickel (1983).

64. See, generally, Cohen (n.d.).

65. There is a small "supply-side" argument that Chrysler produced some cars that enhanced demand. We set this aside, because it is both unlikely to be a significant factor in any case, as well as because if Chrysler excelled at this dimension, it almost certainly would not have required a bailout in 1980!

66. American Motors was still in existence, as was DeLorean Motor Company.

Given this, it seems obvious upon reflection—which is different from saying that it was clearly understood either then or now—that bailing out Chrysler in the early 1980s meant that Chrysler sold more cars than otherwise and that General Motors and Ford sold fewer.[67] Assuming that Chrysler was the least efficient producer in 1980 (which seems reasonable in light of the 1970s—and even more so in hindsight), this story has dramatically different implications when the focus is on the efficient use of assets rather than on the preservation of jobs. From the perspective of the efficient use of assets, rescuing Chrysler was a mistake. From this perspective, we want efficient producers,[68] which Chrysler was not. Oligopoly concerns aside, it would be preferable to shift production from the inefficient Chrysler to the more efficient General Motors and Ford. Chrysler would lose jobs (or close), but General Motors and Ford would presumably increase employment (as well as purchases from suppliers) as they picked up the market share previously held by Chrysler.

But this shift is exactly wrong if the focus is on "preserving jobs." Efficient producers usually are those who have figured out how to make something at the lowest cost, which often implies equal outputs with fewer inputs—including human capital inputs. If one's highest priority is to "save jobs," it means, rather perversely, throttling back on the efficient producer and propping up the inefficient producer. Moreover, the jobs that are "saved"—those of Chrysler— are highly concentrated and visible, while the jobs that are "lost"—cutbacks by General Motors and Ford—are harder to attribute to a single event (or to the government's intervention itself).[69] A political focus on "jobs" has every incentive to favor the inefficient over the efficient—which is dramatically at odds with the other recognized, and firmly entrenched, concern of bankruptcy policy with the efficient use of assets.

With this, we can now see clearly what occurred in Chrysler's 2009 bankruptcy proceeding—albeit with some inexplicable "nodding" by the judiciary (until the final Supreme Court action vacated all that had happened before).[70]

---

67. See Hickel (1983): "Chrysler has increased its market share *not* by making inroads into foreign competition, but by taking customers away from other domestic manufacturers."

68. Here, we are speaking relatively—among the "Big Three." The reason for the import restrictions was based largely on the enormous efficiencies of Japanese manufacturers at this time, particularly in terms of quality, over domestic manufacturers.

69. Hickel (1983): "Unrepresented and unheard was a huge 'invisible' constituency [that] included current and future laid-off Ford and General Motors workers, who never understood that their tax dollars were being used to destroy their own jobs in order to save jobs at Chrysler."

70. While the bankruptcy judge's opinion permitting the sale under dubious procedures and restrictions was affirmed in a hasty decision by the Second Circuit, *In re Chrysler LLC*, 576 F.3d 108 (2d Cir. 2009) (argued on June 5, 2009, decided on June 5, 2009, with an opinion issued after-the-fact on

Chrysler, again almost certainly the least efficient producer, was faced with extinction by the reality of a market that seemed at that time hugely overbuilt in terms of capacity. (Annual capacity for the United States—domestic and foreign—was running in excess of 17 million vehicles, while steady-state demand, at least over the foreseeable future, was perceived to be running closer to 10 million to 13 million vehicles. Pulling close to a quarter of capacity out of the system was going to be painful, no matter how it occurred. Jobs were going to be lost. Dealers were going to be shuttered. Suppliers and communities were going to feel the impact.) Economic reality dictated that the question was not going to be "whether," but "who."

But—just as in the 1980s—the insistent political focus on "saving jobs" meant rescuing the least efficient producer.[71] Had Chrysler been liquidated, perhaps through a sale of some or all of its assets to Fiat or another buyer, its then-existing secured creditors (protected in a liquidation by the absolute priority rule) may well have done better. In addition, the more efficient producers—Ford and others (now often with U.S.-based plants)—would have continued, without the ancillary need to reduce capacity (and jobs!) nearly as much as in the world where Chrysler was rescued. By saving Chrysler, the government may well have saved jobs, but only in the Orwellian universe where it makes sense to punish the more efficient because they produce using fewer jobs than the less efficient. The government saved Chrysler jobs—a concentrated and identifiable group. To say that the government "saved jobs" overall both ignores the repercussions felt by

---

August 5, 2009—when its reasoning could hardly contradict its already-issued judgment), the Supreme Court, on December 14, 2010, granted certiorari, vacated the Second Circuit's opinion and directed that the Second Circuit dismiss the suit as moot. *Ind. State Police Pension Trust* v. *Chrysler LLC*, 130 S.Ct. 1015 (2010). As a consequence, the Second Circuit's opinion has no precedential value. *United States* v. *Munsingwear*, 340 U.S. 36 (1950). This rather remarkable step—since the Supreme Court in July had issued, and then lifted, a stay, following the Second Circuit's ruling (and prior to the Second Circuit's written opinion justifying that ruling), allowing the sale to be consummated, 129 S.Ct. 2275 (2009)—has led some to speculate that the Supreme Court's vacating the Second Circuit opinion six months after the court lifted the stay allowing the sale to go forward "was an expression of its disagreement with the Second Circuit's interpretation of the requirements of § 363(b)" (David 2010, p. 27). This is plausible, since at the time the Supreme Court lifted the stay and allowed the transaction to be consummated, the Second Circuit had not yet written its opinion explaining its reasons for affirming the bankruptcy judge's decision to allow the sale to go forward as then structured. When the Second Circuit wrote its opinion, it is possible that members of the Supreme Court recognized its flaws and hence took a later opportunity to vacate the opinion. Speculation, yes—but *hopeful* speculation!

71. That it did so by almost certainly subverting bankruptcy priority rules along the way is a part of this sad story. See Roe and Skeel (2009); see also www.scribd,com/doc/14952818/Objection-to-Chrysler-Sale-Motion (brief filed on May 4, 2009, in the Southern District of New York bankruptcy court by Chrysler's non-TARP secured lenders).

other manufacturers in responding to a reduction in demand (and capacity) from 17 million vehicles to between 10 million and 13 million vehicles and takes credit for the jobs that *are* saved by propping up the least efficient producer!

What does this story have to do with bankruptcy and its role in economic growth and recovery? The result in Chrysler's 2009 bankruptcy occurred only because the government strong-armed the bankruptcy process, and the judicial system did not resist. But the story is deeper than this. The government's intervention in Chrysler can be seen as a direct response to the changes in practice that made it more plausible to use market valuations for Chrysler's assets. Perhaps a going-concern sale that played by neutral competitive bid rules would bring in less value than a sale of the Jeep brand to one firm, the sale of various real estate owned by Chrysler to a variety of local buyers, and the sale of one or two of Chrysler's most efficient plants to other automotive companies. But the government made it impossible to determine this. Even if the judicial system was not as slow to respond to this abuse of bankruptcy law and policy as it seemed to be, the government may have had its way anyway. Most of the secured lenders to Chrysler were the recipients of funds from the Troubled Asset Relief Program (TARP). Whether through government pressure on those lenders in that capacity or through the various other hats that the government wears (through the Justice Department, the SEC, the Occupational Safety and Health Administration, the Internal Revenue Service, and numerous other pressure points), it is a political reality that the government had an enormous ability to shape outcomes,[72] while claiming that it was not a "bailout" but a justified intervention to "save jobs."[73]

We know of no effective response to this, other than transparency and a belief that the judicial system, more likely than not, ultimately will "get it right." That response may already be taking shape with respect to the 2009 Chrysler rescue. This is particularly so in the context of current reorganization proceedings, where market sales have become commonplace, making judicial asset valuations unnecessary. One can, and should, insist on clear procedures that maximize bids— that insist on a true bidding process. Recognizing the complexities of adequate

72. See Mark Roe, "A Chrysler Bankruptcy Won't Be Quick," *Wall Street Journal,* May 1, 2009 (http://online.wsj.com/article/SB124113528027275219.html): "Worse, there could be a legal fight over whether the vote of Citibank and the other 'big four' creditors . . . —who together hold 70 percent of Chrysler's debt—should be counted toward the two-thirds threshold that would bind the company's other forty-two creditors. The Bankruptcy Code requires that the votes of creditors be given in 'good faith.' It won't be hard for the smaller creditors to argue that Citibank and other TARP recipients' votes aren't in full good faith. In agreeing to Treasury's offer of 32 cents for each $1 of their debt, the objectors would say, Citibank and some others were influenced by the fact that Treasury was keeping them afloat with federal subsidies. If this type of litigation begins, it won't be easily resolved."

73. Precisely as occurred in the 1980 Chrysler bailout.

information, the "lemons" problem, and the "winner's curse,"[74] bidding procedures can still go a long way toward minimizing these problems and, at the same time, minimizing abuses of the process, such as by artificial constraints on competing bids, which the government insisted on in Chrysler. Markets and judicial oversight cannot magically get everything right, but the process can be set up to maximize the possibilities that abuses will be minimized. The question is not whether it is perfect, but how it compares to alternatives. Given that the alternatives to market valuations are judicial valuations or, it seems, government intervention in one way or another, we believe that the focus should be on making the market mechanisms as effective as possible, buttressed by judicial oversight and review.

At the same time, the lessons from practice that have evolved away from the 1978 Bankruptcy Code's envisioned structure—one of disclosure, voting, and judicial umpiring—suggest that it may be appropriate to streamline Chapter 11's approval rules so as to make them more amenable to a quick judicial reorganization rather than an outright sale.[75] Particularly when coupled with mandatory living wills, streamlined procedures can both protect what needs to be protected and minimize the use of procedures for purposes of delay. While complex firms (particularly without pre-bankruptcy planning) may need the full exclusivity period,[76] most firms with living wills should need significantly less time.[77] Moreover, competing plans—or the pressure of possible competing plans—may go a long way toward reducing the use of Chapter 11 as a delaying mechanism, without needing to resort to going-concern sales under Section 363.

Thus, especially if some of our earlier proposals were implemented, we would favor significantly reducing the exclusivity period—to a presumptive thirty to sixty days—which would both enhance pre-bankruptcy planning and add a dose (or threat) of competition into the reorganization process, without requiring Section 363 sales. We would likewise favor reducing the following solicitation and voting period to a presumptive additional thirty days. With streamlined disclosure and solicitation rules, these proposals would go a long way toward making the original structure contemplated in 1978 "competitive" again with the evolving practice toward market-based sales.

---

74. Ayotte and Skeel (2006, p. 465).

75. Some useful ideas are contained in Bussel and Klee (2009).

76. Lehman Brothers filed its plan of reorganization on the last day of the statutorily allowed eighteen-month exclusivity period. Of course, not only was Lehman Brothers extraordinarily complex, it had done zero pre-bankruptcy planning.

77. Indeed, the increasing use of "prepacks"—prepackaged reorganization plans available as the firm files—is a significant step in confirming the direction we are proposing here as a matter of statutory limits.

Concluding Comments

Creating a world in which bankruptcy maximizes its contribution to economic growth and recovery would be aided by a clear understanding that one can only ask bankruptcy to do so much. If its primary purpose is to allocate assets to their highest-and-best use, it probably should not be asked, as a matter of independent policy, to save jobs as well. Rather, that concern should be the focus of other legal rules and government policies, whose advantages and trade-offs are open and accessible, rather than hidden in a complex and (speaking politically) difficult to understand procedure. If the government were to provide assistance (whether training grants or other forms of economic assistance) to workers who lost their jobs as a result of the liquidation of Chrysler, that decision could be argued on its own merits. The irony of the failure to do so is that the workers in other auto manufacturing firms who inevitably lost their jobs as a result of the Chrysler bailout never had the opportunity for a discussion about similar assistance to them.

References

Adler, Barry. 1992. "Bankruptcy and Risk Allocation." *Cornell Law Review* 77: 439–89.

———. 1993. "Financial and Political Theories of American Corporate Bankruptcy." *Stanford Law Review* 45: 311–46.

———. 1995. "A Re-Examination of Near-Bankruptcy Investment Incentives." *University of Chicago Law Review* 62: 575–606.

Adler, Barry, Douglas Baird, and Thomas Jackson. 2007. *Cases, Problems, and Materials on Bankruptcy,* 4th ed. New York: Foundation Press.

Ayotte, Kenneth, and David A. Skeel Jr. 2006. "An Efficiency-Based Explanation for Current Corporate Reorganization Practice." *University of Chicago Law Review* 73 (Winter): 425–68.

Ayotte, Kenneth, and David Skeel. Forthcoming. "Bankruptcy Law as a Liquidity-Provider." *University of Chicago Law Review.*

Baird, Douglas. 1987. "Loss Distribution, Forum Shopping, and Bankruptcy: A Reply to Warren." *University of Chicago Law Review* 54: 815–34.

———. 2004. "The New Face of Chapter 11." *American Bankruptcy Institute Law Review* 12 (Spring): 69–99.

Baird, Douglas, and Thomas Jackson. 1984. "Corporate Reorganizations and the Treatment of Diverse Ownership Interests: A Comment on Adequate Protection of Secured Creditors in Bankruptcy." *University of Chicago Law Review* 51 (Winter): 97–130.

Baird, Douglas, and Robert Rasmussen. 2002. "The End of Bankruptcy." *Stanford Law Review* 55: 751–89.

Block-Lieb, Susan. 1991. "Why Creditors File So Few Involuntary Petitions and Why the Number Is Not Too Small." *Brooklyn Law Review* 57: 803.

Bradley, Michael, and Michael Rosenzweig. 1992. "The Untenable Case for Chapter 11." *Yale Law Journal* 101: 1043–89.

Bussel, Daniel, and Kenneth Klee. 2009. "Recalibrating Consent in Bankruptcy." *American Bankruptcy Law Journal* 83, no. 4: 663–748.

Casey, Anthony. 2011. "The Creditors' Bargain and Option-Preservation Priority in Chapter 11." *University of Chicago Law Review* 78, no. 3: 759–807.

Coffee, John. 2011. "Systemic Risk after Dodd-Frank: Contingent Capital and the New Regulatory Strategies beyond Oversight." *Columbia Law Review* 111: 795–847.

Cohen, Stephen. n.d. "The Route to Japan's Voluntary Export Restraints on Automobiles." Working Paper 20. American University, School of International Service (www.gwu.edu/~nsarchiv/japan/scohenwp.htm).

David, Fred. 2010. "Interpreting the Supreme Court's Treatment of the Chrysler Bankruptcy and Its Impact on Future Business Reorganizations." *Emory Bankruptcy Developments Journal* 27: 25–70 (www.law.emory.edu/fileadmin/journals/bdj/27/27.1/David.pdf).

Duffie, Darrell, and David Skeel. 2012. "A Dialogue on the Costs and Benefits of Automatic Stays for Derivatives and Repurchase Agreements." In *Bankruptcy Not Bailout: A Special Chapter 14,* edited by Kenneth E. Scott and John B. Taylor, ch. 5. Stanford, Calif.: Hoover Institution.

Hickel, James K. 1983. "The Chrysler Bail-Out Bust." Research Report prepared for the Heritage Foundation, July (www.heritage.org/research/reports/1983/07/the-chrysler-bail-out-bust).

Jackson, Thomas. 1982. "Bankruptcy, Non-Bankruptcy Entitlements, and the Creditors' Bargain." *Yale Law Journal* 91, no. 5: 857–907.

———. 1985. "Translating Assets and Liabilities to the Bankruptcy Forum." *Journal of Legal Studies* 14: 73–114.

———. 1986. *The Logic and Limits of Bankruptcy Law.* Harvard University Press.

Jackson, Thomas, and David Skeel. 2012. "Dynamic Resolution of Large Financial Institutions." *Harvard Business Law Review* 2: 435–60.

Rasmussen, Robert. 1994. "The Ex Ante Effects of Bankruptcy Reform on Investment Incentives." *Washington University Law Quarterly* 72, no. 3: 1159–211.

Ritholtz, Barry. 2009. *Bailout Nation: How Greed and Easy Money Corrupted Wall Street and Shook the World Economy.* Hoboken, N.J.: John Wiley and Sons.

Roe, Mark. 1984. "Bankruptcy and Mass Tort." *Columbia Law Review* 84: 846–992.

Roe, Mark, and David Skeel. 2009. "Assessing the Chrysler Bankruptcy." *Michigan Law Review* 108: 727–72.

Schwartz, Alan. 2005. "A Normative Theory of Business Bankruptcy." *Virginia Law Review* 91, no. 5: 1199–265.

Skeel, David. 1993. "Markets, Courts, and the Brave New World of Bankruptcy Theory." *Wisconsin Law Review* (March): 465–521.

———. 1998. "The Law and Finance of Bank and Insurance Insolvency Regulation." *Texas Law Review* 76, no. 4: 723–80.

———. 2001. *Debt's Dominion: A History of Bankruptcy Law in America.* Princeton University Press.

———. 2003. "Creditors' Ball: The 'New' New Corporate Governance in Bankruptcy." *University of Pennsylvania Law Review* 152: 917.

Skeel, David, and Thomas Jackson. 2012. "Transaction Consistency and the New Finance in Bankruptcy." *Columbia Law Review* 112 (January): 152–202.

Warren, Elizabeth. 1987. "Bankruptcy Policy." *University of Chicago Law Review* 54, no. 3: 775–814.

JAY R. RITTER 4

Reenergizing the IPO Market

From 1980 to 2000, an annual average of 310 operating companies went public in the United States. During 2001–12, on average, only 99 operating companies went public.[1] This decline occurred in spite of the doubling of real gross domestic product (GDP) during this thirty-three-year period. The decline was even more severe for small-company initial public offerings (IPOs),

Some of the content of this article overlaps with my testimony before the U.S. Senate Banking Committee on March 6, 2012 (Ritter 2012). The analysis of this paper draws heavily on my joint work with Xiaohui Gao and Zhongyan Zhu (Gao, Ritter, and Zhu 2014), Martin Kenney and Don Patton (Kenney, Patton, and Ritter 2012), and Stefano Paleari, Andrea Signori, and Silvio Vismara (Vismara, Paleari, and Ritter 2012 and Ritter, Signori, and Vismara 2013). I wish to thank Leming Lin for research assistance. For comments on an earlier draft, I wish to thank Barry Silbert, Harry DeAngelo, François Degeorge, David Weild, and participants at the Kauffman Foundation Summer Legal Institute on July 23–25, 2012; the Brookings, Nomura, Wharton conference on Reconstructing and Revitalizing Japan's Financial Sector on October 26, 2012; the Kellogg School conference on Security Market Auctions and IPOs on November 2–3, 2012; and the Brookings Institution conference on Promoting Innovative Growth on December 3, 2012.

1. "Operating-company" initial public offerings (IPOs) exclude closed-end funds, real estate investment trusts (REITs), special-purpose acquisition companies and other blind-pool offers, oil and gas limited partnerships, American Depositary Receipts (ADRs), unit offerings, penny stocks (IPOs with an offer price below $5 per share), small best efforts offers, bank and savings and loan IPOs (most of which are conversions of mutual into stock companies), and stocks not listed on Nasdaq or the American or New York Stock Exchanges. Table 15 of "Initial Public Offerings: Updated Statistics" on my website (http://bear.warrington.ufl.edu/ritter) gives the year-by-year number of IPOs excluded for each of these reasons.

Figure 4-1. *Number of IPOs in the United States, by Size of Firm, 1980–2012*[a]

Number of IPOs

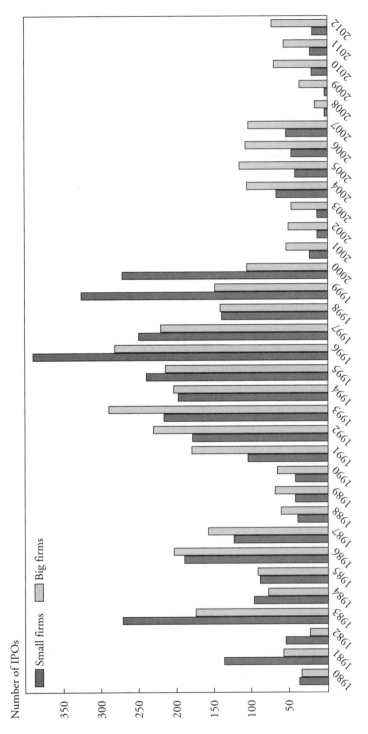

Source: Reproduced from Gao, Ritter, and Zhu (2014).
a. Small firms are defined as having pre-IPO annual sales of less than $50 million (2009 purchasing power) and big firms as having pre-IPO sales of more than $50 million (2009 purchasing power).

for which the average volume dropped 83 percent, from 165 IPOs a year during 1980–2000 to only 28 a year during 2001–12. Figure 4-1 illustrates the pattern on a year-by-year basis for both small and big companies. Small and big companies are defined on the basis of inflation-adjusted (2009 dollars) annual sales in the twelve months prior to going public, using a cutoff of $50 million to define small and big.

Many commentators have been alarmed at this prolonged drop in small-company IPOs, since it is the conventional wisdom that companies going public create many jobs. The *Wall Street Journal* editorial page has bought into this argument, as has Congress, culminating in the April 2012 passage of the Jumpstart Our Business Startups (JOBS) Act.

The JOBS Act is intended to encourage the funding of small businesses, primarily by easing various securities regulations. The JOBS Act, among other things, encourages crowdfunding; eliminates restrictions on general solicitation (that is, permits advertising securities offerings to the general public); creates a category of firms, emerging growth companies, defined as firms with less than $1 billion in annual sales, and for their first five years as public companies exempts them from certain regulations, including some of the Sarbanes-Oxley regulations; increases the number of shareholders of record from 500 to 2,000 before public disclosure requirements are triggered; eliminates "quiet period" restrictions that had prohibited the analysts working for underwriters from publicly making buy and sell recommendations at the time of an IPO; raises the Regulation A limit on securities offerings for which there are fewer regulatory requirements from $5 million to $50 million; and requires the SEC to conduct a study on "the impact that decimalization has had on the number of initial public offerings."

In this paper, I address why IPO volume, and especially small-company IPO volume, has been so depressed for more than a decade. The conventional wisdom is that the main culprits are a combination of heavy-handed regulation, especially the Sarbanes-Oxley (SOX) Act of 2002, a decline in analyst coverage of small firms, and lower stock prices since the 2000 technology bubble burst. I present an alternative explanation—the economies of scope hypothesis—that has very different policy implications. I also discuss the effect of tick sizes on the IPO market, as this is the current focus of policy recommendations from the SEC's Advisory Committee on Small and Emerging Companies. I then discuss the number of jobs created by companies going public and the effect of alternative venues for cashing out and raising capital, SecondMarket and SharesPost. Lastly, I offer some thoughts on what can and should be done to reenergize the IPO market.

Heavy-Handed Regulation

The most common explanation for the decline in IPO activity is a series of regulatory changes, with the Sarbanes-Oxley Act of 2002 shouldering the greatest blame. Motivated by the securities frauds perpetrated by WorldCom and Enron, Section 404 of SOX requires external audits of the internal control systems of publicly traded companies to ensure that their financial reports are accurate.[2] Following complaints that the Section 404 compliance costs were excessively high for small firms, at the end of 2007 small firms were exempted from many of the requirements.

If SOX costs were a major impediment to going public for small companies, small-company IPOs should have rebounded after 2007. Of course, the Panic of 2008 would have delayed this rebound, but 2010, 2011, and 2012 saw fewer, not more, small-company IPOs than in each year from 2004 to 2007. Furthermore, evidence from Europe suggests that heavy-handed regulation has not been the prime deterrent of small-company IPOs.

Following the success of London's exchange-regulated Alternative Investment Market (AIM), all of the major continental European stock exchanges have created second markets for small companies that are exchange regulated (that is, unregulated). Companies going public on these second markets have been exempt from many investor protection regulations.[3] In these papers, we document that public market investors have earned very low long-run returns on second-market IPOs in Europe; new listing volume on these markets was very low during 2008–11; and few of these companies have been reporting positive earnings per share, in spite of being exempt from many regulations applying to companies traded on the main markets.[4]

This evidence suggests that SOX has not been the primary reason that the volume of small-company IPOs has been low for more than a decade in the United States, although this does not mean that heavy-handed regulation has had no effect on IPO volume. It is difficult for regulators to strike the right balance between investor protection and efficient capital raising.

---

2. At their peak, Enron's market capitalization was over $60 billion and WorldCom's was over $180 billion. Enron declared bankruptcy in December 2001, and WorldCom declared bankruptcy in July 2002, wiping out equity investors.

3. See Vismara, Paleari, and Ritter (2012) and Ritter, Signori, and Vismara (2013).

4. IPO activity in Europe during 2011–12 was depressed partly by the Euro Zone crisis, which was associated with low stock returns on many European markets.

Analyst Coverage and IPO Activity

Many people have argued that the SEC's Regulation FD in 2000 and the Global Settlement in 2003, along with other regulatory and technological changes, have contributed to the decline in analyst coverage for small stocks.[5] The implicit assumption, which I find to be very plausible, is that analyst coverage results in greater awareness of a stock's existence. The resulting increase in the number of potential investors leads to greater demand and a higher price relative to the price of other stocks that receive less attention.[6]

If there were more analyst coverage, what would be the effect on the IPO market? To quantify the answer, there are two steps. First, how much does analyst coverage boost a stock's price? Second, what is the sensitivity of IPO volume to increases in public market valuation?

Demiroglu and Ryngaert analyze 549 initiations of coverage on Nasdaq-, Amex-, and New York Stock Exchange (NYSE)–listed stocks that had no reported sell-side analyst coverage prior to the initiation.[7] These initiations occurred during 1997–2005, and 88 percent of the stocks had a market capitalization below $250 million. They report an average announcement effect of 5 percent. Assuming that this is a permanent increase (conditional on continued coverage by an analyst after the original initiation of coverage), we can take this as the valuation effect of analyst coverage.[8]

Gao, Ritter, and Zhu report the results of a regression that has the quarterly number of IPOs scaled by real GDP (in trillions of dollars a year using 2009 purchasing power) as the dependent variable and, among other variables, the lagged log of the market-to-book (MB) ratio for small firms as an explanatory variable.[9] The coefficient on the natural logarithm of the MB ratio is 3.33. This coefficient

---

5. Regulation FD refers to fair disclosure and mandates that companies disclose material information to all recipients simultaneously, rather than leaking the information to favored analysts.

6. For analyst coverage to boost the market value of all stocks, at least some investors would have to decide to move a higher proportion of their assets into stocks from other asset classes as a result of analyst coverage.

7. Demiroglu and Ryngaert (2010).

8. Several considerations must be kept in mind when interpreting this number. First, initiations are typically "buy" recommendations, in that an analyst who evaluates an uncovered firm and is not enthusiastic is more likely not to initiate coverage than to initiate coverage with a negative recommendation. Thus the announcement effect may overstate the effect of coverage itself. Second, additional coverage is likely to have a decreasing impact. For example, for a firm that is already covered by twenty-two analysts, the twenty-third analyst is likely to have little impact. Third, the 5 percent announcement effect for a sample of primarily very small firms is likely to be higher than for a larger company.

9. Gao, Ritter, and Zhu (2014).

implies that an increase in the MB ratio by 5 percent—for example, from 2.00 to 2.10—would result in 3.33 × [ln(2.10) − ln(2.00)] = 0.162 more IPOs per quarter per $1 trillion of GDP. With 2012 real GDP of approximately $15 trillion, this calculation predicts that 2.43 more IPOs per quarter, or ten per year, would occur if small-company stock prices were 5 percent higher due to more analyst coverage. Thus a lack of analyst coverage is unlikely to account for a large proportion of the drop from 310 IPOs a year in 1980–2000 to 99 in 2001–12.

Market Conditions

As discussed above, IPO volume is higher when stock prices are higher. During the eleven years from 1990 to 2000, the quarterly average MB ratio for small firms, lagged by two quarters, was 3.89. During the twelve years from 2001 to 2012, the quarterly average MB ratio was 3.16. Using the coefficient of 3.33 on the lagged logged MB ratio, as discussed above, the drop in the average MB ratio implies 3.33 × [ln(3.89) − ln(3.16)] = 0.692 fewer IPOs per quarter per $1 trillion of real GDP, or forty-two fewer IPOs per year in an economy with real GDP of $15 trillion per year. A full unit drop in the MB ratio from 3.0 to 2.0 is associated with a drop of eighty-one IPOs per year. Thus the market conditions hypothesis can partly explain why IPO volume was lower in 2001–11 than in 1996–2000, but has trouble explaining why IPO volume was lower than in 1980–95, when both price-to-earnings (PE) and MB ratios were relatively low in comparison with 2001–12.

The Nasdaq index peaked in March 2000 and has not come close to this level since then. However, 2000 was not the peak of IPO activity. As shown in figure 4-1, 1996 had more small-company IPOs than any other year during 1980–2012, and only 1993 had more large-company IPOs than 1996. Yet 1996 was not the peak year for valuations. Indeed, one measure of market valuations, the Shiller PE ratio, computed as the ratio of the level of the Standard and Poor's (S&P) 500 index divided by a ten-year moving average of the inflation-adjusted earnings of the S&P 500, shows a surprisingly low correlation with scaled IPO activity, as shown in figure 4-2.

Market upturns (as proxied by increases in the Shiller PE ratio) are typically accompanied by increases in IPO volume, and market downturns are immediately followed by a drop in IPO activity. Yet the level of the market, as measured by the Shiller PE ratio, has very little correlation with IPO activity. Indeed, starting in 1997, IPO activity has been much lower than might be suggested by market valuations. In unreported results, a very similar pattern to that of the Shiller PE ratio is displayed if the MB ratio on small stocks is graphed. So whether MB

Figure 4-2. *Scaled Quarterly Volume of IPOs and Shiller PE Ratio in the United States, 1975–2012*[a]

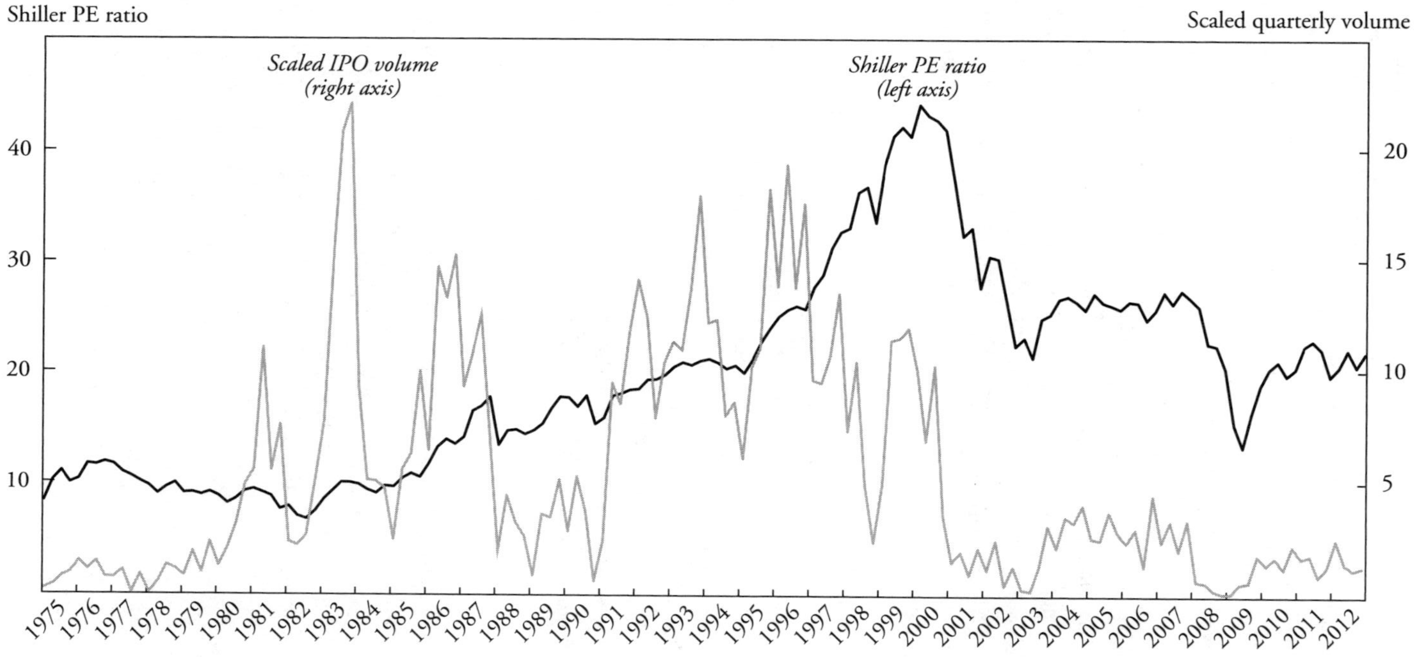

Source: Shiller PE ratio is the CAPE (cyclically adjusted price-earnings) ratio taken from Robert Shiller's website at www.econ.yale.edu/~shiller/data.htm. Scaled IPO volume is from Gao, Ritter, and Zhu (2014).

a. The Shiller PE ratio is computed as the ratio of the S&P 500 index divided by the inflation-adjusted ten-year moving average of S&P 500 earnings. Scaled IPO volume is the quarterly number of initial public offerings divided by annual real GDP, in trillions of 2009 dollars. The period plotted is the first quarter of 1975 through the fourth quarter of 2012.

or PE ratios are used, there has been a sixteen-year drought in IPO activity relative to what might be expected.

The Economies of Scope Hypothesis

In "Where Have All the IPOs Gone?," Xiaohui Gao, Zhongyan Zhu, and I posit that a gradual structural change has been occurring for the last few decades that favors big firms at the expense of small firms.[10] We argue that getting big fast is more important than it used to be, at least in some industries such as the technology industry, and that globalization and improvements in communication technology are behind the change. The implication is that being a small independent company and growing organically (that is, internally) is increasingly an inferior business strategy compared to an alternative strategy of getting big fast, which frequently can be accomplished most efficiently through mergers and acquisitions. This hypothesis implies that young firms are now more likely to make acquisitions or sell out in a trade sale than to go public.

In our paper, we present a body of facts consistent with our economies of scope hypothesis.[11] We show that small companies, whether recent IPOs or more seasoned firms, are increasingly unprofitable and that the frequency of being acquired within three years of going public has increased over time, with the uptrend starting in the early 1990s. Other authors have shown an uptrend in the frequency of acquisitions by companies that have recently gone public. We also show that small-company IPOs have produced low stock returns for public market investors in the last three decades, including within each of four subperiods that we examine. In a companion paper, Andrea Signori, Silvio Vismara, and I show that these patterns were also present in Europe in the 1995–2011 period.[12]

If the U.S. IPO market is broken for small companies, but being a small independent firm is still attractive, we might expect to see many small U.S. firms going public abroad. In fact, as documented by several studies, only a few U.S. firms each year have gone public abroad.[13] Vismara, Paleari, and Ritter document that investors earned low returns on European IPOs from 1995 to 2006 that listed on Europe's markets catering to emerging growth companies.[14] Furthermore, 95

---

10. Gao, Ritter, and Zhu (2014).

11. Gao, Ritter, and Zhu (2014).

12. Ritter, Signori, and Vismara (2013).

13. See Ritter, Signori, and Vismara (2013, table 4).

14. See Vismara, Paleari, and Ritter (2012, table 5). We report that the average three-year buy-and-hold abnormal return relative to the FTSE Euromid index is –19 percent for 1,725 second-market IPOs from 1995–2006.

percent of the listings on London's AIM were "placings," restricted to qualified institutional buyers. Most of these IPOs were for very small amounts, and no liquid market ever developed. The reality is that very few of the IPOs listed on AIM would have qualified for Nasdaq listing.

The economies of scope hypothesis predicts a gradual drop in small-company IPO activity over time, rather than the abrupt fall that occurred between 2000 and 2001. The abrupt fall can be explained largely by the collapse of the Internet bubble.[15] Market valuations during 2001–12 were not sufficiently depressed, however, to be able to explain the long-term downward trend in the volume of small-company IPOs. Figure 4-2, which graphs the Shiller PE ratio, illustrates the inability of market valuations to explain the low IPO volume in the last decade. As the figure shows, a shortfall in IPO volume began to emerge in 1997.

Excessive Direct and Indirect Costs of Going Public

One issue that has gotten very little attention in the United States is the high direct and indirect costs of going public associated with high investment banking fees and the underpricing of IPOs. As noted in a recent *Journal of Finance* article, almost all moderate-size IPOs in the United States pay investment banking fees of 7 percent, whereas in Europe they typically pay fees in the vicinity of 4 percent.[16] Additional legal, auditing, and prospectus printing costs, as well as the opportunity cost of management time, add several percentage points to the costs, although these other costs have a large fixed component and are smaller in percentage terms for larger offerings. Furthermore, there is the indirect cost of selling stock for less than its subsequent market price. In the last decade, the average U.S. IPO had a first-day return of 11 percent, measured from the offer price to the first-day closing price. For a moderate-size IPO with an offer price of $10 per share, the firm thus nets at most $9.30 for a share that trades, on average, at $11.10 in the market. This $1.80 gap is 16 percent of the expected market price of $11.10. Since a typical IPO sells 30 percent of the shares outstanding, at least 0.16×30 percent = 4.8 percent of the post-issue market value of the firm is lost in the process of going public.

Now, I am not arguing that the costs of going public should be zero, nor am I arguing that issuing firms receive nothing in return for the fees that investment

---

15. Gao, Ritter, and Zhu (2014).

16. See Abrahamson, Jenkinson, and Jones (2011). The authors calculate that differences in legal costs can account for approximately 0.5 percent of the 3.0 percent gap in underwriting fees between the United States and Europe.

bankers are paid. But the costs of going public do seem to be higher than they need to be. I continue to be puzzled by why more companies do not hire WR Hambrecht + Co to conduct an IPO auction. WR Hambrecht + Co is willing to charge lower fees, and auctions can result in less expected underpricing.[17]

Perhaps one of the reasons that issuing firms are fairly complacent about the opportunity cost of underpricing is that they are unaware that with book building, the procedure used to sell most IPOs in the United States, Europe, and Japan, the economic incentives of underwriters are misaligned with those of issuers. Specifically, although the gross spread and other direct costs are required to be disclosed as underwriter compensation, the SEC has never insisted that the soft-dollar revenue (that is, commissions in excess of direct execution costs on other trades) received by underwriters in return for allocating underpriced IPOs to hedge funds and other clients be disclosed. The ability to collect soft-dollar revenue on underpriced IPOs creates an incentive for underwriters to recommend a lower offer price than they otherwise would when book building is being used. As Supreme Court Judge Louis Brandeis stated, "Sunlight is said to be the best of disinfectants."

Once a company is public, it is subject to not only SOX requirements, but also the threat of shareholder class-action lawsuits, which result in higher directors' and officers' (D&O) insurance premiums than if the company were private. As many commentators have noted, the current legal system, in which a company pays for the misdeeds of company executives, hits shareholders twice—both from the effect of correcting an accounting misstatement, for example, and from either higher D&O payments or money that the company pays in a settlement. In general, the executive or executives who are responsible for the misdeed bear only part of these costs, reducing the deterrence effect of lawsuits. Furthermore, a cost is associated with discovery and lawsuit defenses whether or not a company has engaged in a misdeed.

Although the direct and indirect costs of going public are high and public firms have higher ongoing legal costs, it is not clear that those costs were higher in the last decade than in the 1990s. Thus these costs do not explain the drop in IPO volume in the last decade.

Minimum Tick Sizes

Section 106(b) of Title 1 of the JOBS Act mandated that the SEC conduct a study of the impact of low tick sizes on the IPO market, resulting in the July

---

17. See Degeorge, Derrien, and Womack (2010).

2012 *Report to Congress on Decimalization*.[18] The study concluded that there was insufficient evidence to recommend mandating a minimum tick size. In their September 2012 Grant Thornton white paper, Weild, Kim, and Newport state that a minimum tick size "in sub-$2 billion market value stocks will bring life back to capital formation and, with it, innovation, job growth, and U.S. competitiveness."[19] They propose that a minimum tick size, perhaps $0.10 per share, should be mandated for small-cap stocks.

Tick size is the minimum increment in which a security can trade. Until 1997, when stocks started trading in sixteenths, the tick size for U.S. stocks was one-eighth of a dollar, with prices such as $12.00, $12.125, and $12.25. Consequently, the minimum bid-ask spread was one-eighth. Until May 1994, however, many Nasdaq stocks had bid-ask spreads of $0.25 because market makers colluded and avoided "odd eighth" prices such as $12.125, 12.375, and $12.625. Following the move to decimalization in 2001, the tick size fell to $0.01.

A higher minimum tick size than the size that market participants would otherwise voluntarily arrive at is equivalent to a transaction tax, with one important caveat. Instead of the government receiving the revenue from an explicit tax, market makers receive the revenue from a higher tick size, which can create economic incentives to market a stock, boosting the price. However, a higher tick size would generate more revenue only if the increase in revenue per transaction more than offset the smaller number of transactions associated with a higher cost of transacting.

Weild and Kim, in both their 2012 white paper with Newport and their previous white papers, make a distinction between tick sizes, bid-ask spreads, and what they term the "bankable spread."[20] They define the bankable spread as "the portion of a spread that market makers can reasonably rely on to compensate themselves for their investment in capital, research, and sales support. In today's electronic order-driven market, as a rule of thumb, the bankable spread is generally equivalent to the tick size."[21] They argue that a major reason for the decline in the volume of small-company IPOs has been a change in market structure that has resulted in a decline in bankable spreads, which in turn has reduced

---

18. SEC (2012).

19. Weild, Kim, and Newport (2012).

20. Weild and Kim (2008, 2009) and Weild, Kim, and Newport (2012).

21. Weild, Kim, and Newport (2012, p. 6). The quoted spreads on small-cap stocks, however, are typically larger than the tick size of a penny per share. Bessembinder (2003, table 1, panel b) reports that the volume-weighted average quoted spread for large-cap Nasdaq stocks declined from $0.0701 per share to $0.0162 per share between the predecimalization period of January 8–26, 2001, and the postdecimalization period of April 9–August 31, 2001, with the average quoted spread declining for small-cap Nasdaq stocks from $0.127 to $0.0798 per share.

the economic incentive for equity salespeople to market a stock and has caused the collapse of the IPO "ecosystem" composed of, among other parts, boutique underwriters and regional investment banks.[22] The decline in bid-ask spreads started with the end of collusion by Nasdaq market makers in 1994. The decline in bankable spreads has been facilitated by technological changes, the SEC's Order Handling Rules in 1997, Regulation ATS in 1998, the move to decimalization in 2001, and Regulation NMS in 2005.[23]

Weild and Kim, however, make no effort to quantify how much a higher tick size would boost the market price of small-cap stocks and the number of IPOs. They merely provide selected facts, such as the reduction in the number of investment banks since 2000 and the decrease in tick sizes in the last fifteen years, that loosely coincide with the decrease in the number of small-company IPOs since 1996. They do not discuss other facts that could also have a causal effect on the volume of small-company IPOs, such as the decline in the profitability of small companies and the low returns earned by public market investors on small-company IPOs.

What evidence would support the claim that the decrease in small-company IPO activity is due to the decrease in tick sizes and the decline in the IPO ecosystem? I can think of two testable predictions. First, if low public market valuations are behind the drought in small-company IPO activity, I would expect a decrease in venture capital funding of start-ups due to the lack of this attractive exit path. Second, I would expect to see a decrease in public market small-company valuation multiples relative to large-company valuation multiples.

The evidence from the venture capital industry is unambiguous: during 1980–94, according to the National Venture Capital Association (NVCA) yearbooks, venture capital investment never exceeded $4.5 billion per year in nominal terms, or $10 billion a year in 2012 purchasing power. During 1995–2012, inflation-adjusted venture capital investment was greater than $10 billion every year, peaking at more than $100 billion in 2000 and exceeding $20 billion a year in almost every year since then.[24] In the last decade, most venture capital exits were via trade sales. It appears that venture capitalists are willing to continue

22. Weild and Kim (2008, 2009) and Weild, Kim, and Newport (2012).
23. Regulation ATS refers to alternative trading systems, which are nonexchange venues for matching buyers and sellers, and NMS refers to the national market system.
24. Dow Jones VentureOne reports slightly different numbers from year to year, but the patterns are the same. For example, VentureOne reports $32.6 billion of new commitments in 2011. In general, when a fund is raised, limited partners make commitments to invest capital when it is requested, and most of the money is then invested over the following five years.

funding new technology and biomedical start-ups even without an active IPO market for small-company IPOs.

The evidence from public market valuation multiples is illustrated in figure 4-3, which shows the PE ratios for publicly traded small firms (less than $1 billion in inflation-adjusted annual sales) and big firms (greater than $1 billion). The ratios are computed using only firms with positive earnings before extraordinary items and are calculated for each year as the sum of market values divided by the sum of earnings.[25] For twenty-nine out of thirty-two years, the small-firm PE ratio was higher than the big-firm PE ratio. There has been no deterioration of the small-firm PE ratio relative to the big-firm PE ratio since 1996, in spite of the decrease in tick sizes and in the number of analysts covering small-cap stocks.[26] Thus the evidence in figure 4-3 offers no support for the hypothesis that the volume of small-company IPOs dropped due to declining tick sizes, since the implied drop in small-company valuations did not occur.

That said, the contraction of the IPO ecosystem has undoubtedly had some effect on the volume of small-company IPOs. Quantifying the effect is difficult because causality goes in both directions: having fewer small-company IPOs has resulted in a smaller infrastructure, and a smaller infrastructure has resulted in fewer IPOs. If smaller investment banks were earning economic profits on trading IPOs in the aftermarket due to higher bankable spreads, they would have an economic incentive to take more companies public; that is, there would be a lower threshold for taking a company public and providing analyst coverage. Given the low long-run returns on small-company IPOs, however, public market investors might not be willing to pay a sufficiently high price to make it attractive for a firm to go public rather than sell out in a trade sale.

25. Appendix table 4A reports the number of companies with positive earnings per share (EPS) each year and reports the time series of PE ratios using two different calculations: the ratio of aggregate market value divided by aggregate earnings, as reported in figure 4-3, and the median PE ratios. Similar patterns are present when the definition of small and large firms is changed from using a $1 billion cutoff (2011 purchasing power) to a $250 million cutoff (2009 purchasing power), as is done in Gao, Ritter, and Zhu (2014). The patterns are also similar when earnings after extraordinary items are used. The patterns are different, however, when the sample includes all firms, rather than just firms with positive EPS. In some years, the median small firm has negative earnings and the aggregate earnings numbers are either negative or near zero. As a result, the ratios jump from positive to negative or to extremely high ratios in some years when the denominator is positive but near zero.

26. One might expect an increase in small-firm PE ratios after 2005 due to the change in the expensing of employee stock options. This increase in reported expenses would, everything else the same, lower reported earnings, even though this accounting change did not affect cash flows. The conventional wisdom is that small companies, and especially tech companies, were more intensive in the granting of employee stock options.

Figure 4-3. *PE Ratios in the United States, by Size of Firm, 1980–2011*[a]

PE ratio

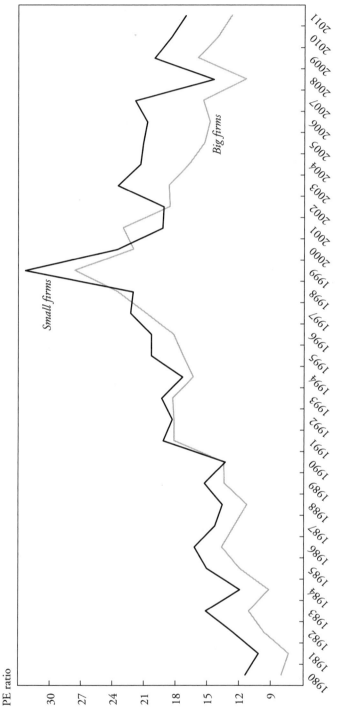

Source: See appendix table 4A.

a. Price-earnings ratio of small-company (annual sales less than $1 billion, 2011 purchasing power) and big-company stocks (annual sales greater than $1 billion, 2011 purchasing power) with positive EPS (before extraordinary items) traded on the Amex, Nasdaq, or New York Stock Exchange with Compustat EPS data available. The price-earnings ratios are computed as the sum of the market values divided by the sum of the earnings for, respectively, small and big companies with positive earnings per share.

The Effect of SecondMarket, SharesPost, and Crowdfunding on IPO Activity

In the last few years, two markets for private companies have sprung up, Second-Market and SharesPost. Both of these markets attempt to bring together buyers and sellers of stock in private companies, including companies, venture capitalists, and employees on the sell side and investors (individual and institutional) on the buy side of the market.[27] As with most illiquid markets where there is private information, buyers have had to worry about adverse selection.[28] For some stocks, however, notably Facebook before its May 2012 IPO, there have been many transactions, and pre-IPO investors and employees have been able to cash out some or all of their stakes before the company is listed.

The JOBS Act increased from 500 to 2,000 the number of shareholders of record that triggers public reporting requirements. Furthermore, the JOBS Act exempted employees from the count. By making these changes, many private companies that did not want to allow existing shareholders to sell shares to other investors for fear of triggering public reporting requirements are now far below the threshold for triggering reporting requirements. These regulatory changes and the development of these secondary markets have reduced the benefits of going public and thus, everything else the same, may result in a reduction in the number of IPOs.

The JOBS Act also encouraged crowdfunding, the concept that a large number of investors each should be able to invest a small amount of money in a company that is, they hope, early in its lifecycle. I say hope because some companies that are early in their lifecycle end up having very short lifecycles before they go out of business. Crowdfunding has obvious collective-action problems, since each investor has little incentive to devote substantial resources to doing due diligence. It appears likely, however, that intermediaries will be created to do some screening. I am of the opinion that it is unlikely that investors will earn high average returns on crowdfunding investments, although the returns may be higher than the –30 percent earned on purchases of state lottery tickets.

27. In 2007, Goldman Sachs set up a private marketplace for unregistered shares (Rule 144a securities), Goldman Sachs Tradable Unregistered Equity trading platform, or GSTrUE. After quickly attracting two large private companies that each issued close to $1 billion in shares, the venue failed to attract additional issuers and liquidity dried up. GSTrUE appears to have been supplanted by the Portal Alliance, a marketplace formed in 2009 by Nasdaq OMX, Goldman Sachs, and other Wall Street firms that has failed to attract issuers.

28. SecondMarket requires the company to give approval to allow its shares to trade, allows it to determine who is permitted to buy or sell its shares, and requires it to provide financial statements and other disclosure to approved buyers and sellers at the time of a transaction.

IPOs and Job Creation

In a recent Kauffman Foundation report, Martin Kenney, Donald Patton, and I document employment and revenue growth for U.S. companies that went public from June 1996–December 2010.[29] For the 2,766 domestic operating-company IPOs in this period, we find that the average company added 822 employees after its IPO. In the ten years after going public, the average company increased employment 60 percent, amounting to a 4.8 percent compound annual growth rate (CAGR).[30]

These numbers can be used to calculate the number of jobs that would have been created if the average annual volume of domestic operating-company IPOs between 1980 and 2000 had continued during 2001–12 rather than collapsed. In 1980–2000, an average of 296 domestic operating companies per year went public, whereas an average of only 90 domestic operating companies per year have gone public since then, a difference of 206 IPOs per year.[31] Over the twelve-year period from 2001 to 2012, this amounts to a shortfall of 2,472 IPOs. Multiplying 2,472 missing IPOs by 822 jobs per IPO results in a figure of 2.03 million jobs that were not "created" due to the IPO shortfall. This calculation assumes that these employees would have been sitting at home watching television if they had not been hired by the recent IPO firm and that the roughly $100 million raised per IPO would not have been invested in anything else. But, in a mechanical sense, 2.03 million jobs were "lost."

In the lead-up to passage of the JOBS Act, a widely reported statistic was that companies going public create huge numbers of jobs after the IPO, with only 8–10 percent of a company's subsequent number of employees on the payroll before the company went public. For example, slide 11 of the IPO Task Force presentation to the Senate Banking Committee on October 11, 2011, reported,

29. See Kenney, Patton, and Ritter (2012).

30. The 60 percent cumulative average growth in employment and 4.8 percent CAGR numbers are based on the 1,857 IPOs from June 1996 to December 2000. The numbers are computed as the increase in the aggregate employment of the 1,857 firms relative to their aggregate employment at the time of the IPO. The average company had 1,303 employees at the time of the IPO. Because of the lack of small-company IPOs during 2001–10, the average pre-IPO employment for the full population of 2,766 IPOs from June 1996 to December 2010 was 1,830 employees.

31. During 2001–12, an average of nine foreign non-ADR IPOs occurred in the United States each year, which is why there was an average of ninety-nine operating-company IPOs and ninety domestic operating-company IPOs. During 1980–2000, an average of fourteen foreign-company non-ADR IPOs occurred each year, which is why there was an average of 310 operating-company IPOs and 296 domestic operating-company IPOs a year. In Kenney, Patton, and Ritter (2012), we calculate 1.88 million jobs lost because we use a number of 298 domestic IPOs during 1980–2000 rather than 296, and we did our calculation for the eleven years ending in 2011 rather than the twelve years ending in 2012.

"92 percent of job growth in a company occurs post-IPO." This number, some-times rounded off to 90 percent, was repeated in several *Wall Street Journal* arti-cles and op-ed pieces.[32]

The 92 percent job growth number comes from reports paid for by the NVCA, an industry trade group. The annual reports, entitled *Venture Impact: The Economic Importance of Venture Capital-Backed Companies in the U.S. Economy,* are produced by consulting firm IHS Global Insight.[33] The 92 percent (or 90 per-cent) number has been used with statements that if the volume of IPOs in 1996 had continued in the years since then, rather than the lower number of IPOs that actually occurred, as many as 22.7 million more jobs would have been cre-ated. For example, the IPO Task Force report presented to the U.S. Treasury and the U.S. Senate Banking Committee in late 2011 by IPO Task Force chair Kate Mitchell used the 22.7 million jobs figure.[34] Where did this number come from?

It comes from a 2009 Grant Thornton White Paper in which Weild and Kim make five assumptions that are different from those used in my 2.03 million jobs lost number.[35] They also report other, lower, numbers based on alternative assumptions about employee growth rates and benchmark numbers of IPOs, but their high-end estimate is the number that has typically been repeated, without qualifications.[36]

First, they make the reasonable assumption that IPO volume should be propor-tional to real GDP, and since the U.S. economy has grown over the last thirty years, one would expect IPO activity to rise rather than be flat. My number, which assumes that IPO activity would be constant over time, is conservative in comparison.

Second, they assume that each IPO that did not occur would have had 1,372 employees before going public and that post-IPO employment would grow at a

---

32. See, for example, the interview with Kate Mitchell, IPO Task Force chair and former NVCA chair, in "How Silicon Valley Won in Washington," *Wall Street Journal*, April 7, 2012. The article states, with-out questioning, "To sell politicians on the benefits of allowing start-ups to grow into public companies, the task force pointed to research showing that when such firms go public, more than 90 percent of job creation happens *after* the IPO." Also, Delaware Governor Jack Markell, in his opinion piece, "Restarting the U.S. Capital Machine," *Wall Street Journal*, March 1, 2012, states, "In fact, 92 percent of a typical company's employment growth occurs after the IPO."

33. See, for example, IHS Global Insight (2011).

34. IPO Task Force (2011).

35. Weild and Kim (2009, pp. 26–27).

36. Exhibit 27 of Weild and Kim's report computes thirty-six separate numbers for job creation based on alternative assumptions regarding the pre-IPO number of employees, the CAGR of employment, and the benchmark number of IPOs (1998 actual, 1991–95 average, and 1996 actual), resulting in estimates varying from 1.1 million jobs to 22.7 million jobs. They then state, "Though 22 million may seem to be a staggering number on its own, we believe it is a reasonable estimate in the context of long-term historical employment growth in this country" (Weild and Kim 2009, p. 27).

CAGR of 17.8 percent, a number that implies employment growing by 415 percent in the ten years after an IPO (and approximately 900 percent in fourteen years). They base the 17.8 percent a year number on a "select" group of twenty-five venture capital–backed IPOs from 1996 and later. In other words, they assume that thousands of companies that did not go public would have grown as fast as a select group of highly successful venture capital–backed companies such as Google if they had! This assumption has a huge impact on their calculations.

Third, they assume that the normal level of IPO activity is that of 1996, the peak of the IPO market, and that the volume should grow from this level.[37] The assumption that the peak year of 1996 is normal biases their number upward. Furthermore, their count of 803 IPOs in 1996 apparently includes 110 penny stock and unit IPOs as well as 64 foreign-company IPOs.[38] Thus they implicitly assume that the average penny stock IPO had 1,372 pre-IPO employees and increased its employment 415 percent in the following decade. In other words, they assume that it would be just as big and successful as the average "select" venture capital–backed IPO.

Fourth, they assume that the IPO shortfall started in 1997, rather than in 2001, and that more than 1,500 additional firms would have gone public in 1997–2000 and then increased their employment by 17.8 percent a year for more than a decade. This 1997–2000 shortfall assumption, combined with the 17.8 percent CAGR assumption, adds at least 9 million lost jobs to their 22.7 million total.

Fifth, their calculation ends in an earlier year than mine, so the difference in per year numbers is even larger than the 22.7 million versus 2.03 million numbers suggest.

In sum, the number of 22.7 million jobs lost is based on one reasonable assumption and three indefensible assumptions.[39] The exact number of jobs lost through a shortfall in IPO activity, however, is not something that can be

37. Weild and Kim (2009, p. 26).

38. See tables 14 and 15 of "Initial Public Offerings: Updated Tables" on my website at http://bear.warrington.ufl.edu/ritter for a decomposition of how many IPOs take place in the United States every year. For 1996, my count is 675 operating-company IPOs, including 32 non-ADR foreign listings, for a total of 643 domestic operating-company IPOs that are not penny stock or unit IPOs.

39. Weild, Kim, and Newport (2012, p. 26) back away from the extreme number of 22.7 million jobs, stating, "We estimate that this dearth of IPOs has cost the United States as many as 9.4 million additional jobs that might have been created after companies go public. If we add the private market effect (our best estimate of the multiplier effect in the private market when more companies go public), the number of additional jobs increases to 18.8 million (see Exhibit 6)." The 9.4 million jobs number is based on an assumption of annual 2.57 percent U.S. real GDP growth and 822 post-IPO jobs created per IPO, with the 822 jobs number coming from Kenney, Patton, and Ritter (2012). They retain the assumptions that there were 803 IPOs in 1996 and that this is the benchmark year for normal IPO activity.

calculated through mechanical computations. If one company goes public and raises capital that is used to hire new employees, capital is taken from some other activity in the economy, and, unless the company only hires people who would otherwise be unemployed, the net number of jobs created in the economy is less than the number added by this firm. Incidentally, to the best of my knowledge, none of the sources quoting the 22.7 million jobs lost number has pointed out that with a civilian labor force of 154.5 million and 12.8 million unemployed in August 2012, any number of jobs lost above 12.8 million would create a negative unemployment rate unless the labor force expanded.[40]

What Should Be Done?

Well-functioning labor markets and capital markets can help to allocate resources to their most valued uses and thus boost standards of living. A strong case can be made that the private returns for investments that lead to technological advances underestimate the social returns. A well-functioning IPO market can facilitate the financing of young growth companies, partly by being a conduit for raising capital, but also by providing an exit for pre-IPO investors who invested with the anticipation of eventually having a liquid market in which to sell some or all of their stock. Not all IPOs are the same, however. I would argue that a restaurant chain adding employees is largely just taking business away from competing restaurants, with little effect on the economy. However, a biotechnology company that develops a drug that cheaply prevents diabetes, resulting in fewer workers taking early retirement or incurring large medical costs, would have large social benefits.

IPOs are merely one way in which pre-IPO shareholders achieve either immediate or future liquidity and by which private companies raise money. Thus public policy toward IPOs should be determined as one element of policies to create and maintain well-functioning capital markets that, in the absence of externalities, fund positive net present value (NPV) investments and do not fund negative NPV investments. Tax policy and investor protection policy cannot be separated from policies aimed at the efficient raising of capital. If venture capitalists and their limited partners were earning very high rates of return during the last decade, if very little money was being invested by venture capitalists, or if public market investors were earning very high returns on investments in small-company IPOs, I would be more concerned about a shortage of capital being a

40. The civilian labor force and unemployment numbers are found in table 1 on the Bureau of Labor Statistics website (www.bls.gov/news.release/laus.htm).

problem for emerging growth companies. Instead, my biggest concern is the lack of profitability of these companies.

If the reason that many small companies are not going public is that they will be more profitable as part of a larger organization, then policies designed to encourage companies to remain small and independent have the potential to harm the economy rather than boost it. Not all emerging growth companies should stay private or merge, however, and to the degree that excessive burdens associated with going public, and being public, result in less capital being raised and invested wisely, standards of living are lowered.

In thinking about the JOBS Act, one should keep in mind that the law of unintended consequences will never be repealed. It is possible that, by making it easier to raise money privately, creating some liquidity without being public, restricting the information that stockholders have access to, restricting the ability of public market shareholders to constrain managers after investors contribute capital, and driving out independent research, the net effect of the JOBS Act might be to reduce the flow of capital into young high-technology companies or the number of IPOs of small emerging growth companies.

I do not think that the JOBS Act will result in a flood of companies going public. The main reason why fewer small companies have been going public is that they are finding it difficult to earn a profit. The JOBS Act does little to solve this problem. Nor do I think that noticeably higher economic growth and job creation will result from the JOBS Act.

I also do not see any reason to set minimum tick sizes for firms with sales or market caps below some threshold. Indeed, the evidence from other countries that have created second markets, with less stringent criteria than Nasdaq and the NYSE impose, is not promising. As documented elsewhere, investors in these markets have earned very low returns.[41]

What should be done? I suggest three policy changes that, I believe, would have a modest effect on encouraging more IPOs. More important, I think that these proposed changes would improve standards of living by encouraging innovation and allocating capital and labor more efficiently.

First, I would lower the costs of going public by encouraging the use of auctions rather than the use of book building. If the costs of going public eat up 5 percent of firm value, on average, quantitatively these costs are of the same

---

41. See Vismara, Paleari, and Ritter (2012) and Ritter, Signori, and Vismara (2013). In the United States, the American Stock Exchange's Emerging Company Marketplace (ECM) was created in 1992 but failed to attract many new listings before it closed in 1995. See Aggarwal and Angel (1999) for a discussion of the ECM.

order of magnitude as the lower level of share prices from a lack of analyst coverage. The specific suggestion that I am making is for the SEC to interpret its existing regulations on the disclosure of underwriter compensation less narrowly and require the disclosure of soft-dollar commission revenue that is generated when underwriters use book building. The average level of IPO underpricing would fall. Investment bankers are opposed to reforms that might lead to lower gross spreads or less underpricing. Investment bankers have a lot of political influence, especially with Republicans.

Second, I would reform the legal system to discourage class-action lawsuits that do not have solid grounds, and I would shift the defendants from the companies (and their shareholders) to the individuals who are responsible for the actions. Plaintiff attorneys, and many defense attorneys and consultants, are opposed to this change, for not only do they benefit from the existing system, but they also do not want to reduce the amount of malfeasance to zero, for then they would make no money. These attorneys have a lot of political influence, especially with Democrats.

Third, I would reform the copyright and patent system. A book by Adam Jaffe and Josh Lerner, *Innovation and Its Discontents*, provides a cogent analysis of the problems with our current system of patenting.[42] Patents and copyrights are designed to create temporary monopoly power so that a creator can capture part of the benefits of an innovation. But current copyright law in the United States gives exclusive rights to receive royalties for seventy years after the death of the creator. The great-grandchildren of dead authors and musicians, and the owners of many existing patents, are opposed to this change. At the other extreme, intellectual property rights are not effectively enforced in China, India, and many other countries, with the result that firms based in the United States and other countries are unable to capture economic returns on their investments.

In summary, I do not know what the optimal level of IPO activity is in the United States or any other country, nor do I think that it should necessarily be the same now as it once was. I believe that a long-term change has been occurring in which getting big fast is now more important than was once the case, at least in certain industries. Because merging is sometimes the most efficient way of getting a successful new technology to market quickly, I do not view the increase in trade sales and the decrease in IPO activity as necessarily alarming.

---

42. Jaffe and Lerner (2004).

Appendix Table 4A. *Number of Publicly Listed Firms in the United States with Positive EPS and the Median and Aggregate PE Ratios, 1980–2011*[a]

	Small firms			Big firms		
Year	Number	Median PE1	Aggregate PE2	Number	Median PE1	Aggregate PE2
1980	2,365	9.62	11.38	953	7.89	7.98
1981	2,493	9.70	10.12	899	7.38	7.28
1982	2,306	12.74	12.55	809	9.76	9.61
1983	2,565	15.31	15.13	820	11.38	11.07
1984	2,587	12.74	11.92	848	9.97	9.17
1985	2,410	15.73	15.04	785	13.04	11.94
1986	2,491	16.43	16.22	783	14.52	13.64
1987	2,625	14.05	14.27	875	12.17	12.46
1988	2,508	13.35	13.57	906	11.57	11.25
1989	2,367	14.42	15.26	884	13.01	13.40
1990	2,342	12.87	13.30	855	12.66	13.44
1991	2,405	17.77	19.16	819	17.23	18.14
1992	2,668	18.09	18.31	798	17.68	18.15
1993	2,995	18.65	19.31	903	18.54	18.27
1994	3,199	16.07	17.34	1,071	15.11	16.35
1995	3,192	18.23	20.31	1,115	16.28	17.31
1996	3,354	18.71	20.31	1,256	17.19	18.20
1997	3,256	19.48	22.28	1,325	19.26	20.83
1998	2,868	16.35	22.04	1,291	18.61	23.52
1999	2,590	16.21	32.31	1,338	16.39	27.60
2000	2,200	13.97	23.54	1,317	16.32	22.00
2001	1,783	19.10	19.23	1,113	20.65	23.00
2002	1,734	16.79	19.12	1,101	16.94	18.54
2003	1,813	22.40	23.49	1,300	19.12	18.63
2004	1,936	22.12	21.34	1,459	18.49	16.74
2005	1,877	21.89	21.08	1,463	17.51	15.29
2006	1,837	21.75	20.70	1,523	17.76	14.78
2007	1,673	21.06	21.84	1,406	16.68	15.42
2008	1,308	14.14	14.41	1,178	12.34	11.38
2009	1,329	19.28	20.03	1,193	16.70	15.93
2010	1,564	19.20	18.40	1,348	16.61	14.00
2011	1,437	17.22	17.08	1,342	15.14	12.73

Source: Sample firms are Amex, Nasdaq, and NYSE firms listed on Compustat by the Center for Research on Security Prices with positive earnings per share (EPS before extraordinary items). Firms with Standard Industrial Classification codes between 6000 and 6199 (banks and savings & loans) and between 6700 and 6799 (closed-end funds, REITs, and SPACs) are excluded.

a. Small firms are defined as those with fiscal-year sales of less than $1 billion in 2011 dollars, using the U.S. Consumer Price Index, and big firms are defined as those with more than $1 billion in sales. PE1 is the median price-earnings ratio, and PE2 is the ratio of the aggregates, calculated as the sum of undiluted earnings divided by the sum of market values for, respectively, small or big firms. For companies with multiple classes of shares outstanding, all share classes are used. Market values are calculated as of the end of the fiscal year, so, for example, the 1999 numbers reflect the prices for December 31 for companies with a December 31 fiscal year, but June 30 for companies with June 30 fiscal years.

References

Abrahamson, Mark, Tim Jenkinson, and Howard Jones. 2011. "Why Don't U.S. Issuers Demand European Fees for IPOs?" *Journal of Finance* 66, no. 6 (December): 2055–82.

Aggarwal, Reena, and James J. Angel. 1999. "The Rise and Fall of the Amex Emerging Company Marketplace." *Journal of Financial Economics* 52 (May): 257–89.

Bessembinder, Hendrik. 2003. "Trade Execution Costs and Market Quality after Decimalization." *Journal of Financial and Quantitative Analysis* 38 (December): 747–77.

Degeorge, François, François Derrien, and Kent L. Womack. 2010. "Auctioned IPOs: The U.S. Evidence." *Journal of Financial Economics* 98, no. 2 (November): 177–94.

Demiroglu, Cem, and Michael Ryngaert. 2010. "The First Analyst Coverage of Neglected Stocks." *Financial Management* 39, no. 2 (Summer): 555–84.

Gao, Xiaohui, Jay R. Ritter, and Zhongyan Zhu. 2014. "Where Have All the IPOs Gone?" *Journal of Financial and Quantitative Analysis,* forthcoming.

IHS Global Insight. 2011. *Venture Impact: The Economic Importance of Venture Capital–Backed Companies in the U.S. Economy.* Arlington, Va.

IPO Task Force. 2011. "Rebuilding the IPO On-Ramp." Report presented to U.S. Department of Treasury, Washington.

Jaffe, Adam B., and Josh Lerner. 2004. *Innovation and Its Discontents: How Our Broken Patent System Is Endangering Innovation and Progress, and What to Do about It.* Princeton University Press.

Kenney, Martin, Donald Patton, and Jay R. Ritter. 2012. *Post-IPO Employment and Revenue Growth for U.S. IPOs, June 1996–2010.* Kansas City, Mo.: Kauffman Foundation.

Ritter, Jay R. 2012. Testimony before the Senate Committee on Banking, Housing, and Urban Affairs, March 6, 2012 (www.banking.senate.gov/public/index.cfm?FuseAction=Files.View&FileStore_id=a5ded25c-135d-484a-943a-bfa52fba3206).

Ritter, Jay R., Andrea Signori, and Silvio Vismara. 2013. "Economies of Scope and IPO Activity in Europe." Forthcoming in *Handbook of Research on IPOs,* edited by Mario Levis and Silvio Vismara. Cheltenham, U.K.: Edward Elgar.

SEC (Securities and Exchange Commission). 2012. *Report to Congress on Decimalization.* Washington.

Vismara, Silvio, Stefano Paleari, and Jay R. Ritter. 2012. "Europe's Second Markets for Small Companies." *European Financial Management* 18, no. 3 (June): 352–88.

Weild, David, and Edward Kim. 2008. "Why Are IPOs in the ICU?" White Paper. Chicago: Grant Thornton LLP.

———. 2009. "A Wake-up Call for America." White Paper. Chicago: Grant Thornton LLP.

Weild, David, Edward Kim, and Lisa Newport. 2012. "The Trouble with Small Tick Sizes." White Paper. Chicago: Grant Thornton LLP.

PART II

The Japanese Approach

YUTA SEKI 5

Reconstructing and Revitalizing Japan's Financial Sector

THE U.S. ECONOMY is now overcoming the shock from what proved to be a once-in-100-years financial crisis, replete with massive losses on subprime loans and a string of major financial institution failures, headlined by Lehman Brothers. Share prices have recovered significantly, and big lenders are announcing strong earnings. More than four years after Lehman's collapse, however, the main indicators of the real economy, including employment and the housing market, have recovered at a surprisingly tepid pace. In Europe, meanwhile, the sovereign debt crisis and the resulting fiscal austerity have kept real economic growth in negative territory well into 2013.

The economic trends in the United States and Europe point to a vicious cycle among economic agents in which seekers of funding are compelled to deleverage, causing further declines in the price of assets used as collateral. This has resulted in the absence of sectors capable of driving demand and brought on a different sort of stagnation than what is normally seen during a recession. These conditions are reminiscent of the Japanese economy in the 1990s.

Meanwhile, the level of share prices and credit ratings suggests that market participants' faith in the U.S. financial sector has yet to recover sufficiently. This is attributed to lingering problems with nonperforming assets, characterized by a huge inventory of illiquid assets and by put-back claims on delinquent residential mortgages.[1] In fact, the aggregate amount of Level 3 assets held by six banks—Bank of America, Citigroup, Goldman Sachs, JPMorgan, Morgan Stanley, and Wells Fargo—totaled $304.4 billion as of December 2012, equivalent to 43 percent of their Tier 1 capital.[2] Additionally, the recovery of earnings reported by the major U.S. banks has been supported largely by a decline in provisions for loan and lease losses rather than by improvements in their business model. Because net interest margins are being squeezed, profits could disappear quickly if there were to be a new wave of debt defaults. Furthermore, in most of the developed world, it has become more difficult for the government to apply taxpayer funds to resolve financial institutions or adopt measures aimed at stabilizing the financial system, which makes it more likely that the shareholders and creditors of lenders under threat will be required to absorb losses, without the benefit of government coming to the rescue.

It is under these conditions that governments in the United States, the United Kingdom, the Euro Zone, and other developed economies are all moving in the direction of financial reregulation. After the experience of the financial crisis, it is certainly rational to want to try to prevent lenders from taking on excessive leverage. Nevertheless, tightening regulations on financial institutions holding nonperforming assets that are not marked to market or do not reflect their selling price could be meaningless and may even lead to unintended consequences.

For example, tightening capital requirements in an environment where it is difficult for lenders to recapitalize or sell assets could trigger a vicious cycle in which banks become reluctant to lend, causing economic stagnation and leading to the failure of companies with poor cash flow. In recent years regulatory authorities in Europe and the United States have frequently conducted stress tests aimed at eliminating financial instability. Many of these tests apply stress to the factors affecting bank earnings and profitability and measure the negative impact on capital. If the tests do not apply stress to the asset side of the balance sheet

---

1. A mortgage put-back is a demand that the originator of an underlying mortgage or the underwriter of the securitization backed by that mortgage buy back (at face value) the mortgage when there is a material breach of the representations and warranties made in the underlying loan purchase agreement. Normally a material breach of representations and warranties comes to light when a default occurs or when default risk appears imminent. From around 2010 until 2012, government-supported enterprises (GSEs) were aggressively making put-back claims, at the expense of Bank of America and other lenders.

2. A Level 3 asset is the type of asset defined under Statement of Financial Accounting Standards 157 as having no reference price information for determining its fair value; it therefore must be valued using internal prices based on the best obtainable information from the disclosing party. Such assets are significantly less liquid than Level 1 assets, which can be valued using quoted prices for the same type of assets in an active market, or Level 2 assets, which can be valued using quoted prices of the same or similar type of asset in an inactive market.

where nonperforming loans (NPLs) potentially lie, lenders are unlikely to win back the trust of investors and counterparties. These conditions make it easier for a default to occur when a loan matures or is refinanced, particularly for lenders holding a large number of real estate mortgages that cannot be recovered unless their fallen collateral values are realized.

This was the problem that Japan's banking sector faced in the 1990s. For example, the transition to Basel I capital requirements began in fiscal 1988 (ending March 1999), with full implementation in fiscal 1992, during which time Japan's stock market and land values peaked and then fell rapidly, which kept bank managements in a state of constant worry over their ability to meet the minimum capital ratio and overly reluctant to extend credit.

Japan was considered a "land standard" society, in which banks traditionally set the value of real estate carefully as collateral for loans. However, during the bubble years banks turned to excessive lending, using as collateral real estate that had appreciated sharply or was anticipated to appreciate in value. In other words, where loans would normally be written for about 70 percent of the assessed value of the land, in many cases loans were written for a loan-to-value ratio of 120 percent in anticipation of sharp increases in the value. Banks also put such a high priority on the amount of loans written that they wound up lending based on junior liens. Because this practice was widespread, when the borrower's business failed and the loan became uncollectable, the value of the real estate serving as collateral often dropped below the amount of the loan, and the lender holding the junior lien could neither collect on the loan nor seize the collateral, making it difficult to sell. At the same time, because it was often impossible to determine the amount of the uncollectable loans without selling the real estate collateral, lenders often painted overly rosy pictures when self-reporting their loan assets to financial regulators. They would underestimate the total amount of NPLs either by classifying them as normal credit claims or by extending additional credit so that the borrower would have enough funds to make the required payments, thereby making the business look stronger than it really was. With investors widely aware of this practice, banks could not have regained the confidence of financial markets even with the stress tests, and none of the banks aggressively sought to raise capital from the market.

Following a drawn-out and unpleasant debate over whether failed lenders should be bailed out with taxpayer funds, in 2002 Japan's financial regulators came up with and quickly implemented a comprehensive set of policies to fix the NPL problem and rejuvenate the financial sector. The next section reviews and analyzes the primary reasons for the success of the policies implemented by Japan's regulators since 2002.

Reasons for Japan's Previous Lack of Progress in Disposing of Nonperforming Loans

The Japanese financial sector's long struggle with NPLs can be attributed to a variety of factors. From the macroeconomic perspective, and more specifically from the perspective of financial regulations and the nature of financial and real estate transactions, the following four factors are particularly worth noting.

First, the amount of nonperforming loans was extremely large, and the impact was widely spread. The stock market (the Nikkei Average) plunged about 78 percent, from 38,915.87 at its peak at the end of 1989 to 8,578.95 at the end of 2002, while land prices (the urban land price index for commercial land) dropped a precipitous 85 percent, from a peak of 519.4 in 1991 to 89.5 in 2002. Because Japanese banks held a large number of shares in the companies they lent to under the "main bank" system and because the amount of real estate loans had grown dramatically during the bubble years, the impact from the significant decline in asset prices spread.

When it becomes clear that serious problems are present throughout the financial system and that allowing even a single bank to fail could risk the collapse of the entire banking system, bank regulators tend to go soft on the banks and put off implementing solutions (the "too many to fail" problem).[3]

Second, the rules for resolving failed banks were still a work in progress. Up until the 1990s, the "convoy system" and the "banks can't fail" myth were implicit public assumptions, and the robust banking system, a de facto public-private partnership, was lauded as underpinning Japan's economic growth. The flipside of this, however, is that there was virtually no system or infrastructure for the orderly resolution of financial institutions. For example, the Deposit Insurance Corporation of Japan (DICJ), established in 1971, was extremely small in terms of both manpower and funding,[4] and its designers did not envision the need for the orderly resolution of anything but smaller lenders. Additionally, the lack of a legal framework to guarantee the entire amount of deposits (bank liabilities) meant that requiring depositors to take a haircut risked a substantial increase in costs from the societal disruption caused by bank runs, possibly making Japan's regulators hesitant to implement a full-fledged resolution process. Not only that, there were no established procedures for the valuation and disclosure of nonperforming loans.

---

3. See Ikeo (2009).
4. For example, in fiscal 1995, the DICJ had fifteen employees and only ¥386.5 billion in policy reserves.

Third, although real estate loans were routine in the banking industry, there was no legal framework or experience with debt restructuring, nor was the regulatory environment conducive to structuring new financial products such as securitization, exchange-traded funds, and real estate investment trusts (REITs). Additionally, there were virtually no private equity funds or other alternative investment players in the market. Lacking reorganization procedures like those in Chapter 11 of the U.S. Bankruptcy Code and having no way to pass ownership to distressed debt funds and other specialists by seizing collateral to sell at auctions, in debt-equity swaps, and through securitization, loans for real estate and to construction and real estate companies became locked up on the balance sheets of the banks. This had a stultifying effect on the real economy by preventing redevelopment and reuse of real estate and effectively froze business investment and growth at companies that suffered sudden damage to their credit, turning them into "zombies."

Fourth, it became difficult for banks to raise capital from the market, which further depressed their share price and credit and created a vicious cycle. Meanwhile, because net losses and the consequent decline in capital ratios drew harsh criticism from investors, counterparties, and regulators, the banks recorded minimum charges to the loan loss reserves needed to keep their capital ratios from falling, and this naturally meant that their disposal of NPLs was too little too late.

Once share prices and land prices started to decline, Japan's regulators and bank managements tended to respond too late. In fact, in the summer of 1992, Prime Minister Kiichi Miyazawa, greatly concerned about the impact from rapidly falling asset prices, suggested injecting financial institutions with public funds, but the idea was never realized because of strong resistance from the Ministry of Finance and other government agencies as well as from the media, the public, and even the lenders themselves. In fact, Prime Minister Miyazawa's approval ratings dropped after that, eventually leading in June 1993 to the defeat of the Liberal Democratic Party (LDP) for the first time in nearly forty years. Fixing the NPL problem by injecting public funds remained a political taboo for a long time after that. It was not until about eight years after the bubble collapsed that the major banks received preemptive injections of public funds, first in March 1998 under the Financial Functions Stabilization Act for approximately ¥1.8 trillion and then in March 1999 under the Financial Reconstruction Act for approximately ¥7.5 trillion.[5]

---

5. See Fuchita and Kodachi (2012) for detailed analysis on Japan's policy responses during the 1997–98 financial crisis.

Policy Change in 2001–02: From Special Inspections to the Program for Financial Revival

From the late 1990s until around 2001, when the Japanese economy seemed to be overcoming the financial shocks of 1997–98, asset prices started to recover, and the Nikkei Average momentarily reached 20,000. From around mid-2000, however, the tech bubble in the United States started to collapse and then came the terrorist attacks in September 2001, both of which had a dampening effect on Japan's stock market. During this time, market participants both inside and outside of Japan had very little trust in Japan's banking sector, and it was widely believed that the NPL problem was the biggest cause of the sluggish performance of the economy and financial markets. As pressure to fix the NPL problem got stronger, a major turning point in policy came in fiscal 2001 (ending in March 2002) when financial regulators changed the way banks were administered.

What triggered the change in Japan's financial regulators? In addition to the pressure from market participants, the two finance ministers, Hakuo Yanagisawa and Heizo Takenaka, provided leadership by designing a set of comprehensive policies that received the backing of Prime Minister Junichiro Koizumi, who headed Japan's only long-lived administration over the past twenty years.

Japan's Financial Services Agency (FSA), which was involved in the design and execution of policy, formally began operating in July 2000 as the successor to the Financial Supervisory Agency established in 1998. When the FSA was created, it was claimed to be independent, modeled after the United Kingdom's Financial Services Authority. In fact, it was created in response to public criticism over the government's handling of multiple scandals involving bureaucrats and financial institutions and appears to have resulted from a reorganization of government agencies motivated by politicians who wanted to separate financial supervisory powers from the power of the purse, both of which had been concentrated in the Ministry of Finance.

In December 2000, Hakuo Yanagisawa, the first economy and financial services minister and highly regarded for his administrative skills in taming the financial crisis, was named to that same post again. Minister Yanagisawa, ahead of legislation phasing out unlimited deposit insurance (by establishing a cap on deposit insurance) beginning on April 1, 2002, proved willing to do what it took to strengthen the financial sector as soon as possible, including expediting the resolution of smaller lenders in trouble.

Then in April 2001, Prime Minister Yoshiro Mori resigned and was replaced by structural reformist Junichiro Koizumi, who kept Yanagisawa in his ministerial post while forming a new cabinet. Prime Minister Koizumi pursued an economic policy built around structural reforms, and, unlike previous LDP administrations that had tended to favor demand-side policies and fiscal stimulus, he was a supply-side reformer. He honed in on the financial sector's NPL problem as the most urgent target of his supply-side reform. First, on June 21, 2001, the Council on Economic and Fiscal Policy announced its Basic Policies for Economic and Fiscal Management and Structural Reform, in which it posited the following goal: "Structural reforms with no sanctuaries cause pain in the process of creative destruction, but without structural reform a real economic recovery and sustained growth are not possible. The goal is to fearlessly, unflinchingly, and agnostically eliminate the NPL problem within two to three years."[6]

Additionally, Yanagisawa proposed starting off with the direct write-off and final disposition of NPLs.[7] In other words, rather than the "indirect write-offs" that Japan's bank management tended to favor—namely, increasing loan loss reserves as the quality of loan assets deteriorated—he argued in favor of the court-ordered liquidation of borrowers, the sale of loans, and debt forgiveness by the banks based on the borrower's restructuring plans. He created a foundation for vigorous debate over improving mechanisms and markets for revitalizing businesses. Arguing for the need to make the NPL problem transparent, Yanagisawa also had the FSA conduct special inspections from October 2001 until end-March 2002 to look at the banks' internal assessment of major borrowers. The special inspections moved forward when it came to light that the major banks had classified their loans to Mycal, which filed for bankruptcy in September 2001 with group-wide total debt of approximately ¥1.7 trillion, as "borrowers requiring caution," a relatively sound category. The inspections focused on the management of credit to large borrowers that would have a major impact on both the real economy and the banking sector and attempted to get banks to use consistent loan categories (so that different banks would not categorize loans to the same borrower differently).

The hardline stance taken by Yanagisawa and the FSA had an impact, and the major banks, becoming more aggressive in disposing of their NPLs, recorded large losses for the fiscal year ended March 2002. Meanwhile, the combination of a worsening economy and stricter inspections caused the amount of NPLs held by the major banks to grow to about ¥27.2 trillion as of March 2002, a year-over-year increase of 47 percent. This prompted criticism of Yanagisawa's approach to

---

6. The Council on Economic and Fiscal Policy is a parliamentary organ established within the Cabinet Office to provide a platform for the prime minister to lead the process of forming economic and fiscal policies while also reflecting the opinions of the relevant state ministers and Diet members with expertise in that area. Prime Minister Koizumi considered this to be the most important policy council, and the council proposed the Basic Policy to give the prime minister's Cabinet Office greater influence on the budget formation process.

7. FSA (2001, 2002a).

supervision and resulted in his dismissal on September 30, 2002. Keizo Takenaka, a Keio University professor who had been appointed state minister for economic and fiscal policy, took his place as economy and financial services minister.[8]

On October 30, 2002, one month after taking the job, Minister Takenaka announced the Financial Revival Program.[9] Subtitled "Revival of the Japanese Economy through Resolving the Nonperforming Loan Problems of Major Banks," the program applied only to the major banks and targeted cutting their NPL ratio from 8.4 percent at end-fiscal 2002 to about half of that by end-fiscal 2004.[10] The Financial Revival Program was nicknamed the Takenaka Plan. As explained later, it was a policy package of incentives and systemic support to encourage the major banks to write off their nonperforming loans, taking into account the characteristics of the Japanese market, including inconsistencies in the methods for assessing NPLs and the lack of private equity and securitization markets. At the time, the FSA's public description of the Takenaka Plan was that, although it contained a variety of policy ideas, it had three main tenets: (1) a new financial system framework, (2) a new corporate reorganization framework, and (3) a new financial regulation framework (figure 5-1).

When the Takenaka Plan was announced, it was widely viewed as being full of policies that would produce a hard landing and be harsh on bank management and on existing shareholders and creditors. In fact, it placed great weight on revitalizing borrower firms and real estate collateral, and, when Resona Bank was in crisis, it did not pursue a bankruptcy resolution that would completely wipe out existing shareholders; rather it followed a soft-landing approach. In any case, the major banks' NPL ratio dropped to 2.9 percent by March 20005, achieving the Takenaka Plan's goal of cutting NPLs in half (figure 5-2).

The Way out of the NPL Problem

Figure 5-3 depicts how the policies proposed by the Japanese government in 2001–02 to solve the NPL problem relate to each other. The first feature of importance is that the Japanese authorities were focused on revitalizing both the

8. Yanagisawa was fervent about solving the NPL problem and promoted policies that would produce a hard landing, making it ironic that his efforts to encourage the disclosure of NPLs earned him the reputation of being soft on the banks and not doing enough to reduce NPLs (see Nishimura 2011).

9. FSA (2002b).

10. The NPL ratio is the value of loans requiring disclosure under the Financial Reconstruction Act divided by total credit extended. The Financial Reconstruction Act requires financial institutions to disclose these loans and to place each borrower in one of four categories: bankrupt or de facto bankrupt, in danger of bankruptcy, needs attention, and normal loans (although reporting of loans needing attention is by loan amount rather than by borrower).

Figure 5-1. *Program for Financial Revival (Takenaka Plan)*

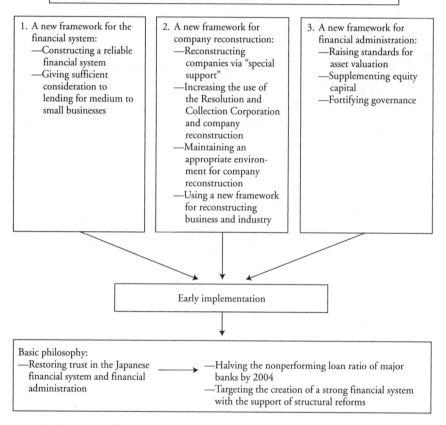

Source: Nomura Institute of Capital Markets Research, based on FSA (2002b).

financial institutions that lent the money and the companies that borrowed it. Because of the absence of the legal structure, markets, and personnel needed to revitalize distressed companies, the policies focused on getting this infrastructure quickly in place. A second feature is that it included multiple policies offering both carrots and sticks to the lenders, ordered in such a way as to give them an incentive to dispose of all of their NPLs. Additionally, the policies aimed to create a virtual cycle whereby the goal of revitalizing the financial institutions enabled those institutions to win trust from the market and recapitalize on their own,

Figure 5-2. *Status of Nonperforming Loans of Major Banks in Japan, 1993–2012*[a]

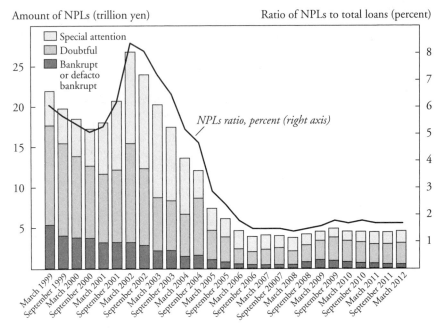

Amount of NPLs (trillion yen)   Ratio of NPLs to total loans (percent)

Source: Japan's Financial Services Agency.

a. Loans are based on the Financial Reconstruction Act; major banks include city banks, trust banks, and the former Industrial Bank of Japan.

while the corporations responded by establishing business models focused on the goal of revitalization while reducing their debt ratios enough to achieve a sustainable financial position.[11]

Promoting the Final Disposition of NPLs

The incentives for financial institutions to dispose of their nonperforming loans comprised several elements.

First, there was a requirement for reporting on progress in implementing business improvement plans. The business improvement plans submitted to the government by banks that received injections of public funds included the rebuilding of businesses and clarification of management responsibility, and the banks were obligated to submit to a quarterly interview about the plan's implementation status. To ensure steady execution of the plan, in the event that the bank is deemed

11. Takenaka (2006).

Figure 5-3. *Sequence of Policies for the Reconstruction Process*

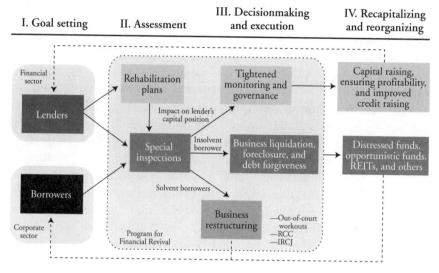

Source: Nomura Institute of Capital Markets Research.

not to be executing the plan properly or a considerable gap between the plan and actual results leads to a decline in market trust, the Rapid Recapitalization Act authorizes the FSA to request reporting on alternative measures and, when necessary, to consider issuing a business improvement order. "Considerable gap" was defined specifically as a level of actual return on equity or net profit that falls short of the target by at least 30 percent and became known as the 30 percent rule.

Because the issuance of a business improvement order questions the responsibility of the management team, often leads to the installation of a new management team, and can lead to the provision of public capital in the form of preferred shares that are converted into common shares, the 30 percent rule was thought to put considerable pressure on the autonomy of bank management. Meanwhile, because of the possibility that lenders would limit additional dispositions to their net operating income in order to keep from reporting losses, in April 2003 the 30 percent rule was made stricter by requiring banks that receive public injections to dispose of NPLs and strengthen profitability at the same time.[12] These measures gave the banks an incentive to dispose of their NPLs quickly in order to protect their management's autonomy in governing the financial institution.

12. Omura and Mizukami (2007) provide a detailed history of the 30 percent rule.

Second, NPL disclosure standards were unified, and special inspections were conducted. Japan's policymakers did not attempt to clarify the scale of bad assets when the real estate bubble first began to collapse, in part because they did not realize how serious the problem was. Additionally, assessing the actual value of bad assets was extremely difficult, even for experts in loan and real estate trading, given that (1) the real estate price cycle became too large in both directions, making it impossible to value real estate used as collateral, (2) the relationship between the credit claim and the debt was complicated by single borrowers having multiple lenders and by the same collateral being used two or three times, and (3) the lack of a market for securitization or loan trading made it difficult to get a reference price for loan assets. The Japanese government first announced the amount of NPLs held by financial institutions in April 1992, but the definition of an NPL as well as the criteria determining which loans were subject to disclosure requirements changed multiple times, and this created distrust both domestically and overseas. The Financial Reconstruction Act of 1998 finally settled on a definition of NPL categories and disclosure requirements,[13] but banks also made disclosures and set aside reserves based on their own assessments (table 5-1). Subsequently there was significant regret both at the banks themselves and at the FSA over their inability to grasp the actual situation, and analysts from foreign capitalized investment banks started estimating that the amount of NPLs was considerably higher than the numbers published by the FSA, creating turmoil.

What changed this situation were the special inspections that began in fall 2001. Special inspections were conducted on all major banks to determine whether the classifications assigned to their large borrowers that had experienced either a rapid decline in market valuation or a sustained period of low valuations were appropriate and whether the amount of provisions taken were appropriate. Because it seemed obvious that the results of the special inspections could lead directly to court-ordered bankruptcy proceedings for borrowers and the confirmation of losses at the banks, the plan created considerable resistance and confusion. However, according to Hirofumi Gomi, FSA commissioner from 2004 to 2007, some bank executives reacted positively at the time, taking a proactive approach to dealing with their large borrowers (Gomi 2012). In addition to proposing stricter asset assessments, compatibility with market values, and standardization of borrower categories for large borrowers, the Takenaka Plan also indicated plans

---

13. Loans requiring disclosure under the Financial Reconstruction Act are classified based on the borrower, but risk-managed loans, a category focused on individual loans, require disclosure under the Banking Act, and disclosure of both categories simply may have confused investors.

Table 5-1. *Bank Asset and Borrower Classification Standards for Self-Assessments*

Large ← Collectability → Small

	Classification of guarantee, collateral[a]			
	Superior collateral (deposit, government bond, other), superior guarantee (public sector guarantee, other)	Ordinary collateral (real estate, other)		No collateral, guarantee
		Estimated disposal value of collateral (70% of market value)	Difference between market value and estimated disposal value of collateral (30% of market value)	
Borrower classification				
Bankrupt[b]	I	II	III	IV
De facto bankrupt[c]	I	II	III	IV
In danger of bankruptcy[d]	I	II	III	III
In danger of bankruptcy, needs special attention[e]	I	II	II	II
Needs attention[f]	I	II	II	II
Normal[f]	I	I	I	I

Financial condition → Insolvent / Solvent

Source: Japan's Financial Services Authority.

a. Category I, assets with no problems in terms of repayment risk or loss of value risk; category II, assets for which there are serious doubts about collection or value; category IV, assets deemed to be uncollectable or without value. III, assets deemed to include a higher than normal repayment risk; category

b. Legally and formally bankrupt, including bankruptcy, liquidation, reorganization, rehabilitation, composition, and suspension of dealings on the bill exchange.

c. In serious business difficulties and considered to be impossible to rebuild, although not yet legally and formally bankrupt.

d. Facing difficulties and failing to make adequate progress on its business improvement plan, so that there is a possibility of falling into bankruptcy in the future.

e. Having problems with lending conditions, fulfillment, or financial conditions.

f. Having strong results and no particular problems with its financial condition.

to resume special inspections in fiscal 2002. The special inspections conducted in 2001 provided a foundation to improve the efficacy of these measures.

The special inspections were significant in four major ways. First, rather than occurring after the fact, they were a real-time check on the banks' borrower categories. They involved a dialogue between the inspector and the bank prior to releasing results and thus constituted a desirable measure for maintaining the trust of market participants at a time when economic conditions were deteriorating. Second, they made it possible to prevent each bank from using a different category for borrowers with large loans from multiple lenders. Ensuring that borrower categories applied to multiple lenders created ample room to use methods of assessing collectability that have theoretical explanatory power. Although these methods were not used as an inspection standard, they sparked research at the working level on the discounted cash flow method and other approaches to valuing businesses and assets.

Third, rules were introduced for removing NPLs from the balance sheet of the banks, along with standards for setting the pace of removal. The emergency economic package announced by the government in April 2001 attempted to implement rules for removing NPLs from the balance sheet of the major banks; specifically, loans in the "in danger of bankruptcy" category and lower were to be removed from the balance sheet within three fiscal years, while loans that were already in those categories were to be removed from the balance sheet within two fiscal years (also known as the three-year rule and the two-year rule, respectively). In addition to these rules, an FSA statement issued in April 2002, "Measures for Developing a Stronger Financial System," required that 50 percent of loans in the "in danger of bankruptcy" category and lower be removed from the balance sheet within one year and 80 percent within two years.

The two- and three-year rules do not have a theoretical basis and, in some respects, are nothing more than psychological targets. However, the FSA and the banks finally had common targets, creating synergy with the Takenaka Plan's special inspections and target of halving the amount of NPLs within two years. This approach of unifying standards for recognizing NPLs and conservatively setting aside provisions helped to give financial markets peace of mind.

Fourth, there was a backstop of public funds. The Takenaka Plan proposed creating a special mechanism for assistance from the government and the Bank of Japan combined, including measures such as the provision of liquidity through special Bank of Japan loans and the injection of public funds needed pursuant to the Deposit Insurance Act (Article 102, para. 1) when individual financial institutions run into business difficulty or become undercapitalized. Meanwhile, for lenders that receive special assistance, it clarifies management's responsibility, requires the permanent stationing of an inspection official, and seeks to strengthen governance, including by separating out new accounts from reorganized accounts.

These measures to deal with a financial crisis express the will of the government to protect financial order even when there are concerns that banks will become undercapitalized as a result of being pushed to dispose of NPLs. Subsequently in May 2003, Resona Bank's use of deferred tax assets as capital was denied by its auditor,[14] which lowered its ratio of equity capital below 4 percent and triggered financial crisis measures. Public funds totaling ¥1.96 trillion were injected into Resona Bank and the management team resigned en masse, but its stock listing was maintained based on the determination that it was not insolvent. The injection of public funds into Resona Bank sparked criticism from both sides, one maintaining that the government was too soft on the banks (that is, opposing the need to bail out a bank with taxpayer funds when nonfinancial corporations are allowed to fail) and the other maintaining that it was too harsh (that is, opposing the government's nationalization of the bank). However, the stock market rebounded significantly on realization that the set of policies provided a backstop for the financial system, marking the start of a recovery in share prices. Additionally, major banks, fearing that the government would intervene by injecting public funds, began to increase their capital ratios.

Creating a System to Encourage Borrowers to Recapitalize

During the process of financial restoration that began in 2001, calls to restore finance and industry made measures to restore corporate borrowers important. However, Japan had little experience with corporate reorganization and needed to create rules along with a specialist organization to enforce them.

Reform of the Bankruptcy Act and the Civil Rehabilitation Act played a major role in this regard. The Civil Rehabilitation Act, largely meant to be applied to smaller firms, significantly reformed the procedures for reorganization. It was promulgated at the end of 1999 and went into effect in April 2000. Likely inspired by Chapter 11 of the U.S. Bankruptcy Code, the Civil Rehabilitation Act aimed to provide speedier and more flexible procedures, increase the likelihood that a corporate borrower would restructure, and raise the incentives for business executives to commit to doing so. In Japan up until then, society and the financial institutions themselves were supportive of the ethical argument for seeking accountability from the companies and managers that were having trouble repaying their debt. However, the idea started to spread that the likelihood that reorganization procedures would be used strategically was, in many respects, desirable from an economic welfare perspective. The financial institutions started studying financial methods, such as debtor-in-possession financing, that increase

---

14. At end-September 2002, deferred tax assets accounted for 76 percent of Resona Bank's shareholder capital.

the effectiveness of the civil rehabilitation process. Furthermore, in September 2001 the financial and nonfinancial sectors cooperated to spell out guidelines for private debt workouts, seeking to come up with a set of best practice standards for reconciling debt claims and for restructuring out of court.

Also playing important roles were the two asset management companies, the Resolution and Collection Corporation (RCC) and the Industrial Revitalization Corporation of Japan (IRCJ).

The RCC was established under the Financial Reconstruction Act by merging the Resolution and Collection Bank, established in September 1996 to dispose of the credit claims of failed credit cooperatives, with the Jusen Resolution Corporation, established in July 1996 to take over the assets of seven failed housing lenders. The RCC's purpose was to resolve quickly the bankruptcies of smaller lenders, collect on their remaining credit claims after the fact, and sell the assets. It was modeled after the Resolution Trust Corporation, established during the savings and loan crisis in the United States. Because the RCC was successful in working through complicated debt claims, it was expected to fill the role of corporate reorganization coordinator, and under the Financial Revival Program of 2002, the RCC strengthened its corporate reorganization division and began encouraging financial institutions to sell their debt claims to it (figure 5-4).

The RCC was very successful in reconciling competing interests and maximizing collections, but it lacked the manpower and experience to reorganize and rejuvenate relatively large corporate borrowers outside of the court system. However, Japan's private sector at the time had virtually no private equity funds specialized in leveraged buyouts. To deal with that, the government passed a special law in April 2003 to establish the Industrial Revitalization Corporation of Japan, giving it two years to purchase debt claims and mandating its closure after five years. The IRCJ received funding from the DICJ and the Norinchukin Bank; the government, with approval from members of the executive and decisionmaking body, the Industrial Revitalization Committee, guaranteed loans from the IRCJ up to a maximum of ¥10 trillion. The IRCJ was staffed primarily with specialists from the private sector. The IRCJ provided assistance in forty-one cases until 2005, particularly by purchasing loans from the three largest banking groups, and continued working to revitalize each company through debt forgiveness, debt-equity swaps, and hands-on consulting. It shut down operations after five years, as planned (figure 5-5).[15]

Thus the IRCJ effectively acted as a buyout fund backed by the government and received high marks for the earnings it was able to generate even during the

---

15. Seki and Iwatani (2001) and Seki (2002).

Figure 5-4. *Expanded Functions of the Resolution and Collection Corporation*

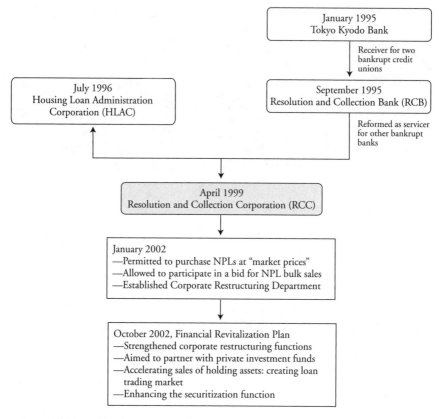

Source: Nishimura (2011).

financial revival process in the 2000s.[16] The forty-one cases handled by the IRCJ did not exclusively comprise large corporate borrowers targeted by the special inspections and the Takenaka Plan, but the amount of loans extended to the companies assisted during the business year immediately prior to the decision to offer assistance totaled approximately ¥4 trillion, more than 10 percent of the ¥35.3 trillion of NPLs held by banks nationwide in fiscal 2002. The experience and human capital built up at the IRCJ contributed to the development of Japan's buyout market after the IRC was disbanded.

16. Okina (2009) and Kinoshita (2011).

Figure 5-5. *Function of the Industrial Revitalization Corporation of Japan (IRCJ)*

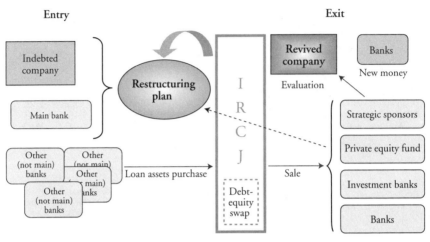

Source: Takagi (2003a, 2003b).

Real Estate Market Liquidity

Also playing an important role in financial revival were the real estate securitization and REIT markets. Of course, the origin of Japan's bubble was the formation of abnormal real estate prices and the excessive creation of credit backed by real estate. Neither the liquidation nor the recapitalization of borrowers was sufficient to achieve progress in writing off nonperforming loans without the help of a reinvigorated market for real estate transactions.

The securitization of real estate loans and other debts in Japan began in 1998 with temporary legislation authorizing the creation of special-purpose companies. The legal framework was put in place with passage of the Asset Securitization Act in 2000. The Revised Investment Trusts Act, which authorized the formation of investment trusts to invest in real estate and securitize the equity, was enacted in 2000, and two REITs were listed on the Tokyo Stock Exchange in September 2001.[17]

As the market was forming after that, traditional nonperforming assets, such as land set aside for failed development projects, were not used for securitization. However, operating properties with relatively favorable locations, including sale and lease-back deals, were securitized. Hence the real estate securitization process itself did not contribute directly to cutting the amount of NPLs in half.

17. Seki (2007).

Figure 5-6. *Issuance of Asset-Backed Securities in Japan, 1998–2011*

Amount of asset-backed securities issued (trillion yen)

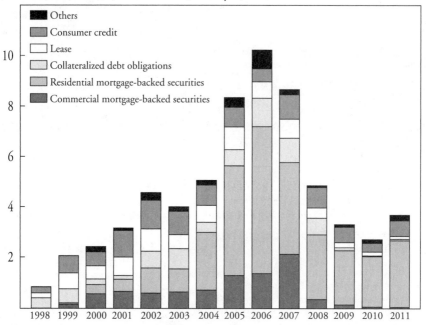

Source: Nomura Institute of Capital Markets Research.

Nevertheless, at a time when the secondary real estate market had virtually dried up as a result of the collapse of the bubble, thereby wiping out the visibility of market prices, the emergence of a securitization market fueled a gradual increase in transactions. The investors in these transactions valued the properties on a cash flow basis on the assumption of holding for the long term; this brought liquidity and transparency to Japan's real estate market, while indirectly creating an environment more conducive to the disposal of properties by large borrowers and lenders (figure 5-6). With the banks still reluctant to lend, this also opened the door to asset-based financing and widened the set of funding alternatives available to many businesses and insurance companies.

Lessons Learned in Japan

One of the lessons learned from Japan's success in solving its NPL problem was that when a collapsing bubble affects both the real economy and asset markets, a solution is unlikely to be reached by focusing exclusively on the soundness of lenders.

Table 5-2. *Factors Affecting Changes in NPLs, 2002–07*

Trillion yen

Factor	Change, April 2002– March 2005	Change, April 2002– March 2007
Changes in NPLs[a]	–25.3	–31.2
Newly generated NPLs due to weakened business activities	20.2	27.3
Upgrade from lower categories	2.0	2.6
Return to normal claims	–9.5	–12.1
Repayment, etc.	–4.3	–5.2
Removal from the balance sheet, etc.	–33.8	–44.1
Bankruptcy process (liquidation)	–2.6	–3.4
Bankruptcy process (reorganization)	–4.2	–5.6
Business improvement by reorganization	–1.8	–2.0
Asset liquidation	–13.5	–17.4
Charge-off	4.5	6.8
Subtotal	–17.6	–21.6
Collection and repayment	–12.1	–16.6
Business improvement	–4.1	–6.0
Subtotal	–16.3	–22.6

Source: Japan's Financial Services Authority (Nishimura 2011).
a. Based on the Financial Reconstruction Law.

Table 5-2 looks at the specific factors causing changes in the amount of NPLs requiring disclosure under the Financial Reconstruction Act since 2002. Based on this analysis, the decline in NPLs was helped substantially not only by asset liquidation, but also by returns to normal claims, repayments, and business improvement. In that sense, one reason for the success of Japan's financial revival was that policies to revive corporate borrowers were also adopted, as opposed to focusing only on pushing financial institutions to remove NPLs. Additionally, simultaneously reviving both finance and industry also requires implementing the appropriate macroeconomic policies to stimulate the economy as well as efforts to effect a recovery in demand through structural reform.

Another lesson learned was that using market mechanisms is effective. Ministers Yanagisawa and Takenaka engineered a major change in Japan's administration of its financial system, from the old convoy system to the new segregation policy. The latter tolerates widening differences among the banks while using public funds to intervene where necessary in the management of problem banks and to encourage their revitalization. Looked at from a different perspective, the underlying approach in the Financial Revival Program was to get the relatively stronger banks to dispose of NPLs and recapitalize voluntarily, thereby beginning the process of revitalization with those banks favored by the market. In other words, in the event of a liquidity crisis like the one that occurred in 1998–99, the financial system can be maintained with the combination of public capital injections and deposit insurance, but when the problem is one of nonperforming assets, it is important to leverage the pressure from capital market valuations. The policies adopted by the U.S. government around the time of the collapse of Lehman Brothers—namely, the wide distribution of taxpayer funds through the Troubled Asset Relief Program in October 2008 and the use of stress tests to authorize the repayment of taxpayer funds and voluntary recapitalization in 2009—followed a pattern similar to Japan's financial revival policies.

Additionally, the use of market mechanisms had a major impact on Japan's financial revival by way of reviving corporate borrowers and restoring liquidity to the real estate market. Unlike the United States, Japan had a traditional financial system built around commercial banks and thus had to scramble to put together a legal framework and develop the human capital to be able to take advantage of securitization, reorganization, and other methods. Consequently, it took Japan much longer to solve the problem. China and other countries in Asia also have financial systems based on a commercial bank–dependent model, and they must act soon to develop the capital market mechanisms and players needed to avoid following in the footsteps of Japan's lost decades.

References

FSA (Financial Services Agency). 2001. "The Advanced Reform Program: Financial Sector." Tokyo, October 26 (www.fsa.go.jp/news/newse/e20011026-1.html).

———. 2002a. "Measures for Developing Stronger Financial System." Tokyo, April 12 (www.fsa.go.jp/news/newse/e20011026-1.html).

———. 2002b. "Program for Financial Revival: Revival of the Japanese Economy through Resolving Nonperforming Loans." Tokyo, October 30 (www.fsa.go.jp/news/newse/e20021030.pdf).

Fuchita, Yasuyuki, and Kei Kodachi. 2012. "Managing Systemwide Financial Crises: Some Lessons from Japan since 1990." In *Rocky Times: New Perspectives on Managing Financial Stability*, edited by Yasuyuki Fuchita, Richard Herring, and Robert Litan. Washington: Brookings.

Gomi, Hirofumi. 2012. "Kin'yu Doran [Financial Turmoil]." Nikkei Publishing (in Japanese).

Ikeo, Kazuhito. 2009. "Ginko Hatan to Kantoku Gyosei [Bank Failure and Supervisory Authority]." In *Furyo Saiken to Kin'yu Kiki [Bad Loans and Financial Crisis]*, edited by Kazuhito Ikeo. Keio University Press (in Japanese).

Iwatani, Masanobu. 2000. "Reorganization of Insolvent Companies under the New Reorganization Law." Tokyo: Nomura Institute of Capital Markets Research (www.nicmr.com/nicmr/english/report/repo/2000/2000spr03.pdf).

Kinoshita, Nobuyuki. 2011. "Kin'yu Gyosei no Genjitsu to Riron [Facts and Theories of Financial Administration Policies]." Kinzai Institute for Financial Affairs (in Japanese).

Nishimura, Yoshimasa. 2011. "Kin'yuu Sisutemu Kaikaku Gojunen no Kiseki [50 Years of Financial System Reform]." Kinzai Institute for Financial Affairs (in Japanese).

Okina, Yuri. 2009. "Activity of IRCJ and Banking Crisis in Japan." *Public Policy Review* 5, no. 2 (November): 151–200.

Omura, Keiichi, and Shinji Mizukami. 2007. "Kin'yu Saisei: Kiki no Honshitsu [Financial Reconstruction: Essence of the Crisis]." Nikkei Publishing (in Japanese).

Seki, Yuta. 2002. "The Use of Debt-Equity Swaps by Japanese Companies." Tokyo: Nomura Institute of Capital Markets Research (www.nicmr.com/nicmr/english/report/repo/2002/2002sum03.pdf).

———. 2007. "ETFs and REITs in Japan: Innovation and Steps for Future Growth." In *New Financial Instruments and Institutions: Opportunities and Policy Challenges*, edited by Yasuyuki Fuchita and Robert Litan. Washington: Brookings Press.

Seki, Yuta, and Masanobu Iwatani. 2001. "Management Buyouts in Japan." Tokyo: Nomura Institute of Capital Markets Research (www.nicmr.com/nicmr/english/report/repo/2001/2001win04.pdf).

Takagi, Shinjiro. 2003a. "Industrial Revitalization Corporation of Japan." Presentation at the Forum for Asian Insolvency Reform, Seoul, November.

———. 2003b. "Maximizing Value of Nonperforming Assets." Paper prepared for the Forum for Asian Insolvency Reform, Seoul, November.

Takenaka, Heizo. 2006. "Kozo Kaikaku no Shinjitsu [Truth of Structural Reform]." Nikkei Publishing (in Japanese).

Contributors

FRANKLIN ALLEN
Wharton School, University of Pennsylvania

MARTIN NEIL BAILY
Brookings Institution

JAMES R. BARTH
Auburn University College of Business and Milken Institute

RICHARD J. HERRING
Wharton School, University of Pennsylvania

THOMAS JACKSON
Simon School of Business, University of Rochester

JAY R. RITTER
Warrington College of Business, University of Florida

YUTA SEKI
Nomura Institute of Capital Markets Research

DAVID SKEEL
University of Pennsylvania Law School

GLENN YAGO
Milken Institute

Index

Absolute priority rule, 103, 112
"Actual intent" test, 109
Adjustable-rate mortgages, 35, 55
Affordability of housing, 79–86; and
     government-sponsored enterprises, 48;
     and lease-to-purchase mortgages, 80; and
     property rights, 88; and shared-equity
     ownership, 79–80; and subsidies, 72
Allen, Franklin, 2–5, 20, 25
Alternative Investment Market (AIM), 126
American Recovery and Reinvestment Act
     of 2009, 85
Analyst coverage of IPOs, 11, 127–28
Asset Securitization Act of 2000 (Japan),
     19, 166
Australia: homeownership rates in, 45;
     housing finance in, 36, 81; subprime
     mortgages in, 63
Austria, housing finance in, 36
Automatic stay provisions, 6, 100

Bailouts, 98, 116–20
Baily, Martin Neil, 1

Balance sheet insolvency, 8–9, 107
Bankable spreads, 133–34
Bank Insurance Fund, 32
Bank of America, 150
Bank of Japan, 162
Bankruptcy, 5–11, 97–122; Chrysler case
     study, 116–20; delayed commencement
     of cases, 7–8, 101–10; and economic
     growth, 97–100; economic vs. financial
     failure, 98–99; in Japan, 163–65; and
     jobs, 9–10, 110–15; nonpunitive nature
     of, 7, 101; recommendations, 107–10; of
     subprime lenders, 57
Bankruptcy Act (Japan), 163
Bankruptcy Code of 1978, 112–13, 115, 120
Bankruptcy judges, 113–14
Bardhan, Ashok, 41
Barth, James R., 2–5, 20, 25
Basel I capital requirements, 151
Basic Policies for Economic and Fiscal
     Management and Structural Reform
     (Japan), 155
Belgium, homeownership rates in, 37–38

Bid-ask spreads, 133–34

Book building, 14, 15, 142

Brandeis, Louis, 132

Bright-line rules, 109

Brookings Institution, 1, 20

Building societies, 30

Business improvement plans, 18, 158–59

California, property tax–based financing
in, 85

Canada: homeownership rates in, 4, 65;
housing crisis in, 64–68; housing finance
in, 4; subprime mortgages in, 63, 67

Canada Mortgage and Housing Corporation
(CMHC), 44, 66

CAPC (Community Asset Preservation
Corporation), 77

Capital aggregation, 78–79, 88–89

Capital requirements, 150–51

"Cash flow" test for involuntary bankruptcy,
106

CDOs (collateralized debt obligations), 57,
88

Chapter 7 bankruptcy, 111, 112, 113

Chapter 11 bankruptcy, 103, 112–13, 115,
120, 163

China: housing finance in, 80–81; housing
market in, 25; intellectual property rights
in, 143

Chrysler bankruptcy case study, 10–11,
116–20

Citigroup, 150

Civil Rehabilitation Act of 2000 (Japan),
18, 163

Class-action lawsuits, 15, 143

Clean Energy Works Portland, 85–86

CMHC (Canada Mortgage and Housing
Corporation), 44, 66

Collateralized debt obligations (CDOs),
57, 88

Collectivization of creditors, 8, 103–04,
111–12

Colorado, property tax–based financing in,
85

Commercial banks, 31–33, 36, 45, 55–56,
82

Committee on Small and Emerging Companies (SEC), 125

Community Asset Preservation Corporation
(CAPC), 77

Community Reinvestment Act of 1977
(U.S.), 3, 43, 54, 66

Compliance costs of Sarbanes-Oxley, 12,
126

Copyrights, 15, 143

Council on Economic and Fiscal Policy
(Japan), 155

Covered bonds, 3, 36, 50, 64, 76

"Cream-skimming," 47

Credit analysis: and housing finance, 87–88;
and subprime mortgages, 56, 59; technology innovations for, 73–74

Credit enhancement, 82–83; housing funds,
78

Creditors: bankruptcy shifting ownership to,
6, 99–100, 103–04; and delayed commencement of bankruptcy case, 101–10;
incentives for, 108–09

Crowdfunding, 13, 137

Debtor-in-possession financing, 163–64

Decimalization, 132–36

Deed-restricted housing, 79

Delaware, bankruptcy courts in, 102

Demiroglu, Cem, 127

Denmark, housing finance in, 3, 36, 50,
64, 76

Deposit Insurance Act (Japan), 162

Deposit Insurance Corporation of Japan
(DICJ), 16, 19, 152, 164

Deposit Insurance Fund, 33

Directors and officers (D&O) insurance,
132

Dodd-Frank Act of 2010 (U.S.), 8, 70, 106

Economies of scope hypothesis, 130–31
Edelstein, Robert H., 41
Emergency Home Loan Financing Act of 1970 (U.S.), 48
Employment: and bankruptcy, 9–10, 110–15; IPO market and job creation, 138–41
Energy-efficient home improvement, 84–86
England. *See* United Kingdom
Enron, 126
Enterprise Community Partners, 78
Entrepreneurial innovation, 98
Equal Credit Opportunity Act of 1974 (U.S.), 43, 54
Equity owners: and delayed commencement of bankruptcy case, 101–10; incentives for, 99–100, 108
Europe and European Union: financial regulation in, 150; government involvement in mortgage markets in, 43–44; homeownership rates in, 37–38; housing finance in, 36, 41, 64, 76; housing market declines in, 88; investment banking fees in, 131; IPO market in, 130; sovereign debt crisis in, 149
Executory contracts, 7, 100

Facebook, 137
Fair Disclosure Rule (2000), 11
Fair Housing Act of 1968 (U.S.), 43, 54
Fannie Mae. *See* Federal National Mortgage Association
Federal Deposit Insurance Corporation (FDIC), 3, 32, 107
Federal Deposit Insurance Reform Act of 2005 (U.S.), 33
Federal Home Loan Bank Act of 1932 (U.S.), 32, 47
Federal Home Loan Bank Board (FHLBB), 32, 33
Federal Home Loan (FHL) bank system, 3, 32

Federal Home Loan Mortgage Corporation (Freddie Mac): affordable housing goals of, 48; establishment of, 3; and secondary mortgage market, 43, 44; and securitization, 48, 56–57, 66
Federal Housing Administration (FHA), 3, 43, 45–46, 51, 89
Federal Housing Enterprises Financial Safety and Soundness Act of 1992 (U.S.), 48
Federal Housing Finance Agency, 84
Federal National Mortgage Association (Fannie Mae): affordable housing goals of, 48, 51; establishment of, 3, 45–46; and secondary mortgage market, 43, 44; and securitization, 56–57, 66
Federal National Mortgage Charter Act of 1954 (U.S.), 51
Federal Reserve, 31, 55
Federal Savings and Loan Insurance Corporation (FSLIC), 3, 32
FHA. *See* Federal Housing Administration
FICO scores, 59, 60
Financial Functions Stabilization Act of 1998 (Japan), 153
Financial Reconstruction Act of 1998 (Japan), 18, 153, 160, 168
Financial Revival Program (Takenaka Plan, Japan), 17–20, 154–56, 160–62, 164, 169
Financial Services Agency (FSA, Japan), 17, 18, 154, 156, 159
Financial Supervisory Agency (Japan), 154
Finland: housing finance in, 36; housing market in, 25
Fisher, Lynn M., 41
Fixed-rate mortgages, 89
Foreclosures, 56, 57, 60, 61, 76–77
France: homeownership rates in, 37–38; housing finance in, 36
Frederiksen, D. M., 35
Freeman, Daniel, 28

FSA. *See* Financial Services Agency

FSLIC (Federal Savings and Loan Insurance Corporation), 3, 32

Gao, Xiaohui, 127, 130

Germany: homeownership rates in, 37–38; housing finance in, 3, 36, 41, 50; housing market in, 25; loan-to-value ratios in, 63

Ginnie Mae. *See* Government National Mortgage Association

Global financial crisis (2007–09), 1, 54–68

Global Settlement (2003), 11, 12, 127

Goldman Sachs, 150

Gomi, Hirofumi, 160

Government National Mortgage Association (Ginnie Mae), 3, 43, 56–57, 66

Government-sponsored enterprises (GSEs), 47–50. *See also specific organizations*

Graduated-payment mortgages, 35

Great Depression: and housing market, 55; and savings and loan associations, 3, 31–33

Great Recession, 1. *See also* Global financial crisis

Greece: homeownership rates in, 41; housing finance in, 36

GSEs. *See* Government-sponsored enterprises

Herring, Richard J., 1

HOLC (Home Owners' Loan Corporation), 45, 89

Home Energy Loan Program (HELP), 83–84

Home improvement loans, 83–84

Home Mortgage Disclosure Act of 1975 (U.S.), 43, 54

Homeownership rates: and global financial crisis, 55, 70; and government-sponsored enterprises, 47–48; international comparisons, 37–38, 65; promotion of, 27–29; and sources of funding for home purchases, 35–42

Home Owners' Loan Act of 1933 (U.S.), 32

Home Owners' Loan Corporation (HOLC), 45, 89

Homestead Act of 1862 (U.S.), 28, 86

Homestead Movement, 28–29

Horoi (mortgage stones), 26

Housing Act of 1949 (U.S.), 43

Housing Act of 1961 (U.S.), 51

Housing and Community Development Act of 1974 (U.S.), 46

Housing and Economic Recovery Act of 2008 (U.S.), 78

Housing and Urban Development Act of 1968 (U.S.), 54

Housing and Urban Development Department (U.S.), 66

Housing bonds, 82

Housing finance, 2–5, 25–95; and affordability, 79–86; and capital aggregation, 78–79, 88–89; challenges for, 68–74; and credit analysis, 87–88; and credit enhancement, 82–83; and demand for housing, 71–72; federal government involvement in, 43–54; and foreclosure crisis, 76–77; future innovations for, 74–86; and global financial crisis, 54–68; history of, 26–29; and homeownership promotion, 27–29; and house size, 90–91; and housing bonds, 82; and land trusts, 81; lessons learned, 86–92; organizational innovations for, 81–82; pricing models for, 77; and property logjam, 78; and property tax–based financing, 84–86; recommendations, 86–92; and rental housing, 80; and revolving loan funds, 82; and savings and loan associations, 29–35; and savings models, 80–81; sources of funding for, 35–42; and structured finance, 75–76, 91; subsidies for, 72–73; and supply-side housing innovations, 73; technology innovation for, 73–74; and unsecured home improvement loans,

83–84; for urban areas, 51–54. *See also* Affordability of housing; Housing market; Mortgage market

Housing market: in Canada, 64–68; as challenge for financial restructuring, 70–71; and house size, 90–91; international comparisons, 62–64; in Japan, 19, 166–67; property logjam in, 78; and rental housing, 80; in U.S., 54–61, 64–68. *See also* Housing finance

Housing Partnership Network, 78

Housing provident funds, 80–81

IHS Global Insight, 139

Immigration, 71

India: development rights transfers in, 73; housing market in, 25; intellectual property rights in, 143

Industrial Revitalization Corporation of Japan (IRCJ), 19, 164–65

Information technology, 73–74, 91

Initial public offerings. *See* IPO market

Innovation and Its Discontents (Jaffe & Lerner), 143

Insolvency. *See* Bankruptcy

Intellectual property rights, 15, 143

Interest Rate Control Act of 1966 (U.S.), 33

Investment banking fees, 12–13, 14–15, 131, 142–43

Involuntary bankruptcy petitions, 101–10

IPO market, 11–15, 123–45; and analyst coverage, 127–28; costs of IPO, 12–13, 14–15, 131–32; and crowdfunding, 137; and economies of scope hypothesis, 130–31; and job creation, 138–41; and market conditions, 128–30; and minimum tick sizes, 132–36; recommendations, 141–43; regulation of, 126; and SecondMarket, 137; and SharesPost, 137

IPO Task Force, 138, 139

IRCJ (Industrial Revitalization Corporation of Japan), 19, 164–65

Ireland: homeownership rates in, 45; housing market declines in, 62, 63, 88

Italy: homeownership rates in, 41; housing market in, 25

Jackson, Thomas, 5–11, 21, 97

Jaffe, Adam B., 143

Jaffe, Austin J., 41

Japan, 16–20, 149–70; bankruptcy reform in, 163–65; Financial Revival Program (Takenaka Plan), 17–20, 154–56, 160–62, 164, 169; housing finance in, 1–2, 36; lessons learned, 167–69; and nonperforming loans, 152–53, 156–67; Program for Financial Revival, 154–56; real estate market liquidity in, 166–67; special inspections in, 154–56

Jefferson, Thomas, 27–28

Jobs. *See* Employment

JOBS Act. *See* Jumpstart Our Business Startups Act of 2012

Johns Manville, 98–99

Journal of Finance on investment banking fees, 131

JPMorgan, 150

Jumpstart Our Business Startups (JOBS) Act of 2012, 13–14, 125, 132–33, 137, 142

Jusen Resolution Corporation, 164

Kauffman Foundation, 138

Kenney, Martin, 138

Kim, Edward, 133, 134, 139

Koizumi, Junichiro, 17, 154–55

Land Act of 1796 (U.S.), 28

Land Ordinance of 1785 (U.S.), 28

Land trusts, 79, 81

Land use regulations, 73

Lea, Michael, 63, 68

Lease-to-purchase mortgages, 79, 80

Lehman Brothers, 149, 169

Lerner, Josh, 143

Liberal Democratic Party (Japan), 153
Life insurance companies, 33, 45
Limited-equity cooperatives, 79
Lincoln, Abraham, 27–29
Living will approach, 8, 106
Loan modifications, 71, 79
Loan-to-value (LTV) ratios: in Canada,
    67; and credit analysis, 88; and foreclo-
    sure rates, 60, 74; in Japan, 151; and
    mortgage insurance, 45; and subprime
    mortgages, 56, 63
Local Initiatives Support Corporation, 78
Loss reserves, 32, 150

Market-to-book (MB) ratio, 127–28
MBSs (mortgage-backed securities), 57
"McMansions," 90
MGIC (Mortgage Guaranty Insurance
    Corporation), 46
Microfinance, 81–82
Minimum tick sizes, 132–36
Mitchell, Kate, 139
Miyazawa, Kiichi, 153
MMIF (Mutual Mortgage Insurance Fund),
    45–46
Morgan Stanley, 150
Mori, Yoshiro, 17, 154
Mortgage-backed securities (MBSs), 57
Mortgage Guaranty Insurance Corporation
    (MGIC), 46
Mortgage insurance, 45–47
Mortgage interest tax deduction, 67, 72
Mortgage market, 2–5; federal govern-
    ment involvement in market, 43–54;
    and government-sponsored enterprises,
    47–50; history of, 26; and loan modifica-
    tions, 71, 79; product innovation in,
    45–47; regulation of, 54; and secondary
    markets, 91; and urban housing, 51–54;
    and variable-rate mortgages, 35. See also
    Housing finance

Mortgage stones (horoi), 26
Mutual Mortgage Insurance Fund (MMIF),
    45–46
Mutual savings banks, 30, 33, 45, 81

NACA (Neighborhood Assistance Corpora-
    tion of America), 79
Nasdaq, 127, 128
National Community Stabilization Trust
    (NCST), 77, 78
National Housing Act of 1934 (U.S.), 32,
    43, 45
National Urban League, 78
National Venture Capital Association
    (NVCA), 134, 139
Negative amortization mortgages, 74
Negative equity, 67–68, 70, 79
Neighborhood Assistance Corporation of
    America (NACA), 79
Neighborhood Stabilization Program, 78
NeighborWorks America, 78
Netherlands, housing finance in, 63
Net present value (NPV) investments, 141
New Jersey, foreclosure crisis response in, 77
Newport, Lisa, 133
New York: property tax–based financing in,
    85; savings and loan associations in, 30
New York Stock Exchange (NYSE), 127
Nikkei Average, 16, 152
Nomura Institute of Capital Markets
    Research, 1, 20
Nonperforming loans (NPLs) in Japan:
    and bankruptcy reform, 163–65;
    extent of, 151; final disposition of,
    16–17, 158–63; lack of progress in
    disposing of, 152–53
Nonrecourse mortgages, 4, 61, 79
Norinchukin Bank, 19, 164
NPV (net present value) investments, 141
NVCA (National Venture Capital Associa-
    tion), 134, 139

Oklahoma, savings and loan associations in, 30
Omnibus Housing Act of 1954 (U.S.), 51
Order Handling Rules (SEC), 134
Over-collateralization, 83

Paleari, Stefano, 130
Participation rights, 114
Patents, 15, 143
Patton, Donald, 138
Peer-to-peer lending, 89
Pennsylvania, home improvement loans in, 83–84
Penny stocks, 140
Pension funds, 81
PMI. *See* Private mortgage insurance
Pollock, Alex, 44
Preemption Act of 1841 (U.S.), 28
Preference rules, 6, 105, 109
Prepayment penalties, 4
Pricing models for housing market, 77
Priority rules, 7, 100, 103, 112
Private-label-backed mortgage pools, 56–57, 70
Private mortgage insurance (PMI), 46–47, 49, 54
Program-related investments (PRIs), 78
Property Assessed Clean Energy Program (California), 85
Property rights, 88
Property tax–based financing, 84–86
Put-back mortgages, 149–50

Rapid Recapitalization Act (Japan), 18, 159
Rate ceilings, 33–34
RCC (Resolution and Collection Corporation, Japan), 18–19, 164
Reach-back rules, 100
Real estate investment trusts (REITs), 19, 153, 166

Real-estate-owned (REO) inventory, 77
Recovery through Retrofit Plan, 85
Redlined areas, 54
Regulation ATS (SEC), 134
Regulation FD (SEC), 12, 127
Regulation NMS (SEC), 134
Regulatory environment: and global financial crisis, 150–51; of IPO market, 126; in Japan, 156; of mortgage market, 54, 91
REITs. *See* Real estate investment trusts
Rental housing, 5, 75, 80
Report to Congress on Decimalization (SEC), 133
Reserve requirements, 31, 150–51
Resolution and Collection Bank (Japan), 164
Resolution and Collection Corporation (RCC, Japan), 18–19, 164
Resolution Trust Corporation, 164
Resona Bank, 156, 163
Retirement funds, 81
Revenue Act of 1951 (U.S.), 33
Reverse-annuity mortgages, 35
Revised Investment Trusts Act of 2000 (Japan), 19, 166
Revolving loan funds, 82
Ritter, Jay R., 11–15, 21, 123, 127, 130, 138
Romania, homeownership rates in, 37–38
Russia, development rights transfers in, 73
Ryngaert, Michael, 127

Sarbanes-Oxley (SOX) Act of 2002, 11, 12, 125, 126
Savings and loan associations, 2–3, 29–35; development of, 29–31; failures of, 3, 34–35; and Great Depression, 31–33; growth and diversification of industry, 33–34; housing finance from, 36, 45, 55; in 1980s, 34–35; origin of, 29–31

Savings Association Insurance Fund, 33
Savings models, 80–81
SecondMarket, 125, 137
Section 8 rental assistance, 80
Securities and Exchange Commission
    (SEC), 9, 106, 125, 127, 132–34
Securitization: in Canada, 66; by govern-
    ment-sponsored entities, 48; and housing
    crisis, 56–57, 61, 70, 86; international
    comparisons, 50; in Japan, 19, 153, 166;
    recommendations, 75–76, 91; by savings
    and loan associations, 3
Seki, Yuta, 1, 16–20, 21, 149
Self-Help (organization), 80
Shared-equity ownership, 79–80
SharesPost, 125, 137
Shiller, Robert, 26
Shiller PE ratio, 128, 131
Signori, Andrea, 130
Singapore, housing finance in, 80–81
Skeel, David, 5–11, 21, 97
Soft-dollar revenues, 132, 143
South Carolina, savings and loan associa-
    tions in, 30
SOX. See Sarbanes-Oxley Act of 2002
Spain: homeownership rates in, 41, 45;
    housing finance in, 3; housing market in,
    25, 62, 88
Special inspections, 17, 160, 162
Standard and Poor's (S&P) 500 index, 128
Stock markets, 127, 128–30, 152. See also
    specific exchanges
Stress tests, 150–51, 169
Structured finance, 75–76, 91
Subordinated loans, 16, 83
Subprime mortgages, 56, 57, 59
Subsidies: for housing finance, 43, 72–73,
    74; for mortgage insurance, 54; people-
    vs. place-based, 72–73; for rental hous-
    ing, 5, 75, 80
Summers, Lawrence, 60–61

Supply-side housing innovations, 73
Sweden: homeownership rates in, 37–38;
    housing market in, 25
Switzerland: homeownership rates in,
    37–38; housing finance in, 41

Takenaka, Heizo, 17, 154, 156, 168
Takenaka Plan. See Financial Revival
    Program
Takeout financing, 79
TARP (Troubled Asset Relief Program), 119,
    169
Tax Equity and Fiscal Responsibility Act of
    1982 (U.S.), 33
Tax policy: and housing finance, 43, 74;
    mortgage interest deduction, 67, 72;
    property tax–based financing, 84–86;
    and savings and loan industry, 2–3, 33;
    and subsidies for housing, 72, 80
Tax Reform Act of 1986 (U.S.), 33
Technology innovation, 73–74, 91
Tick sizes, 13, 125, 132–36
Tokyo Stock Exchange, 19
Transportation costs, 90
Truth-in-lending disclosures, 59

Underpricing of IPOs, 13, 15, 132
Underwater mortgages. See Negative equity
United Kingdom: financial regulation in,
    150; homeownership rates in, 37–38, 45;
    housing market in, 25; land use plan-
    ning in, 73; loan-to-value ratios in, 63;
    subprime mortgages in, 63
United States: bankruptcy reform in,
    97–122; financial regulation in, 150;
    foreclosures in, 76–77; homeowner-
    ship rates in, 4, 27–29, 37–38, 45, 65;
    housing crisis in, 54–61, 64–68; housing
    finance in, 25–95; housing market in,
    25, 62, 88; IPO market in, 123–45;
    nonrecourse mortgages in, 61

Unsecured home improvement loans, 83–84

Urban housing: demand for, 71; financing for, 51–54; and house size, 90; and property values, 41

Variable-rate mortgages, 35, 55

Venture capital, 134–35

Venture Impact: The Economic Importance of Venture Capital-Backed Companies in the U.S. Economy (IHS Global Insight), 139

Veterans Administration (VA), 43

Vicinity of insolvency, 7, 102

Vismara, Silvio, 130

Voluntary bankruptcy petitions, 101–10

Wall Street Journal on IPO market, 125

Weild, David, 133, 134, 139

Wells Fargo, 150

Wharton Financial Institutions Center, 1, 20

Wood, John, 26

World Bank Survey IV on bank assets in residential real estate loans, 50

WorldCom, 126

WR Hambrecht + Co, 132

Yago, Glenn, 2–5, 20, 25

Yanagisawa, Hakuo, 17, 154, 155–56, 168

Zhu, Zhongyan, 127, 130

Zone of insolvency, 7, 102

Zoning restrictions, 73

Brookings Institution

The Brookings Institution is a private nonprofit organization devoted to research, education, and publication on important issues of domestic and foreign policy. Its principal purpose is to bring the highest quality independent research and analysis to bear on current and emerging policy problems. The Institution was founded on December 8, 1927, to merge the activities of the Institute for Government Research, founded in 1916, the Institute of Economics, founded in 1922, and the Robert Brookings Graduate School of Economics and Government, founded in 1924. Interpretations or conclusions in Brookings publications should be understood to be solely those of the authors.

Nomura Foundation

Nomura Foundation is a nonprofit public interest incorporated foundation which aims to address social and economic issues involving Japan and the rest of the world by devoting private sector resources to promote international exchanges and the interchange between social science theory and practice. The foundation also provides grants and scholarships to support the social sciences, arts and culture, and up-and-coming international artistic talent. In the area of World Economy Research Activities it sponsors research, symposiums, and publications on current trends in capital markets of advanced and emerging economies as well as on topical issues in global macroeconomic stability and growth. It relies on a network of institutions from Europe, the United States, and Asia to assist in organizing specific research programs and identifying appropriate expertise.

Nomura Institute of Capital Markets Research

Established in April 2004 as a subsidiary of Nomura Holdings, Nomura Institute of Capital Markets Research (NICMR) offers original, neutral studies of Japanese and Western financial markets and policy proposals aimed at establishing a market-structured financial system in Japan and contributing to the healthy development of capital markets in China and other emerging markets. NICMR disseminates its research among Nomura Group companies and to a wider audience through regular publications in English and Japanese.

Wharton Financial Institutions Center, University of Pennsylvania

The Wharton Financial Institutions Center is one of twenty-five research centers at the Wharton School of the University of Pennsylvania. The Center sponsors and directs primary research on financial institutions and their interface with financial markets. The Center was established in 1992 with funds provided by the Sloan Foundation and was designated as the Sloan Industry Center for Financial Institutions, the first such center designated for a service-sector industry. It is now supported by private research partners, corporate sponsors, and various foundations and nonprofit organizations. The Center has hundreds of affiliated scholars at leading institutions worldwide, and it continues to define the research frontier, hosting an influential working paper series and a variety of academic, industry, and "crossover" conferences.